A HISTORY OF
AMBITION IN
50
HOAXES

A HISTORY OF AMBITION IN
50
HOAXES

GALE EATON
Introduction by PHILLIP HOOSE

Tilbury House Publishers
12 Starr Street, Thomaston, Maine 04861
800-582-1899 • www.tilburyhouse.com

First hardcover edition: August 2016
ISBN 978-0-88448-465-3

Library of Congress Cataloging-in-Publication Data

Names: Eaton, Gale, 1947- author.
Title: A history of ambition in 50 hoaxes / Gale Eaton.
Other titles: History of ambition in fifty hoaxes
Description: Thomaston, Maine : Tilbury House Publishers, 2016. | Series:
    History in 50 | Includes bibliographical references and index.
Identifiers: LCCN 2016015590 (print) | LCCN 2016021622 (ebook) | ISBN
    9780884484653 (hardcover) | ISBN 9780884484929 (pbk.) | ISBN
9780884484936
    (ebook)
Subjects: LCSH: History--Miscellanea--Juvenile literature. |
    Hoaxes--History--Miscellanea--Juvenile literature. |
    Ambition--History--Miscellanea--Juvenile literature.
Classification: LCC D10 .E25 2016 (print) | LCC D10 (ebook) | DDC
    001.9/5--dc23
LC record available at https://lccn.loc.gov/2016015590

Text designed by Jonathan Friedman, Frame25 Productions
Cover designed by John Barnett, 4 Eyes Design

Printed in China through Four Colour Print Group, Louisville, Kentucky

15 16 17 18 19 20 4CM 5 4 3 2 1

Table of Contents

Presenting the History in 50 Series

by Phillip Hoose

The *History in 50* series explores history by telling thematically linked stories. Each book in this series includes 50 illustrated narrative accounts of people and events—some well-known, others often overlooked—that, together, build a rich connect-the-dots mosaic and challenge conventional assumptions about how history unfolds. In *A History of Civilization in 50 Disasters*, for example, Gale Eaton weaves tales of the disasters that happen when civilization and nature collide. Volcanoes, fires, floods, and pandemics have devastated humanity for thousands of years, and human improvements such as molasses holding tanks, insecticides, and deep-water oil rigs have created new, unforeseen hazards—yet civilization has advanced not just in spite of these disasters, but in part because of them.

History in 50 is a canny, fun, and logical way to present history. The stories are brief, lively, and richly detailed. They work as narrative and also as bait to lure readers to well-selected source material. History in these books is not a stuffy parade of generals, tycoons, and industrialists, but rather a collection of brief, heart-pounding non-fiction narratives in which genuine calamities overtake us, genuine athletes leap skyward on feet of clay, and genuine discoverers labor bleary-eyed through the night to take us to the depths of the ocean, explore the vast reaches of space, unlock the genetic code, or develop a vaccine that saves millions of lives. It's history that bellows and shivers and roars.

And who doesn't love lists? Making a list of fifty great episodes of any kind invites—*demands*—debate. Even if the events aren't ranked (they're in chronological sequence), something always gets left out. I just finished reading *A History of Civilization in 50 Disasters*. I paged wide-eyed through plagues, eruptions, famines, microbes, and vaccines that worked or didn't. From my reading chair I took on dust storms, meltdowns, and epidemics at all scales that claimed my unwavering attention. When I closed the book and looked up, blinking, my first thought was, "Unbelievable. How have we ever made it through all this?"

But these feelings quickly gave way to a surge of indignation: *Where was the Tri-State Tornado of March 1925?* It's my favorite disaster—one that hit home. Actually a series of twisters, the Tri-State storm ripped through Missouri and Illinois before closing in on my great-grandparents in southwestern Indiana. Seven hundred people were killed in what is commonly ranked as the worst tornado ever. Contemporary meteorologists agreed that it was surely a category five twister, and yet it didn't make the top fifty disasters? I needed to lodge a protest.

But then I realized that my pique was a good thing. The book had made me care. The stories had swept over me and shaken my certainty like the 1906 San Francisco earthquake. And I realized that many readers will have the very same reaction: *Hey, where's my favorite episode?* It will spur debate. I imagine smart teachers asking students to describe their own favorite historical episodes, backing up findings with research. I imagine readers of all ages heading back to their bookshelves to support their arguments.

History is rewarding, but in my experience most people have to be led to it. So-called Reluctant Readers are mainly reluctant to be bored. They require, and deserve, historical material that meets them partway. History with menacing characters, even if some of them are invisible (germs); history replete with tough decisions; crisp episodes that leave you wondering what you would have done in that situation; history moved by people just like us, often from the humblest of origins, struggling in their daily lives while reaching for greatness—that's the history that works for most readers. And that is the history we have in this brilliant new series. The writing is clear and exciting, punchy stories that are, on average, two pages long. I have high hopes for the History in Fifty series, and it gives me pleasure to enthusiastically endorse it. Why? Because it works.

PHILLIP HOOSE is the National Book Award–winning author of *Claudette Colvin: Twice Toward Justice* and *The Boys Who Challenged Hitler: Knud Pedersen and the Churchill Club*.

Introduction

Hieronymus Bosch and/or artists in his workshop painted this conjurer sometime between 1496 and 1520. Like any good magician or hoax artist, the performer is manipulating audience attention—but members of the audience, including the pickpocket, have ambitions of their own.

Ambition is about wanting more—more than food and shelter, more than a humdrum job, more than the bare minimum to get by. Some people want riches and power; some want to create great art or win Olympic gold; some want to find cures for lethal diseases or to understand the universe. Some want these things for themselves and their families; others, for their communities, their nations, or people worldwide.

No matter what form ambition takes, it doesn't stop with wanting. Ambitious people work for the things they want. Some ambitions seize the limelight while others operate the lighting, but whether the ambition is public or private, ambitious people help create the world we live in.

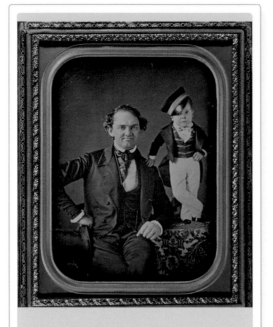

National Portrait Gallery

P. T. Barnum (1810–1891) called himself a "showman." If a fake like the Fejee Mermaid (Chapter 18) would draw crowds, he showcased the fake. Many of his most popular attractions were genuine, like tiny Charles Stratton (a.k.a. General Tom Thumb)—but Barnum advertised him as 11 years old when he was only 4, and taught him to smoke cigars by the time he was 7. Barnum's hype made Tom Thumb an international celebrity.

When ambition stays on the rails, we get *Hamlet*, the *Mona Lisa*, the polio vaccine, the Eiffel Tower. When it runs off the rails, we get war, thievery, assault, murder, greed, lies, cheating, propaganda, slander, cruelty, and hoaxes. In this array of misbehaviors, hoaxes are often the most creative and sometimes—though by no means always—the least harmful. But there never yet was a hoaxster who wasn't ambitious.

P.T. Barnum (Chapter 18) was an ambitious man who made a good living by following Rule #1 for the successful hoax artist: Tell the audience something they want to believe. Barnum called his version of hoaxing "humbug," and he said "there is no sort of object which men seek to obtain, whether secular, moral or religious, in which humbug is not very often an instrumentality."[1] In other words, people use humbug (or hoaxes) to get what they want.

Hoaxes serve many kinds of ambition. They can be used for military advantage, like the Trojan Horse (Chapter 1) or Operation Mincemeat (Chapter 38). They can be used for financial gain, like a Ponzi scheme (Chapter 31), or simply for fun, like National Public Radio's report on the dangers of untapped maple trees exploding in the forest (Chapter 16). Some hoaxsters want to jolt people into reforming the world;

the Spectric School of Poetry (Chapter 30) and the Coalition to Ban DHMO (Chapter 49) made fun of social trends. Other hoaxsters want to fit themselves and their communities more securely into the world as it is; the Kensington Rune Stone (Chapter 25) was all about Scandinavian roots in America, and Anna Anderson (Chapter 33) longed to fit herself into a royal family.

There is something artistic about a fine hoax; like a good novel or a conjurer's trick, it creates an alternative reality. The very word "hoax" probably comes from "hocus pocus," which stage magicians used to say as they pulled rabbits out of their hats. Hoaxsters don't set their work on a stage or between covers, but their creations are no less painstaking. No wonder they're often called con artists, scam artists, or pitch artists. It requires art to graft a false alternative into people's shared everyday reality.

Some hoaxes are meant to be accepted as valid forever, like the *Donation of Constantine* (Chapter 2), while others are constructed for the sheer pleasure of seeing someone's face when the hoax is revealed, like the elaborate plan that gets the guest of honor to a surprise party. A hoax is not successful if nobody believes it, but some pranksters also feel that a hoax fails if everybody believes it. They miss the fun of winking over the fools' shoulders at the clever ones who have figured out the joke and are in the know. Rule #2 for the successful hoaxster: Let the audience feel clever. Don't tell them the whole story you want them to believe; make them work to connect the dots. Give them a mystery, and let them believe the solution was their own idea.

Any hoax can offer a window onto history, giving us a look at what kinds of things people have believed and how truth has been tested. For instance, the invention of printing made some kinds of hoax more difficult. As maps became more standardized and accurate, imaginary islands and dragons vanished from their corners (Chapter 8). People stopped believing that lambs could grow from plants or that there was a race of headless humans with faces on their chests (Chapter 4).

Yet new technologies make new kinds of hoax possible. Printing could be a tool of hoaxing in at least two ways. A printed document (such as a banknote, a will, or a set of credentials) could be a forgery in its own right, or it could be the means of spreading a false story. As readers became familiar with the way scientists talked—or the way journalists talked about scientific discoveries—many judged a story's plausibility by its prose style. One week in 1835, New Yorkers believed there were tailless beavers, winged bat-men, and blue unicorns on the moon (Chapter 16). They never would have been taken in by a taradiddle like that if it hadn't been written in such a fine scientific style.

The fifty hoaxes in this book are taken from the history of European and American politics, warfare, economics, art, literature, and science. Each was designed to serve an ambition, from teasing parents (Chapters 19 and 32) to demonizing a people (Chapter 26). Some of them had unintended consequences, as when listeners panicked during the *War of the Worlds* broadcast (Chapter 37).

But as carefully staged lies, all hoaxes raise questions about *epistemology,* or how we know what we know. Can we trust the evidence of our eyes? Can we trust handwriting analysts, connoisseurs, and chemists to detect art forgeries and faked diaries? Can we trust journal editors to know when scholars fake data?

Good hoaxes make good stories. (No wonder trickster tales have been popular in cultures all over the world.) They also give us a chance to sharpen our wits, as Barnum well knew. When we become a hoaxster's target—as most of us surely will, repeatedly—will we ask ourselves what that smooth-talking pitch artist hopes to gain by getting us to believe his or her story; or why we want to believe; or how well the "hoax" information matches other things we know? Analyzing hoax stories may increase our information literacy and powers of critical thinking—but maybe sometimes it's worthwhile to be fooled. Samuel Taylor Coleridge coined a useful phrase, "the willing suspension of disbelief," for the enjoyment of artistic entertainments that we know are untrue. Those dragons and imaginary islands have vanished from cutting-edge maps of this world, and nobody recently has ridden a tornado from Kansas to Oz, but they're still fun to think about.

The Original Trojan Horse

Three thousand years ago, a hoax ended a war—or so the story goes. For ten years the Greeks besieged the city of Troy. Great heroes fought on both sides, displayed their strength and courage, and died. Children born in Troy learned to walk, talk, do chores, and carry messages as the armies clashed around them. The Trojan War was epic, and even the Greeks got tired of it.

The Greeks could not fight their way past Troy's walls and into the city. Finally—so the story goes—resourceful Ulysses designed a trick to defeat Trojan defenses. The Greeks built a massive wooden horse—as an offering to the goddess Minerva, they claimed—and left it behind when they broke camp, loaded their ships, and sailed away. But the ships hid just out of sight, and inside the horse a strike force of thirty Greeks waited. The Greeks also left behind a gifted young liar named Sinon.[1]

The Trojans ran down to see the abandoned Greek camp. Some rejoiced; others worried. Some thought they should haul the mountainous horse into the city; others thought they should check its contents first or burn it. A wise priest, warning them not to trust Greek gifts, hurled his spear at it.

The skeptics might have saved the city, but then Sinon was dragged in. He thanked the Trojans for capturing him. They were actually rescuing him, he said, since the Greeks had left him behind as a sacrifice. As

Archaeological Museum of Mykonos

One of the earliest known images of the Trojan Horse, the Mykonos vase dates from 670 BC—centuries after the war. It shows
Greek warriors looking out from windows in the horse's side.

for the horse, the Greeks had supersized it for a reason. They'd heard a
prophecy that if the horse was damaged Troy would fall, and the Greeks
would win the war. So they built the horse too large to squeeze through
the city gates without damage.

Sinon's story sounded plausible, and just then two serpents swam
to shore and killed the priest and his sons. People thought Minerva had
sent those serpents as punishment for spearing the horse. Sinon was
right, they thought—damaging the thing was risky. So to avoid hurting
it, the Trojans broke down their own walls and wheeled the horse into
town, celebrating the end of war.

That was the last day of Troy. In the night, Greek warriors burst
out of the horse and helped the entire Greek army into the city. They
burned Troy to ashes.

What Really Happened at Troy?

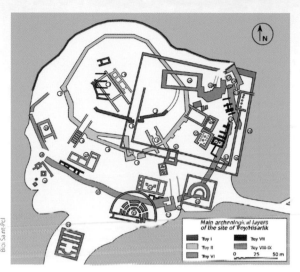

Bibi Saint-Pol

Main archaeological layers
of the site of Troy/Hisarlik

Troy I
Troy II
Troy VI
Troy VII
Troy VIII-IX

0   25   50 m

An archaeological plan of the excavations at Hisarlik shows how successive cities were built on top of each other over the centuries. Troy VI could be the wealthy city described in Homer's epics.

Was there really a Trojan horse? We can't be sure. Many scholars believe that Troy stood at present-day Hisarlik, in Turkey, where cities have been built on the ruins of older cities for centuries. Since the nineteenth century, archaeologists have worked to make the physical evidence match the stories. Fire and slaughter wiped out a city there in the twelfth century BC. Was that the site of the legendary Trojan War?

The twelfth century BC was the end of the Bronze Age. For centuries the eastern Mediterranean had been wealthy. Egyptians, Babylonians, Greeks, and Hittites traded everything from wheat to pottery to swords; their rulers exchanged ambassadors and letters. But suddenly great cities fell, one after another. Some were ruined by earthquakes and others apparently by war. There may have been famines, political upheavals, and invasions by the mysterious Sea People, a group or groups of sea-going raiders possibly originating from the Aegean area. There may have been a perfect storm of disasters, all striking at about the same time. We don't have written records of Greek history from the hardscrabble centuries that followed.[2]

But stories were passed along by bards, and eventually—probably around the eighth century BC—Homer's great epics The Iliad and The Odyssey gave us much of what we know about the Trojan War and its aftermath. The legend of the Trojan Horse was known then; the oldest picture of the Trojan Horse is on a brooch dating from about 700 BC.[3] Virgil's Aeneid told the story in more detail, but Virgil lived in first century BC Rome—more than a thousand miles from Troy and a thousand years after the war. Some modern scholars think the Trojan Horse was really just a kind of battering ram.[4] Maybe. Stories told for a thousand years are bound to change in the telling.

The story of the Trojan Horse describes a classic hoax. It was carefully staged. Sinon's story matched the beliefs of the time: an angry goddess had to be placated. It matched what the Trojans believed about the Greeks: a treacherous lot who would not hesitate to trick their enemy into damaging a holy sacrifice. And best of all, it allowed the Trojans to believe what they truly wanted to believe: the war was over. The scam worked, and it's been an inspiration to spies and special agents ever since.

The Forgery Underlying the Power of Medieval Popes

One of history's most influential hoaxes was a letter called the *Donation of Constantine*. It was forged in the eighth century AD— probably before 777[1]—at a time when few people could read. Passed off as a fourth-century document, it was used to legitimize the political might of popes throughout the Middle Ages. We can still see its after effects. For instance, Pope Adrian IV (the only pope to date who was English) relied on its authority in 1155 when he awarded Ireland to Henry II, king of England.[2] The relationship between England and Ireland remains vexed to this day.

How did Pope Adrian get the right to dispose of an entire country? According to the *Donation*, the Emperor Constantine gave that power to the popes on March 30, 315. Pope Sylvester had cured Constantine of leprosy, a disease that in those times condemned its victims to years of suffering and isolation before killing them. The cure was a miracle. Sylvester also taught Constantine the doctrine of the Trinity and baptized him.[3] A grateful Constantine bestowed imperial gifts on the papacy: lands and power in the Western Roman Empire and authority over all other bishops. Then, humbly leaving Rome to be God's capital on Earth, the emperor moved his political capital east to Constantinople.

Of course, Constantine did not really write the letter. The forger— probably an eighth-century clerk in the papal chancery—may have thought the emperor *should* have written it.[4] Constantine probably never even had leprosy, but the legend of his miraculous cure by Sylvester had been well known in Rome for centuries.[5] True or not, people believed it, so they believed the forged letter, too. This helped the eighth-century popes, who needed allies closer than Constantinople.

They found a strong ally in France, where Pope Zachary helped Pepin establish a new line of kings. Pepin in turn promised to recapture lands that had been taken by other rulers and restore them to the popes.[6] Pepin gave Zachary the Papal States,[7] but where did Pepin get the right to make that gift? The forged *Donation of Constantine* gave his generosity both a precedent and a legal basis.

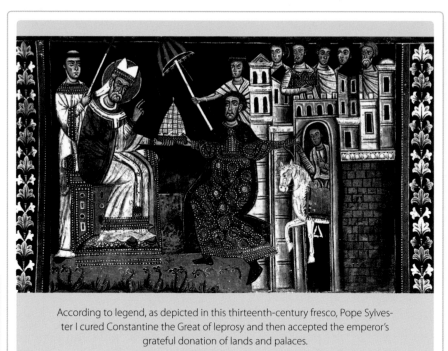

According to legend, as depicted in this thirteenth-century fresco, Pope Sylvester I cured Constantine the Great of leprosy and then accepted the emperor's grateful donation of lands and palaces.

Pepin's son Charlemagne (768–811) continued the alliance, and in 800 Pope Leo III crowned him in Rome, making him the Holy Roman Emperor. Again, it was the *Donation of Constantine* that gave Leo

Constantine, Christian Emperor of the Greek East and the Latin West

Capitoline Museums

Constantine the Great was revered in medieval Europe as the Roman emperor who adopted Christianity. From AD 306 to 337 he ruled an empire that stretched from Britain to Egypt, circling the Mediterranean. His people were diverse, and they spoke many languages—but most of what they wrote down was Greek (in the east) or Latin (in the west).[12] Those were the languages citizens needed to get by in life, as people today need Mandarin, Spanish, and English.

To administer such a vast and complex government, an emperor needed administrative support. Diocletian (284–305) had appointed a co-emperor to share his rule and two junior emperors as well; Constantine's father was the junior emperor in the west. This system (called the Tetrarchy, or rule of four) was unstable, and after being acclaimed emperor by troops in Britain, Constantine was embroiled in civil wars until 324. Before a battle in 312, he reportedly saw a cross of light in the sky and the Greek words, "In this sign conquer." He ordered his troops to display the Christian symbol on their shields and went on to victory.[13]

The empire's people practiced many religions, but most gave outward respect to the official state religion, which worshipped many gods (including the emperor). Jews and Christians resisted—and in 303, Diocletian and his co-emperors launched a harsh persecution of Christians. Constantine officially ended this in 313 with the Edict of Milan, ordering tolerance for all religions. He became the first Christian emperor, and was baptized on his deathbed.[14]

The Western Roman Empire fell in 476, and the Eastern Roman Empire was too weak and far away to rule Europe. But Constantine still had immense prestige in the Middle Ages, and historians used his story to legitimize their own religious and political ideas.

the theoretical power to bestow or withhold an empire. It stated that kings in medieval Europe were subordinate to popes.

For centuries nobody dared question the fraud. Not everybody approved—the poet Dante, for one, saw the donation as a source of evil and corruption—but the *Donation of Constantine* justified the wealth and influence of the Church.

Eventually, Renaissance scholars exposed the hoax. Nicolas of Cusa detected it in 1433, and in 1440 Lorenzo Valla wrote that the "falsely believed and lying *Donation of Constantine*" was "not even likely."[8] Constantine had fought hard to win the empire and wasn't the type to give it away.[9] Valla also pointed out anachronisms in the text. How could Constantine have moved to Constantinople in 315 when he didn't start building it until 324? And language changes over time. How could Constantine, writing in the fourth century, have used the language of the eighth century? Constantine could not have written the *Donation*. In proving it, Valla pioneered a new way of analyzing and understanding language.[10]

The *Donation of Constantine* helped shape a world. So did Valla's proof that it was a forgery, which Martin Luther read in 1520—eighty years after Valla wrote it. Luther was locked in conflict with the pope—a conflict that helped start the Reformation, dividing all of Europe into Catholic and Protestant camps. Luther's reading of Valla strengthened his belief "that the papacy had for generations attempted to despoil and usurp the empire."[11] So the very same forgery that had helped shore up the popes' worldly power for so long became a factor in the movement to limit it.

A Letter from the Mythical Prester John

How exciting! News from the fabled Indies! An emissary came from India in 1122, followed in 1145 by rumors of a great war lord—a longed-for ally in the fight for the Holy Land. Finally, in 1165, came the letter.

Twelfth-century Europe was hungry for news from the east. Between 622 and 750, Muslims conquered all but the northern fringes of the Mediterranean world. Lands that had been part of the old Roman Empire—including what we now call Spain, Morocco, Libya, Egypt, Syria, and Turkey—became part of a triumphant new Islamic culture. The ancient trade routes were disrupted, and Christian Europe was cut off from the rest of the world. Europeans no longer knew just where the "Indies" were: India, or some other place between Ethiopia and Indochina?

Prester John rules East Africa in the atlas made by Portuguese cartographer Diogo Homem for England's Queen Mary in 1558.

Before the First Crusade (1096–1099), Islamic powers ringed Europe from southern Spain and northern Africa to Syria and Turkey. By 1100, Christians occupied a fringe of small "Crusader States" along the eastern Mediterranean, including Jerusalem; but the Seljuk Empire still separated them from the Indies. Could an ally to the east help Europeans overcome the Seljuks?

Thomas Lessman

Then, in 1095, Pope Urban II called for a Crusade. It was time to seize back control of Jerusalem, he said; time to bring the Holy Land under Christian control. For the next two centuries, Europeans launched one Crusade after another. They fought; they picked up new ideas from their Muslim enemies; and their interest in what lay beyond Islam kept growing.

The emissary turned up at the pope's court in Rome in 1122, and said he represented Patriarch John of India.[1] All Europe knew that the Apostle Thomas had worked miracles and founded a Christian congregation in far-off India. The emissary described a rich and exotic country, but was he an impostor? Pope Callixtus II wasn't sure, though the man swore on a Bible that he was telling the truth.[2]

In 1145, early in the Second Crusade (1145–1147), a Syrian bishop told a German colleague the story of a great warlord. A Christian prince, a descendant of the Magi, had defeated a Muslim army in Central Asia. He was known as Prester John. He was both king and priest, and he would lead an army to help his fellow Christians in the Holy Land.[3] In reality the warlord was probably the Mongolian Yeh-lü Ta-shih, who defeated the Seljuks near Samarkand in 1141.[4] News did get garbled in those days, when communication traveled no faster than men on horseback. Sadly for the Europeans, the Second Crusade fizzled out unsuccessfully. No help came from the Indies.

So in 1165, when Prester John wrote to Byzantine Emperor Manuel I Comnenus (1143–1180), Europe took notice. The letter was rude and boastful. Prester John said he was the Lord of Lords, the supreme ruler of the Three Indies, served by seventy-two kings. He had fabulous treasures. His very bed was made of sapphire.[5] He called the Byzantine emperor a mere "governor" and offered him a position as major-domo. Outrageous! But copies of the letter circulated around Europe.[6]

The letter was a hoax—but who perpetrated it, and why? Was it meant to encourage the Crusaders or to improve their morals? Was it written by a northern European to put the Greek Orthodox Byzantines in a bad light? Maybe the writer forgot his original motives and was carried away by his imagination as he wrote. His wild tales of riches and marvels seized readers' imaginations, too. The Indies were as unreachable then as Mars is now, and stories of Prester John were like science fiction.[7]

Whatever the forger planned, the hoax did have consequences. It entered into the calculations of Henry the Navigator and Columbus. It helped motivate an age of European exploration and expansion. The search for Prester John went on for centuries and became a search for riches.

Imagining the World

More than distance, ignorance separated twelfth-century Europe from East Asia—Europeans simply didn't know what was out there.

Travel was difficult. For most people it meant walking—through woods, across fields, or along unpaved roads—covering maybe 20 miles in a day. So while some left their villages on business, or made pilgrimages to shrines around Europe, or joined the Crusades and fought in the Holy Land, most people never went far from home. Most Europeans had to base their ideas about the Indies on hearsay.

Wikimedia.org

This "T and O" diagram of the world, printed in 1472, puts east (Oriens) at the top. The three continents are separated by a T of waters—the Don on the left, the Nile on the right, and the Mediterranean below. Around this inhabited world, the O represents the Ocean Sea.[8]

What did they imagine? A simple way to think about the world in those days was a "T" and "O" diagram, with east at the top, Jerusalem in the center, and Ocean encircling three continents peopled by the sons of Noah: Shem (Sem), Ham (Cham), and Japheth (Iafeth). Everyone knew there was more to the world than you could see on that map. But what was it really like?

Maps improved after the invention of printing. A printed map is standardized; all the copies are the same. Explorers could compare printed maps to real coastlines, find the mistakes, and correct them.[9] But the printing press did not come into use until the 1400s. In the meantime, books and writing materials were fantastically expensive, and most people—even if they knew how to read—didn't do much of it. Writing was associated with religion and government. It was a tool of authority.

So twelfth-century Europeans were both ignorant of the East and fascinated by the very idea of it. That combination of ignorance and fascination made them likely dupes for hoaxes involving the Indies. And the use of writing—a prestigious technology at the time—gave the hoax an air of authority. Willing believers and cutting-edge technology: what more does a hoax artist need?

Did Marco Polo Really Go to China?

This miniature from an early manuscript shows some of the ways
Marco Polo traveled: boat, camel, and elephant.

Wikimedia.org

Marco Polo (1254–1324) is famous for going to China. His *Description of the World*, probably written in 1298,[1] reported first hand on Mongolia, China, India, and Sumatra. To travel so far from Italy took dangerous months or years by foot, camel, or ship. The Crusades (and the Prester John forgery, Chapter 3) had piqued European interest in Asian goods: silk, flax, and cloth-of-gold; silver, rubies, and lapis; dates, pistachios, and spices. All these and more were traded along the ancient

A. Omer Karamollaoglu

Marco Polo said he ran many missions for Kublai Khan (1215–1294), the Mongol conqueror of China.

Silk Road, usually by Persians and other middlemen. In Polo's time, Italian merchants had begun to go farther afield and handle more of the routes themselves, setting up trading posts in distant ports. They needed information.

According to the prologue of the *Description*, Marco's father and uncle, Maffeo and Niccolo Polo, traded in Constantinople in 1260 and went on to trading posts on the Black Sea and the Caspian Sea. Eventually they reached Karakorum, the capital of the Mongols, and met the great Kublai Khan. They were gone for ten years, and didn't stay home for long. In 1271, they took young Marco back to Karakorum with them. For the next seventeen years he "never ceased to travel on special missions" for the Khan.[2] These were years in which the Mongol Empire fell into four parts, but Kublai's portion was still huge. It reached from the Black Sea to the Pacific, and after 1279 it included all of China.[3] Kublai sent Marco far and wide, and the homesick Polos did not see Venice again until 1295.

Italy wasn't a single nation then. Venice was at war with Genoa—another Italian trading city—and Marco Polo soon became a prisoner of war. In a Genoese prison he told his travel stories to a man named Rustichello, who made them a best seller. Polo's *Description* was copied and recopied in a dozen languages, and it was still popular 200 years later—Christopher Columbus took a copy to the Americas in 1492. But scribes and translators left some things out and added others; at least 143 versions appeared between the fourteenth and nineteenth centuries.[4] It's hard to know exactly what was in Polo's original version.

Polo seems to have said nothing about the Great Wall of China, or the practice of foot-binding, or the popularity of tea, and Chinese records say nothing about Polo.[5] Was he really there? Omissions don't prove that he wasn't. The Great Wall of China as we know it was built in the sixteenth century, under the Ming Dynasty; earlier walls were less prominent and might not have impressed Polo. He probably associated more with foreigners (including the Mongol conquerors) than with the Chinese themselves, so he might not have seen much of foot-bind-

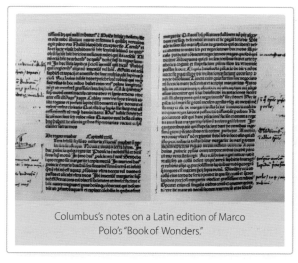

Columbus's notes on a Latin edition of Marco Polo's "Book of Wonders."

ing and tea-drinking. Or, if he did mention these things, copyists may have dropped them from later manuscripts.[6]

And while some details may have been dropped, others may have been added. Some versions of the *Description* make implausible claims for the Polos: that they helped win the siege of Hsiang-yang, for instance, or that Marco governed Yang-chou for three years. Did copyists add these details, or did the Polos overstate their own importance?[7]

The *Description* is full of information about the mining of asbestos, the diplomatic and commercial contacts between Yuan China and southern Asia, and other matters that medieval traders would have wanted to know. If Marco Polo never went to China, it's a hoax, but a remarkably useful one.

Mandeville's *Travels*

He said he was an English knight from St. Albans, but scholars doubt it; there's little contemporary evidence that "Sir John Mandeville" existed. He said he was writing his own experiences, but now we know he plagiarized earlier writers; whoever he was, he compiled more stories than he wrote. He said he'd seen men and women with heads like dogs, and men without mouths who lived on the scent of apples, and ants digging for gold in Ceylon. Manuscripts of his work began to appear in the 1350s or 1360s, and, like Polo's *Description of the World*, Mandeville's book became a medieval best seller.[8] Like Polo's book, Mandeville's was copied and translated so often that we can't even be sure of its original language; it was often bound into volumes with other travel manuscripts, including Polo's; and it was referred to by Columbus.

Woodcut from the Nuremberg Chronicle, 1493

Mandeville claimed that in Ethiopia he saw the Sciapods, who hop everywhere and shade themselves from the desert sun with their single big feet. In *The Voyage of the Dawn Treader*, C. S. Lewis called them Monopods. Was Mandeville writing fantasy?

Mandeville's book was obviously riddled with falsehoods, and they can't all be blamed on copyists, but was it a hoax? According to one recent scholar, it was "certainly as up to date a factual account of the world as its author knew how to make it," and it served as an authority on the East for generations.[9] It also had a viewpoint that appealed to Europeans at the time. Mandeville found that religions around the world resembled Christianity in some respects; he concluded that people everywhere could be brought to perfect faith by "the preaching and teaching of Christian men." Crusades to take back the Holy Land were fading into ancient history as he wrote, but the Age of Exploration lay ahead. Columbus and those who came after would repeat Mandeville's message: the people they found "could easily be made Christians."[10] Hoax or not, Mandeville's *Travels* had an impact.

The World's Most Mysterious Book

The Voynich Manuscript has one great claim to fame: it's a book nobody can read. Its many illustrations hint that it's about plants and stars. It might be an early science book or something occult. But it's written in an unfamiliar alphabet and an unidentified language. Among its past owners and would-be readers:

* John Dee, astrologer and spy for Elizabeth, Queen of England. Around 1586, Dee reportedly sold a book for 600 gold ducats. The book was "nothing but Hieroglyphicks," his son recalled, and Dee could not "make it out."[1]

* Rudolf II, Holy Roman Emperor. Around 1586, he paid 600 ducats for a book—supposedly by Roger Bacon (English philosopher, scientist, and Franciscan friar, 1214–1292). It was entirely in cipher.[2]

* Athanasius Kircher, a Jesuit scholar famous for translating Egyptian hieroglyphics (although his translations were all wrong). Around 1666, a friend sent him an indecipherable book once owned by Rudolf II.

* Wilfred M. Voynich, London book dealer and expert on medieval manuscripts. He bought the book (with a letter to Kircher) from a Jesuit collection in 1912 and sent photographed pages to about twenty of the world's top cryptologists.

* William R. Newbold, university professor. In 1921, he announced that the manuscript was indeed Bacon's work.

* John M. Manly, university professor. In 1931, he showed fatal errors in Newbold's reading and concluded that Bacon could not possibly have written it.[3]

According to a 2009 carbon analysis, the manuscript was written on fifteenth-century parchment long after Bacon died.[4] We don't know who wrote it or in what language. Could it be in an unknown "north Germanic dialect"[5] or "an extinct dialect of the Mexican language Nahuatl"?[6] Scholars disagree.[7] Some think it might be an invented language. It could simply be gibberish produced by an autistic monk.[8]

Or it could be a hoax. Psychologist Gordon Rugg argued in 2003 that a sixteenth-century con artist could have created the book in just three or four months to fool Emperor Rudolf—those 600 ducats

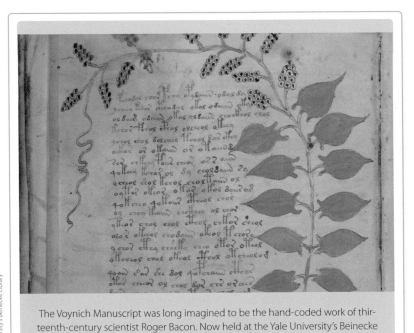

The Voynich Manuscript was long imagined to be the hand-coded work of thir-teenth-century scientist Roger Bacon. Now held at the Yale University's Beinecke Library, it is written on parchment dating from the fifteenth century.

Yale University's Beinecke Library

A Question of Motives

Ashmolean Museum, Oxford

John Dee, astrologer to Queen Elizabeth I of England, admired Roger Bacon. Did he try to decipher the Voynich Manuscript under the impression that it was Bacon's work?

Why have investigators assumed that the Voynich Manuscript is written in cipher? Partly because it looks like a language, and partly because so many fifteenth- and sixteenth-century Europeans had reasons to hide information. For instance:

• Nations had political and military secrets. Elizabeth's spy-master, Sir Francis Walsingham, used ciphers—and John Dee worked for Walsingham.

• Merchants had trade secrets. So did alchemists (Chapter 9), who used codes and allegorical language to make sure only qualified readers would understand their experiments.

• Scientists arrived at research findings that contradicted Church doctrine. To silence dangerous scientists, the Church might forbid them to teach and publish (like Roger Bacon in the thirteenth century), keep them under house arrest (like Galileo in the seventeenth), or worse.

• Protestants, heretics, and suspected witches could be burned alive for their deviations from Church doctrine.

Spies, witches, merchants, alchemists, astronomers, all had good reasons to encode their messages, so it's reasonable to guess that an unreadable manuscript is in cipher.

would be worth about $30,000 today.[9] Or an earlier hoaxster could have produced the book for some other reason. Maybe a healer or magician carried it from village to town, using it as a prop to give people an impression of his learning.

Most investigators still believe there's a real message coded in the manuscript. In 2014, linguist Stephen Bax announced that he had deciphered ten words—in two years. It was just a beginning, he admitted, but it showed "that the manuscript is not a hoax, as some have claimed." He saw it as "probably a treatise on nature, perhaps in a Near Eastern or Asian language."[10]

Later in 2014 Sukhwant Singh asserted that the book is written in a mix of ancient languages from the Sindh region of what is now Pakistan. He said it is a compilation of knowledge passed down through the generations from one "Holy Man" to the next, and was carried to Europe by the Romani.[11] Maybe. Impolitely known as "gypsies," the Romani migrated to Europe in the Middle Ages.[12]

If the Voynich Manuscript was written to deceive an audience, then it was a truly elaborate piece of fakery. But unless or until a translation of the work gains general support, we can't be sure what its purpose was. What if the book was written for an audience that understood it? Or what if it was written with no thought of an audience at all?

Invented Languages

Would anybody really invent a language? Yes. In the nineteenth century, L. L. Zamenhof constructed Esperanto. He wanted to create an easy-to-learn language that didn't belong to any one nation and could "foster peace and international understanding between people with different languages."[13] Others may invent languages for pleasure or intellectual curiosity. J. R. R. Tolkien invented both languages and scripts, and then he invented the elves, dwarves, and hobbits of Middle Earth to speak them.[14] Who would have taken on such an elaborate project in the fifteenth or sixteenth century, and why?

Books on display at the 2008 World Esperanto Congress.

Ziko van Dijk

Was Lambert Simnel a Lost Prince?

On May 24, 1487, an unlikely event took place in Dublin, Ireland. A ten-year-old calling himself Edward of Warwick was crowned king of England. Shouldn't that have happened in London?

He had princely manners and claimed to be a nephew of the late kings Edward IV and Richard III. Anglo-Irish residents of Dublin cheered him in the streets. Then, with the earl of Lincoln and other backers, the boy's army invaded England.

Crowning a king of England in Ireland was unheard of, but crowning a new king of England was almost routine in the 1400s. There had been Henry V (1413), Henry VI

Hailed as Edward of Warwick, rightful king of England, Lambert Simnel was carried through the streets of Dublin to his coronation.

(1422), Edward IV (1461), Henry VI again (1470), Edward IV again (1471), Richard III (1483), and Henry VII (1485). The dates point to a story. Henry VI was only nine months old when his father died, leaving him king of England and head of the House of Lancaster. Young Henry lost a war with France and suffered a mental breakdown. His cousins, the House of York, thought they could do better, and civil war broke out in England: the Wars of the Roses. In 1471 it seemed that the white rose of York had finally beaten the red rose of Lancaster.

But the Yorks were a dysfunctional family, plagued by disappearances and rumors of murder. Edward IV had two brothers, George and Richard. George was executed for treason in 1478, leaving his three-year-old son, Edward of Warwick, under the protection of Richard. Edward IV died in April 1483 (of pneumonia or typhoid or poison or overeating), leaving his two sons under the protection of Richard. By the end of June, Richard was king of England. His three nephews disappeared from public view.

Reenacting the Battle of Stoke Field, where supporters of alleged impersonator Lambert Simnel failed to overcome the forces of King Henry VII.

Mark Abel

In 1485, Henry VII—Henry Tudor—ousted Richard at the Battle of Bosworth Field. Henry was descended from the Lancasters, and he married a York. He hoped he could unite the families and end the civil wars. But anybody who wanted to topple him would support Richard's nephews, if they could be found. As long as they lived, they were a danger.

So when word of the boy in Ireland reached him in February 1487, Henry promptly called a Great Council—a meeting of important advisors and leaders. He told them the boy was an impostor, a craftsman's son named Lambert Simnel. An Oxford priest had trained the boy to

Henry Tudor's Claim to the Throne

National Portrait Gallery

Henry VII was the first Tudor king of England—but did he have a right to the throne? His father had royal blood, but it was French. Henry's mother had English royal blood, but it was illegitimate.

In theory the law of succession was simple: the crown passed from a king to his eldest legitimate son. If that son died childless, the second son (and his descendants) would be next in line.[5] But what if a king had no children, or only daughters? (Henry I left England to his daughter Matilda, and from 1135 to 1154, her cousin Stephen fought her for it.) What if a rightful king turned out to be a disastrous king? (Richard II,

Henry VII holds the Tudor double rose, combining the white rose of York and the red of Lancaster.

Henry VI, and Richard III were all seen as dreadful kings—especially by those who seized their crowns.)

Henry VII did not have a strong claim to the throne by right of descent, but he seized it by right of conquest. Then he held onto it by persistent nation-building; he was an able ruler. Rightful heir or not, Henry VII left England stronger than he found it.

impersonate royalty and taken him to meet Yorkist supporters in Ireland. The priest confessed this to the Council. It was all a Yorkist conspiracy, Henry said. He brought out a boy he said was the real Edward of Warwick, alive and in good health.[1] All was done to convince the world that the *real* state of affairs was open and aboveboard.

But was it? To this day, people wonder what truly became of Richard III's nephews. Did Richard have them murdered? Did Henry? Was the pretender's name really Lambert Simnel? (It sounds like a joke; a simnel is a fruit cake.) Did the priest come up with the whole idea, or were powerful Yorkists behind it from the beginning? The sources are sketchy and unreliable.[2] Henry had his agents destroy at least one record, the acts of the 1487 assembly leading to that Dublin coronation.[3]

On June 16 the rebels met Henry's forces at the Battle of Stoke and lost.[4] The Earl of Lincoln was killed, and Lambert Simnel became a scullion boy in Henry's kitchens. The other boy's fate is unknown.

The History of Crowland Abbey: A Forged Source?

One primary source for the Wars of the Roses may itself be a partial hoax: the history of Crowland (or Croyland) Abbey.[6] It records the abbey's life over hundreds of years, and has been used to study many facets of medieval life, ranging from agricultural productivity to England's Jewish community. But nineteenth-century scholars concluded that much of it was a forgery[7] intended to prove Crowland's ownership of lands also claimed by Spalding Priory.

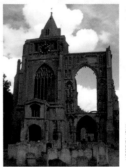

Crowland Abbey, founded in the eighth century, has been destroyed, rebuilt, and restored over the centuries. Are its records a reliable source for the Wars of the Roses?

Calling for a reassessment, a twentieth-century scholar wrote, "Most communities found it expedient to forge at some time in their history," but the monks of Crowland had claimed only lands that already belonged to them.[8] They were not trying to rewrite history, but to replace documents that had been lost to time.

Michelangelo Fakes an Antiquity

Imagine finding an unknown work by Michelangelo, the artist who painted the ceiling of the Sistine Chapel. His great marble statues *David* and *Pietà* are famous, but some of his works are lost. His statue of Pope Julian II was melted down for ammunition;[2] other pieces are rediscovered at rare intervals. A battered fountain in New York City was identified as a Michelangelo in 1996,[3] as was a pair of bronze panther riders in an English museum in 2015. "You have to be pretty brave to even contemplate that they could be work by an artist of the magnificence and fame and importance of Michelangelo," said a museum authority.[4] But if you're right, the works are suddenly more valuable and look even more beautiful than they did before.

But in 1495, Michelangelo was only a gifted young artist in Florence, competing with Italy's other gifted young artists for good jobs. Wanting to sell a new sculpture for the highest price he could, he tried to pass it off as the work of somebody more respected.

And who was more respected? The sculptors of ancient Rome. Centuries had battered the splendid marble buildings and statues of Rome. Pope Gregory the Great (540–604) ordered that "images of demons" should be destroyed. The Roman gods were considered demons then, and their broken statues made handy building materials or ships' ballast.[5] But 900 years later, anybody who found a Roman statue would dig

Domenico Fetti

Cupid sleeps like a statue in the lower right-hand corner of Domenico Fetti's *Vertumnus and Pomona*. Fetti was the Duke of Mantua's court painter, and would have seen Michelangelo's *Sleeping Cupid*. Ruth Rubinstein suggests that this could be a picture of it—the best we have.[1]

it up carefully. Collectors paid lavishly for ancient marbles, and artists studied them for inspiration. Even copies had market value.[6]

The young Michelangelo studied a collection in the Medici garden, where there was an antique *Sleeping Cupid*.[7] Perhaps his own *Sleeping Cupid* was a copy of that one; he had copied other classical statues. His work was as good as any ancient Roman's—and when he heard that it would fetch a better price if people thought it *was* an ancient Roman's, he made it look like an antique. A dealer, Baldassare del Milanese, bought it for 30 ducats and sold it to Cardinal Riario, an avid collector, for 200 ducats.[8]

In the end, nobody seemed completely happy with that deal. Michelangelo thought Baldassare should share some of the profit; Baldassare refused. Then Riario began to suspect his *Cupid* was made by a modern Florentine, not an ancient Roman after all, and he returned it to Baldassare for a refund. Michelangelo offered to buy it back; Baldassare refused.

Was that what Michelangelo hoped for all along? Perhaps he even helped expose the hoax. He lost money in the short term, but the scandal enhanced his reputation for artistry; wealthy patrons began offering him jobs. Indeed, Cardinal Riario invited him to Rome. The not-so-ancient *Cupid* helped launch Michelangelo's career.[9]

The *Cupid* was acquired in 1502 by Isabella d'Este, who said that "for a modern piece" the *Cupid* had "no equal."[10] It was bought for Charles I of England in the 1630s, and there the trail goes cold. Much of the royal art collection was lost when the Palace of Whitehall burned in 1698.[11]

Could Michelangelo's *Sleeping Cupid* have survived? Probably we will never know. But if anybody finds it and proves its identity, its value will be increased because it was made by Michelangelo. Things have changed since he could raise the price of his work by pretending it wasn't his.

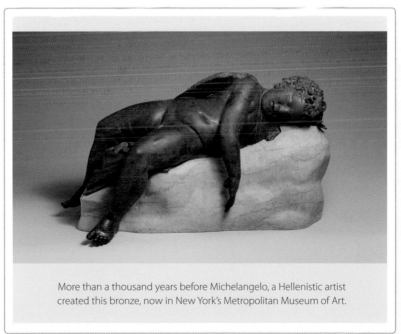

More than a thousand years before Michelangelo, a Hellenistic artist created this bronze, now in New York's Metropolitan Museum of Art.

Metropolitan Museum of Art

A Patriotic Monk Glorifies His Hometown

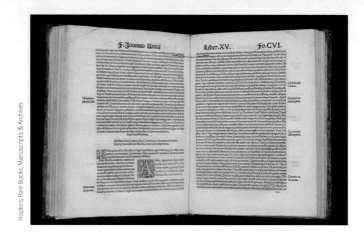

Hopkins Rare Books, Manuscripts, & Archives

Michelangelo was a great sculptor, but he was not much of a scam artist compared with Annius of Viterbo (1432–1502), a Dominican monk and loyal booster of his hometown in Italy. In 1493 he dug up not one but several carefully planted marble statues illustrating the area's legendary past.[12] But in the Annius version of history, it wasn't only pagan gods who distinguished the place. He forged documents in "ancient Chaldean, Etruscan, and Egyptian"— languages he didn't even know—and then wrote translations and commentaries to "prove" that the Biblical Noah had ended up right there in Viterbo.[13] It was easier to get away with such forgeries when most people couldn't read their own language (let alone ancient Etruscan), but critics doubted Annius from the beginning, and he was widely discredited before 1600.

A Mythical Island Appears on Maps of the North Atlantic

Was it a hoax, or did a Venetian navigator visit America long before Columbus? According to the story, Nicolò Zeno set sail for England and Flanders in 1380, a century after those earlier Venetians, the Polos, explored Asia and served Kublai Khan. Blown off course and wrecked on Frislanda, he was saved by Zichmni, ruler of the "Porlanda" islands and the "Duchy of Sorant," who was invading Frislanda, "an Island much larger than Ireland." Zichmni hired Nicolò as his navigator, and Nicolò recruited his brother Antonio. After Nicolò died in 1394, Antonio sailed with Zichmni west from Greenland to find the rumored shores of Estotiland and Drogeo.[1] (They found cannibals in Drogeo.)

Antonio's papers moldered in the family archives for more than a century. Another Nicolò Zeno, as a boy, even tore some of them up. But in 1558 he published a narrative based on surviving letters, and to help readers understand it, he included his ancestors' navigational chart.

The chart was not perfect,[2] but it seemed more complete than other maps of the North Atlantic. Mercator and Ortelius, two influential cartographers, put "Frisland" on their maps. In 1570 Ortelius also showed Estotiland, which he identified with Labrador.[3] (But if Estotiland was Labrador, Drogeo would have been Newfoundland. Were there cannibals in Newfoundland?)

England took notice. Since Portugal and Spain claimed all southerly trade routes, England hoped to find another route to China.[4] Explorer

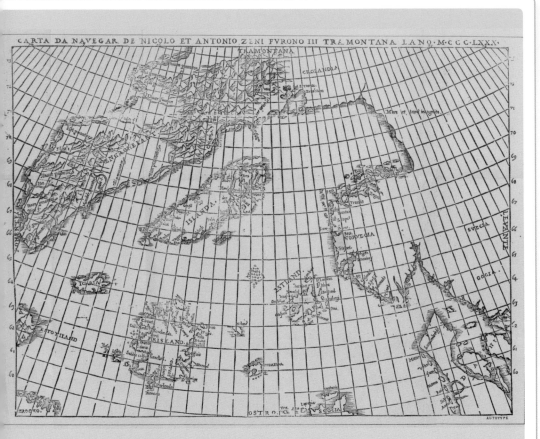

CARTA DA NAVEGAR DE NICOLO ET ANTONIO ZENI FVRONO III TRE MONTANA L A NO·M·C C C·LXXX·

In 1558 Nicolò Zeno published a copy of his ancestors' navigational chart. Supposedly made a century before Columbus, it was good enough to mislead legitimate mapmakers and hapless explorers.

Martin Frobisher searched for the Northwest Passage, carrying Mercator's 1569 map along for reference.[5] Like Columbus, who carried Marco Polo's misleading narrative, Frobisher drew some false conclusions as he tried to match what he saw with what he'd read. Where was Frislanda?

A sixteenth-century map could be wrong without being a deliberate hoax. Sailors then had no way of determining longitude at sea; they could not know exactly how far west a new island was. Explorers drew maps of the coastlines they found, but drawing an accurate map is not easy. And even a good map could get distorted when copied by hand before the invention of print. With printed maps, what was discovered could stay discovered.[6]

It took nearly 200 years to get past the influence of the Zeno map,[7] and even then, scholars struggled to match what they saw in that chart and narrative to what they found in other sources. Where was Frislanda, really? Many nineteenth-century scholars argued for the Faroe Islands, but one said Iceland,[8] while another said it was Friesland, on the European mainland.[9] And who was Zichmni? Many identified him with Henry Sinclair, Earl of the Orkneys.[10] The younger Nicolò just misread the unfamiliar word "Sinclair" (or "D'Orkney") in old handwriting, they said. Some even thought "Sinclair" could sound like the Wabanaki culture god "Glooscap," which would prove he'd been to America—wouldn't it?

In 1898, Frederic William Lucas, a British lawyer and amateur geographer, proved the story was a fabrication when he uncovered literary sources for the Zeno narrative and earlier maps used to create the brothers' chart. Then Antonio da Mosto checked Venetian archives and clinched the case: the elder Nicolò Zeno did not die in the north in 1394, because he was facing embezzlement charges in Venice at the time.[11]

What was the motive? Nicolò the younger may have wanted to glorify his ancestors or his hometown—Columbus was supposed to have come from Genoa, the rival of Venice—while

A Nova Scotia monument commemorates Henry Sinclair's alleged landing.

Dennis Jarvis

users of the map may have had more practical motives. (The English used maps to claim North American land rights.)[12] And scholars of today who still argue for the narrative's truth, even if there's no Frislanda, may be lured by the story's romance or the sheer fun of solving puzzles.

Athanasius Kircher's map of Atlantis, in the middle of the Atlantic Ocean. The map is oriented with south at the top.

The Atlantic Ocean has always been full of mythical islands. Some were huge. Atlantis, which (according to Plato) lay beyond the Pillars of Hercules and sank beneath the sea more than 11,000 years ago, was supposed to be larger than Asia and Africa combined.[13] Some were tiny and quick to vanish—if you land on a whale (as St. Brendan reportedly did), it may submerge; an iceberg could melt out from under you or drift away so you can't find it on your return journey. Farthest to the north lay Thule, a challenging destination ever since the fourth century BC. Like Frislanda, it moved about on the charts and has been identified with various places: Norway, Orkney, Shetland, Iceland, or Greenland. (Nazi occultists believed Thule was the birthplace of the Aryan race, but they got this idea from the Oera Linda book, a nineteenth-century hoax.)[14]

Some mythic islands were known to Renaissance mapmakers from throwaway lines in ancient texts. Others may have been mirages, and—considering how difficult it was to determine the exact location of an island without knowing longitude—the same landmass could appear more than once on a map. Buss Island, known from Frobisher's 1578 voyage, could have been the southern tip of Greenland.[15] However an island myth began, it was hard to disprove in those days before GPS and Google Maps.

Secrets of an Imaginary Alchemist

Modern chemistry is a science. Chemists observe phenomena, develop theories to explain them, and test their theories. They also communicate their methods and findings openly. Openness lets new scientists build on established work, and that is how science progresses.

Before chemistry came alchemy, a more secretive pursuit. It flourished in the Roman Empire as early as the third century AD, developed in Islamic countries during the Middle Ages, and was reintroduced to western Europe in the twelfth century. Alchemists had high ambitions, seeking to turn lead into gold and to discover an elixir of life.

Hopes of riches and long life often give rise to fraud, and al-Jawbari's *Revelation of Secrets* warned against alchemical cheats and swindles as early as 1220.[1] False alchemists would hide gold in charcoal to make it look as if their work was successful and deserved funding. They would talk people into giving them enough gold to make a substance that would transmute other metals into gold—and then they would leave town, taking the gold with them. Pope John XXII issued a decretal against crooked alchemists in 1317, but to little avail.[2]

Meanwhile, honest alchemists worked with dyes, mining, and other crafts. Like modern chemists, they observed, experimented, and tested.[3] Their theories were wrong; they didn't know about atoms, so they didn't realize that each metal was a separate element. Instead, they thought all metals were made of mercury and sulfur in various proportions. If lead and gold were made of the same things, why couldn't lead turn into gold?

To protect trade secrets and dodge trouble with Church and state authorities, they hid their meaning in coded language and allegorical stories so only fellow alchemists would understand them. As an added precaution, alchemists often wrote under pseudonyms—often "the names of revered (and safely dead) figures,"[4] but sometimes made-up names.

One famous alchemical hoax had nothing to do with stolen gold and everything to do with plagiarism and fake identity. An important treatise of 1604, the *Triumphal Chariot of Antimony*, told how to prepare

Roy G. Neville Historical Chemical Library, Chemical Heritage Foundation

In this woodcut from Valentine's *Of the Great Stone*, the rooster symbolizes gold, the fox symbolizes acid, and a non-alchemist should think twice about an experiment that involves the dragon.

many compounds of antimony and how to use those compounds in medicine.[5] The author was supposedly a German monk named Basil Valentine (which means "mighty king") who lived in the 1400s. His

An alchemist in his laboratory, painted by David Teniers the Younger (1610–1690).

Chemical Heritage Foundation

books were first published after 1599, when they were found in the Erfurt (Germany) chapterhouse (the monks' meeting space).[6]

Modern scholars doubt that Valentine ever existed. No record of him has been found in the monastery rolls,[7] and his references to his own life seem anachronistic.[8] So who wrote the *Triumphal Chariot*?

The simplest and most plausible answer is that it was written or co-authored by its publisher and editor, Johann Thölde, a chemist himself and owner of a saltworks in Thuringia.[9] (By 1600, alchemists were adding salt to their mercury and sulfur.) Thölde wrote a four-part work about salts called *Haliographia* (1603–1618), with three volumes under his own name and the fourth under the name "Basilius Valentinus."[10] He knew enough to write the parts of *Triumphal Chariot* that weren't plagiarized.

Whoever Basil Valentine really was, his greatest crime was copying the ideas of Paracelsus (1493–1541).[11] Since Valentine supposedly lived earlier, it was Paracelsus who became known as a plagiarist.

By the 1600s, chemistry was separating from alchemy. Robert Boyle, Isaac Newton, and other important thinkers drew on alchemy for some of the ideas and techniques that fed the Scientific Revolution (the beginning of which is often traced to the publication in 1543 of Nicolaus Copernicus's *On the Revolutions of the Heavenly Spheres*), but the way they practiced science was changing.

Paracelsus, Scientific Rebel

Musée de France

The famous doctor Paracelsus outraged conservative physicians and scientists. They were quick to believe that he'd plagiarized the work of Basil Valentine, but did Basil Valentine ever exist?

Paracelsus (1493–1541) was a great physician who outraged the medical experts of his day. He had no respect for authority. He threw out treatments that doctors had used for centuries and relied on direct observation to figure out what worked best. His adopted name "Paracelsus" implies that he put himself on a level with Celsus, a famous first-century doctor. His real name was Philippus Aureolus Theophrastus Bombastus von Hohenheim, and his enemies thought he was bombastic. But he founded the discipline of toxicology, and he was an important chemist. He drew his information not just from ancient theorists, but from sources like mine workers who applied chemical processes.[12] Like his phantom rival Valentine, Paracelsus was the author (or supposed author) of many books published after his death.

The Stagecraft of Athanasius Kircher

Athanasius Kircher was not a modest man. As a Jesuit priest, he always praised God and Mary for saving him from drowning, galloping horses, gangrene, sectarian violence, and other dangers. But he praised himself for his knowledge of mathematics, science (which in those days was called "natural philosophy"), and ancient languages. He called himself "master of a hundred arts," and he loved impressing rich patrons and fellow scholars with his brilliance.

He was born in Germany in the seventeenth century. Witches were burned then; Protestants fought Catholics and each other; and the Thirty Years' War (1618–1648) ripped through Europe like a plague, leaving death and poverty behind it. You could risk your life by saying the earth circled the sun: Galileo was tried in 1633. But literacy was on the rise, and knowledge was exciting. The printing press, new in the 1450s, was filling Europe with books—Kircher would write more than thirty of them.[1] Books printed in modern languages such as French, German, and English meant that you didn't have to learn Latin before learning to read.[2]

Kircher learned Latin, Greek, and Hebrew. He also learned Arabic, Syriac, Coptic, and (he said) even ancient Egyptian. He deciphered hieroglyphics (he said) with the help of an ancient rabbinical work that he didn't show to other scholars and a printed illustration that depicted the original Egyptian markings incorrectly. How could you trust Kircher's translations?[3] But a friend even sent him the Voynich Manuscript to decipher (Chapter 5).

Kircher had the soul of a stage magician—or a hoax artist. He would take great pains to create a dazzling effect. In 1633, he showed off a clock powered by a sunflower seed that was drawn unerringly to the sun. (The clock was really a compass, powered by a hidden lodestone. To make it tell time, you first had to know the time.[4]) He enjoyed creating illusions, from talking statues to magic lantern displays that drove cats crazy.

From the book *Mundus Subterraneus*, written in 1664

With interests ranging from Egyptology to volcanology, Athanasius Kircher knew a lot, believed more, and may have fallen victim to more hoaxes than he perpetrated.

Though such parlor tricks made him look like a fraud, Kircher's love of science was genuine. In 1638 an earthquake swallowed the town where his boat was about to land. Some would avoid shaky ground after this, but Kircher wanted to know how earthquakes work. Were Italy's volcanoes connected underground? He climbed into the crater of Vesuvius for a look around, and began to imagine the earth as "a kind of organism"—his word for it was *geocosm*.[5]

He was interested in everything, from what caused plague (his microscope showed the blood of victims "crowded" with tiny worms)[6] to why the Tower of Babel could never have reached the moon (building it would have taken five million lifetimes and more bricks than Earth could supply).[7] He mapped Atlantis (Chapter 8).

Kircher's Museum: A Scientific Distraction?

Athanasius Kircher's professional base for much of his life was the Collegio Romano, where he taught mathematics and Asian languages, conducted research, and presided over his own museum. The seventeenth century was an era of "Cabinets of Curiosities" or "Wonder Rooms,"[11] where kings or merchants or scientists gathered marvels from the worlds of art and nature. Exotic birds and skeletons and paintings would squeeze in around butterflies

Kircher's vast collection of obelisks, classical busts, and curiosities took up space in the Collegio Romano. When his superiors told him to consolidate, it nearly broke his heart.

and arrowheads and geodes. Kircher's museum "included the 'tail and bones' of a mermaid, which Kircher told visitors he obtained on Malta, and a brick from the Tower of Babel"[12] Some of the exhibits were devices he made himself, and he delighted in showing them off to visitors. P.T. Barnum (Chapter 18) would have loved it.

Today's museums are usually more specialized than Kircher's. Wild jumbles still exist—there's even a Museum of Jurassic Technology with a hall devoted to Kircher. But more typically, we have museums of art and museums of science, museums devoted to the history of television or witchcraft or the age of sail.

Today's science is far more specialized than Kircher's, and far more systematic. Kircher thought about ears, magnets, perpetual motion, and networked fire at the heart of the earth. He marveled at all kinds of things, and wanted to collect and study them all. He lived at a time when old ideas about the universe were being questioned. Over his lifetime a new approach to scientific research was gradually accepted—an approach that emphasized direct observation and patiently repeated experiments.[13] Kircher, quick to observe and speculate, was less apt to narrow his focus to a single line of experiments. Did this make him easier to fool?

From *Magnes*, written in 1643

Kircher said his sunflower seed clock worked because the sunflower was always attracted to the sun. But actually, to make it work he had to have a magnet, and he had to know the time already.

Even when his objects of study matched those of later scientists (like Newton, Hooke, and Leibnitz), his methods and conclusions didn't. He used experiment to debunk Paracelsus and the alchemists, but he still recommended an amulet of dried toad powder to ward off plague, and snakestone to draw out the poison of a snake bite.

Hoaxster or not, Athanasius Kircher was rumored to be the target of hoaxes.[8] One Andreas Müller reportedly "concocted an utterly unintelligible manuscript, then sent it to Kircher with a note saying it had come from Egypt, and asking for a translation. Kircher apparently produced one right away."[9] It must have been fun to trick the author of a book called *The Great Art of Knowing*, a man who studied the world "not as it was, but as it could and must have been."[10]

Dr. Beringer Reads Lying Fossils

Some hoaxes are personal, and some are downright cruel, like the trick played on Johann Bartholomew Adam Beringer (1667–1740). Beringer was dean of medicine at the University of Würzberg, in Germany, and personal physician to the prince-bishop. He was an able and respected but annoying man. He certainly annoyed two of his colleagues—J. Ignatz Roderick (Professor of Geography, Algebra, and Analysis) and Georg von Eckhart (Privy Councillor and Librarian to the Court and to the University). They thought he was "arrogant and despised them all,"[1] and they hatched a plot to humiliate him.

Knowing that Beringer paid three teenagers to bring him fossils from a nearby mountain, Roderick carved stones to resemble fossils that only an enthusiast like Beringer would believe: carvings of a dragon, a pomegranate, and a lion.[2] The hoaxsters then recruited one of the teens, Christian Zänger, to deliver some of the stones to Beringer and bury the rest where Beringer or the other youths, Niklaus and Valentin Hehn, would find them. It was a good deal for Zänger—he got paid by the hoaxsters and paid again by Beringer. When he reported a delivery, the hoaxsters laughed uproariously and paid Zänger extra.[3]

For a while, everyone was happy. Beringer, a pious man, marveled at how these unique stones revealed "the transcendence of God in lowly things."[4] His familiar mountain became a source of wonder to him. Besides the delicately petrified animals and plants that fossil hunters had found elsewhere, Beringer saw fossils carrying the images of heavenly bodies: suns, moons, stars, and comets with streaming tails. He saw fossils engraved with the name of God in Latin, Arabic, and Hebrew.[5] Skeptics warned him the stones might be forgeries, but he led them on a "pleasant jaunt to the site" to dig up marvels of their own. Didn't that prove it?

Admittedly, there were clues all along that the stones *were* fakes, and Beringer even noticed some of them. The fossils appeared on broken stones, but were hardly ever broken themselves. They fit on their individual pieces so well, Beringer said, "that one would swear they are the work of a very meticulous sculptor."[6]

The Teylers Museum in the Netherlands displays fake fossils made in 1725 to deceive Dr. Beringer.

When Beringer started writing a book, the conspirators tried to confess. Roderick even carved some new fakes and delivered them personally, trying to show Beringer how he'd been fooled. But Beringer thought the confession was the real hoax. He said Roderick was a scholarly nobody, a bitter man given to "calumny and imposture" who was "shamelessly" casting doubt on the genuine stones by copying them.[7] So Beringer published the book, submitting his findings "to the scrutiny of wise men," he wrote, "desiring to learn their verdict."[8] In his openness, at least, he was truly scientific.

Centuries later, Beringer was remembered as a fool, the victim of a schoolboy prank. It was said he died of shame when the hoax was

Interpreting Fossils in 1725

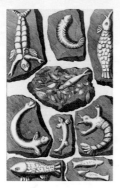

Dr. Beringer's book included images of the "fossils" he so admired. These small animals fit neatly onto their pieces of stone—almost, Beringer marveled, as if a "meticulous sculptor" had put them there

Fossils are traces of living creatures—animals, plants, and other organisms—preserved in rock. Some are tiny, like microbes; some are large, like dinosaurs. They were formed in various ways. Some are just molds of creatures that decayed, leaving no other trace; others look as if mineral had replaced their living tissue, turning them to stone. Some contain bits of feathers, teeth, and even DNA.[10]

It is unlikely that a lizard could be fossilized without losing the soft tissue from between its toes, and unlikelier still that a spider's web could be fossilized. No modern geologist would be fooled for a moment by Roderick's animal carvings. And obviously comets and letters cannot be fossilized, as they are not organisms to begin with.

But in the eighteenth century, thinkers were still debating what fossils were and what they might "teach us about the age of the earth, the nature of our planet's history, and the meaning and definition of life."[11] Maybe Beringer argued the question with Roderick and Ekhart. Maybe they had adopted newer views and were annoyed by Beringer's stubborn defense of positions that struck them as irrational.

Beringer was wrong, but not completely irrational. He thought the natural cause of fossilization didn't have to be organic. He thought it probably

This external mold of a bivalve, found in Ohio, is one kind of fossil.

involved "the refraction, distortion, and confusion" of light, as in mirrors. In that case, fossils wouldn't have to be the size of the objects whose images they preserved, and they wouldn't have to be plants or animals. In this way, Beringer explained the images of stars, comets, and even Hebrew letters—there was an "ancient Jewish cemetery" near the mountain.[12]

revealed by a "fossil" with his own name on it.[9] But what he really did in 1726 was sue the hoaxsters—we know about their "big laugh" from court testimony. In the end it was Roderick and Eckhart who had to leave town. Beringer lived on for another 14 years and published two more books.

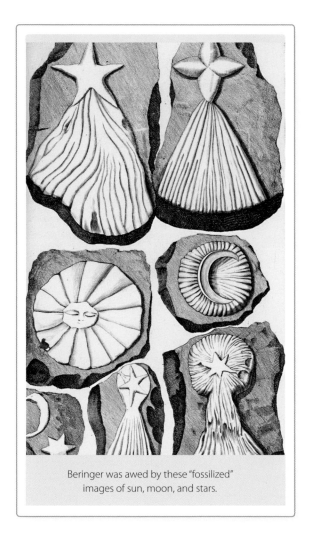

Beringer was awed by these "fossilized" images of sun, moon, and stars.

An Ancient Bard Awes the Literary World

In 1760 an unlikely best seller took Britain by storm. *Fragments of Ancient Poetry* evoked the ancient culture of Scotland—a culture the English had forcibly repressed. The Scots rebelled against English rule twice in the 1700s, and after putting down the second rebellion in 1746, the English moved to outlaw Scotland's traditions. Everything that marked the Scots as Scots became illegal, from wearing kilts to speaking Gaelic. Anti-Scottish feelings rose high in England, and Scots—especially Highlanders—were considered rude and primitive.

For the Scots, it was a time of national grief and dashed hopes. People felt displaced in their own country. But by 1760, other Europeans were also feeling displaced. The Industrial Revolution brought machines to the workplace and a growing nostalgia for the way life used to be.[1]

So *Fragments of Ancient Poetry* found an eager audience. The translator, James Macpherson (1736–1796), said he had often heard the poems recited. They were a treasure carried in human memory, handed down orally; some were supposedly composed by Ossian, the great poet who had lived 1,500 years earlier.[2] Macpherson said he had merely translated them into English.

Macpherson knew that the great Greek epics might have been woven from shorter poems handed down orally for generations like the Scottish ballads.[3] After college, he began collecting Highland poetry.

Roger Griffith

Front door of Ossian's Cave at The Hermitage, Scotland.

When the playwright John Home asked for an English translation of one poem, Macpherson gave him "The Death of Oscur." Although based on two traditional ballads, it was less a translation than an original adaptation.

Home loved it, and so did his literary friends. They kept asking for more, and they organized funding to help Macpherson find it.[4] In August 1760 he set out into the Highlands to gather manuscripts and oral transcriptions, and soon published *Fingal* (1761) and *Temora* (1763), epics based on the collected material.

Ossian had been a blind bard like Homer, Macpherson said. Ossian was also a character in the stories—son of the legendary Finn McCool and father of the heroic Oscur. His works quickly became an international sensation; his longing for lost times resonated with readers:

"Here shall I rest with my friends by the stream of the sounding rock. When night comes on the hill, when the wind is upon the heath; my ghost shall stand in the wind, and mourn the death of my friends. . . ."[5]

Macpherson rendered the poems in a rhythmic prose that sounded a little like Milton or the Bible. Ossian might have been a rude pagan bard, but his work was right in line with eighteenth-century taste. Thomas Jefferson called him "the greatest poet that ever existed," and Napoleon carried the poems with him on campaign.[6]

But the famous Samuel Johnson, who loathed Scotland, said Ossian was a hoax. If Macpherson had really translated the poems, why wouldn't he produce the manuscript? "Stubborn audacity is the last refuge of guilt," Johnson said,[7] and Ossian is remembered as "one of the most controversial and influential forgeries in the history of eighteenth-century letters."[8]

Was Johnson right? Traditional poems, songs, and stories really did exist, and Macpherson did collect them. Some people then and now consider that he was guilty of nothing worse than adapting his material rather freely in an effort to

Ossian on the bank of the Lora, invoking the Gods to the strains of a harp, as painted by François Pascal Simon Gérard in 1801.

restore it to what he believed must have been its original state.[9]

Would readers have found poems by a modern Macpherson as beautiful as the same poems by an ancient Ossian? (Would Italians in 1496 have found a statue by the living Michelangelo as beautiful as one by an ancient Roman?) If 24-year-old James Macpherson set out to hoax the world, maybe it was his way of gaining recognition for a talent that didn't quite fit the world as he found it. Between a Scottish past and an English future, he offered a melancholy dream.

England and Scotland

In *After Culloden-Rebel Hunting*, painter John Seymour Lucas shows British troops rounding up rebellious Scots. (Later in the eighteenth century, Scots would help Redcoats put down another uprising against England--in the American colonies.)

England and Scotland have shared a monarch since 1603, when James VI, the Stuart king of Scotland, became James I of England. But Protestant England was hard on the Stuarts, with their Catholic sympathies. King Charles I was executed during the English Civil War (1642–1651). King James II (James VII of Scotland) was deposed by the "Glorious Revolution" in 1688—a revolution that made it illegal for a Catholic to rule England.

In 1707 the Acts of Union joined the two nations, with England, richer and more populous, as the dominant partner. Scotland chafed under foreign rule, especially after the 1714 death of the last Stuart monarch, Queen Anne. The new king, George I, was a German who wouldn't have been in line for the throne of Great Britain if he hadn't been a Protestant, while the son and grandson of James II were Catholic. In 1715 and again in 1745, the Scots rose in support of the Stuarts. The 1746 English victory at Culloden ended any hope of a restoration, and the English attack on Highland culture embittered the Scots. The grief and loss expressed in Ossian's third-century poems struck a raw nerve in 1760.

Benjamin Franklin Pretends to Be the King of Prussia

It was in the newspaper, but could Londoners really believe that item about cod and whale fisheries in the Great Lakes? How would sea creatures get so far inland? One reader wrote in an enthusiastic description of "the grand Leap of the Whale" up Niagara Falls, "one of the finest Spectacles in Nature!"[1]

This sarcastic reader was Benjamin Franklin (1706–1790), visiting England from the Colonies in the 1760s. Known as a scientist and a politician, Franklin studied electricity, mapped the Gulf Stream, and invented bifocals. He was a genius. And, as a retired newspaperman, he knew how to use a printing press.

One of his favorite tools for swaying opinion was the literary hoax. At the age of 16, he snuck an article into print under the name of "Silence Dogood." Later he wrote an almanac under the name of "Poor Richard." In 1755, after arguing with a stubborn friend, he printed up an extra chapter of *Genesis* and tipped it into her Bible to prove that God favored tolerance.[2] And in 1790, just weeks before dying, he published an imaginary Algerian pirate's justification for kidnapping European Christians and selling them into slavery—the same justification Americans used for enslaving Africans.[3]

In October 1773, a British newspaper printed an outrageous demand from Frederick the Great, King of Prussia, that England pay taxes to Prussia. Frederick claimed that England had been settled by ancient Prussians and was therefore a colony with obligations to its parent country. He demanded that England repay Prussia for its aid against France in the Seven Years' War (1756–1763). He said all ships carrying goods to or from England must stop in Prussia to be taxed. The English must cease all trades that competed with Prussian interests: they must stop producing iron, wool, and hats. Prussian criminals, if not hanged, would be transported to England to help populate that country.[4]

Franklin, in England at the time, was chatting with friends over breakfast when a Mr. Whitehead came running in with that day's paper in his hand, crying, "Here's news for ye. Here's the king of Prussia

In this 1767 portrait by David Martin, Franklin is well dressed to do business with British aristocrats.

Benjamin Franklin's Witch Hoax

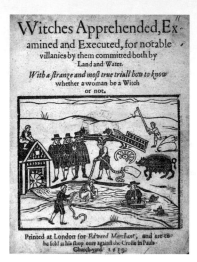

Benjamin Franklin belonged to the Age of Enlightenment, but many people in his time still believed in witchcraft, as described in this 1613 book before the English settled in Virginia and Massachusetts.

After the Salem (Massachusetts) witch trials of 1692, nobody in the Thirteen Colonies was brought to justice for witchcraft. Ben Franklin, born less than 20 years later, lived in the Age of Enlightenment—or so we like to believe. So when the *Pennsylvania Gazette* reported on a witch trial in New Jersey In 1730, the tone was humorous; the reporter (probably Franklin) assumed nobody could still believe in the old superstitions:

BURLINGTON, Oct. 12. Saturday last at Mount-Holly, about 8 Miles from this Place, near 300 People were gathered together to see an Experiment or two tried on some Persons accused of Witchcraft. It seems the Accused had been charged with making their Neighbours Sheep dance in an uncommon Manner, and with causing Hogs to speak, and sing Psalms, &c. to the great Terror and Amazement of the King's good and peaceable Subjects in this Province; and the Accusers [were] very positive that if the Accused were weighed in Scales against a Bible, the Bible would prove too heavy for them. . . . [7]

How much of this really happened? The court records are lost, but witchcraft was still a hanging offense in New Jersey and elsewhere. Pennsylvania adopted a law against it in 1718, and Franklin's effort to repeal that law in 1754 was unsuccessful.[8]

claiming a right to this kingdom." Everybody stared, including Franklin, but Whitehead suddenly looked at him and said, "I'll be hanged if this is not some of your American jokes upon us."[5] He was right.

In America, where the Seven Years' War was called the French and Indian War, the English had beaten the French at great expense. Now they were trying to recover war costs from the Americans, but Americans argued that Parliament couldn't justly tax them, since they were not represented in Parliament. Americans resented having their ships searched and their competitive trade restricted—just as the English would, if Prussia claimed dominion over them.

Franklin had written that royal proclamation while trying to negotiate tax relief and other concessions for the Colonies. He tried to win peace with humor. It didn't work—the American Revolution began in 1775—but at least Franklin enjoyed his joke.

It wasn't his last attempt to influence the English by hoax diplomacy. In 1777, Franklin set up a printing press in France, where he represented U.S. interests during and after the Revolution. Franklin wanted England to pay American civilians for war damages, and in 1782 he printed a "supplement" to a Boston newspaper. It featured a letter from an imaginary military officer describing British-incited atrocities by the Iroquois. Franklin intended this "scalping letter" to underline British responsibility for harm both to colonists and Native Americans. Sadly, it had quite a different effect. Printed and reprinted well into the nineteenth century, it was accepted as factual and fed hostility toward Native Americans.[6] A hoax is a dangerously unpredictable weapon.

The Potemkin Village: More Than Just a Pretty Façade

A Potemkin village is the quintessential hoax: a prosperous-looking settlement consisting only of false fronts, slapped up to make the place look good. The 1940s Nazi concentration camp at Theresienstadt has been called a Potemkin village: it was designed to pass Red Cross inspection, but prisoners who didn't die there of malnutrition or disease were sent on to die at Auschwitz. More recently, the term has been used for a North Korean village built to encourage South Korean defection, a fake trading floor built to impress Wall Street visitors to Enron's Houston headquarters, and other cosmetic touch-ups from Caracas (Venezuela) to Cleveland (Ohio) to Sochi (Russia).[1]

The Potemkin village is named after Prince Grigory Potemkin, a favorite of the Russian Empress Catherine II. During her reign (1762–1796) Russia expanded to the west and south, winning vast territories from Poland and the Ottoman Empire. In 1783, Catherine annexed Crimea, and in 1787 she enjoyed a long-planned tour of her new possessions.[2] Her party traveled by river, which allegedly made it easy for Potemkin—then governor of the territory—to bamboozle her "by putting up cardboard villages on the way and importing thousands of peasant serfs with their implements and cattle in order to create a picture of sham prosperity."[3] But he didn't.

Hermitage

With the help of Field Marshall Grigory Potemkin (1739–1791), Catherine the Great added vast territories to Russia. The cities and towns he established have had an undeserved reputation ever since for flimsy show. Portrait by Johann Baptist Lampi the Elder, circa 1790.

The fake village story was itself a fake, a malicious rumor that circulated at court and was published by Georg von Helbig, a Saxon envoy.[4] Catherine took a number of ambassadors on the trip, but she chose them at least partly for congeniality.[5] The bitter Helbig—like Catherine's bitter son and heir, the Grand Duke Paul—was left behind. They resented Catherine's lover, Potemkin.

But Potemkin was a man of substance, and Catherine's companions—including the French ambassador Ségur and Emperor Joseph II of Austria—saw more than cardboard cutouts. As a military commander and a diplomat, Potemkin helped win this territory; as governor after

1784, he was developing it. Ségur reported that in three years Potemkin had increased the area's population from 204,000 to 800,000 inhabitants, bringing in "Greek colonists, Germans, Poles, invalids, retired soldiers and sailors."[6] The growth has been called "unparalleled in scale, scope, and rapidity" for that pre-railroad era.[7]

Intent on absorbing the annexed lands into Russia, Potemkin was building solid towns, not cardboard villages. Catherine approved his plans for the Black Sea port of Kherson in 1778, and by May 1779 he had brought in thousands of workers, from carpenters to quarrymen; the keels of two warships were already laid down in the Kherson shipyard.[8] Two centuries later, Kherson and other "Potemkin villages" such as Nikolaev, Sebastopol, and Odessa are important cities, with shipyards, naval bases, and hundreds of thousands of residents.[9]

A Tatar cavalry bowman. The Crimean Khanate, ruled by descendants of Genghis Khan, was part of the Ottoman Empire from 1478 to 1774; it was annexed to the Russian Empire in 1783.

Muzeum Narodowe

Potemkin advised Catherine on land grants and strategic tax incentives to encourage settlement and colonization. She issued decrees that made it easier for peasants to move into the south from areas where land was scarce. Military deserters, fugitive serfs, and Cossacks who had fled abroad were offered pardon (for any offense short of murder) if they chose to reenter

Catherine II ruled Russia from 1762 to 1796, extending its boundaries with the help of advisors like Potemkin.

military service, return to their private owners, or move south. Potemkin advised against forcing serfs to return to their owners. "It would be contrary to the well-being of the state," he said; "Poland would benefit by all of them."[10]

What Catherine's entourage saw on that tour of the Crimea was a work in progress, but a work with solid foundations. It is ironic that Potemkin, that indefatigable builder and developer, is remembered for nothing more enduring than a sleazy bit of public relations. His detractors undermined Potemkin's reputation after he and Catherine were gone, and the legend attached to his name is the real hoax.

Newly Discovered Shakespeare Play Jeered by Theater-Goers

William-Henry Ireland adored his father—though he wasn't sure if Samuel Ireland really was his father. They lived in an upscale London neighborhood with Mrs. Freeman (supposedly Samuel's housekeeper and secretary; previously an earl's mistress); four children (two girls and two boys, allegedly not Mrs. Freeman's); and Samuel's collection of books, art, and antiquities that had belonged to royals and other celebrities.

Samuel had interesting friends. The children saw many stage performances, and even got small parts in one at the home of Robert Brinsley Sheridan, a famous playwright. William loved it. But his father, who considered him stupid, left him at school in France until he almost forgot his English. After his brother, Henry, died, William was brought home at last, but called by his brother's name.[1] In his memoir William referred to his father as Mr. Ireland—almost never "my father."[2]

The lonely teen tried to win his father's esteem by literary forgery.[3] Apprenticed to a lawyer, William spent most of his time idle, alone in an office full of old parchment and seals. On December 16, 1794, he gave his father a lease signed by Shakespeare. "It is impossible for me to express the pleasure you have given me," said Mr. Ireland.

So in 1795 William gave his father more and more ambitious Shakespeare memorabilia. He forged a confession of faith (making

Silvester Harding stipple engraving, 1798

William-Henry Ireland, 1775–1835.

Shakespeare a good Protestant) and personal letters (making Shakespeare a loving husband, a modest gentleman, and much appreciated by Queen Elizabeth).

Where was he finding these things? People kept asking him, and to cover his lies he had to lie more.[4] His story was that he had met a stranger, "Mr. H.," who invited him to examine some inherited legal papers and take what interested him. William found evidence deciding a lawsuit in favor of Mr. H., who rewarded him with the Shakespeare material. And who was Mr. H.? He had made William promise never to tell.

Samuel Ireland showed the documents to experts, and William heard them praise Shakespeare's language—which was really his own! It inspired him to even greater creativity. He worked fast, always afraid that somebody would come into the office and catch him in mid-forgery.

He made mistakes. William's Lord Leicester awarded Shakespeare 50 pounds two years after the real Leicester died. William showed properties "abutting" each other from opposite sides of the Thames. But he used old paper and old-looking ink, and his forgeries were not fully exposed until the worst moment possible: March 31, 1796, two days before the opening night of Shakespeare's new play, *Vortigern*.

Yes, William had written a play. Some thought Samuel himself must be the forger, but they knew there was a forger; Edmund Malone proved it in a long exposé published just before *Vortigern*'s premiere.

Vortigern opened to a full house. The jeers and catcalls didn't get bad until the fourth act, when a Saxon warrior fell in battle, the curtain fell on his body, and he started kicking. At the climax, the lead actor played some of William's most dramatic lines for laughs. By the end, the audience booed in earnest. There was no second performance.

William's father never forgave him, and neither did the "republic of letters."[5] Forging currency was a hanging offense in England. Literary forgery was not quite so severe, but this one offended national pride. "For

The legend of Vortigern featured love, war, and dragons; Ireland did his best to make it Shakespeare's.

a forger of no known social, political, or literary authority to appropriate Shakespeare's language was for a usurper . . . to contest and lay claim to the voice of Britain."[6] Although he went on to publish 67 original titles—not including translations to or from the French—William never succeeded financially and was never considered respectable.

Literary Forgery as an Eighteenth-Century Epidemic

Tate

The Death of Chatterton, by Henry Wallis (1856), imagines the end of a 17-year-old poet and forger who influenced the Romantic movement.

The creative forgers of the eighteenth century influenced each other. Macpherson's Ossian (Chapter 12) influenced Thomas Chatterton (1752–1770), and Chatterton inspired William-Henry Ireland. As a boy, Chatterton wandered in the cemetery near his charity school and imagined what Bristol had been like in the fifteenth century, when William Canynge was mayor and Thomas Rowley was sheriff. He read all he could find on almost any subject, and he wrote poetry.[7]

In 1767, apprenticed to a lawyer who left him idle most of the day, Chatterton imagined the world of Rowley and Canynge complete with its own history, geography, and wildly spelled medieval language. He invented biographies for Canynge and Rowley, and as Rowley evolved into a poet and playwright, so did Chatterton. By 1769, "Rowley" had written the historic play *Aella*. It owed more to the work of Shakespeare (1564–1612) than you'd expect from somebody writing in the 1400s, but it contained some lovely original passages. Chatterton offered some of his Rowley pieces (including one he called "perhaps the oldest dramatic Piece extant"[8]) to a London publisher; later, he offered material to writer Horace Walpole and was outraged when Walpole rejected it as a forgery. The next year Chatterton died, either of suicide (he'd threatened it more than once) or accidental overdose (he was treating himself with arsenic and opium).

In the end, Chatterton was writing more in his own voice than Rowley's, and he influenced not just later forgers but a whole literary movement. The Romantic poets Keats, Shelley, and Browning admired Chatterton's work and drew on it. Even Walpole, refusing blame for the 17-year-old poet's death, doubted "that there ever existed so master a genius."[9]

An Astronomer Discovers Intelligent Life on the Moon

Sir John Herschel (1792–1871), son of astronomer William Herschel, was an astronomer himself. He was also a mathematician, chemist, photographer, and botanist—one of the most consulted scientists in the world. In 1833, he took his family to remote South Africa, where he could map the skies of the southern hemisphere, but the world didn't forget him. Charles Darwin consulted with him when the H.M.S. *Beagle* visited Cape Town in 1836.[1] And in 1835, New York City was mesmerized by news of Herschel's latest discovery: life on the moon.

Herschel learned of his discovery months after New York did. It was the Age of Sail, and the electric telegraph didn't come into commercial use until after 1837,[2] so Herschel had no way of knowing that he had invented an incredibly powerful telescope, built it with funding from the king, and set it up in South Africa.[3] He didn't realize that his fictitious assistants had filled an imaginary supplement to the *Edinburgh Journal of Science* with reports of his work, or that the story had been serialized in America.

While Herschel was reading Charles Lyell's *Principles of Geology* and thinking about the gradual evolution of languages and species,[4] New Yorkers were reading about what Herschel saw in his fantastic telescope: the moon's birds and bison, its blue unicorn, its beavers (who walked upright and used fire), and its humans. The humans were about

The *New York Sun* pretended this image of "Lunar animals and other objects" was copied from sketches of Herschel's discovery in the respected *Edinburgh Journal of Science*.

four feet tall, with yellow faces, copper-colored fur, and thin wings. New Yorkers learned to call this new species *Vespertilio-homo*, or "bat-man."[5]

The Sun ran installments for almost a week, starting on August 25, 1835.[6] A couple of Yale professors investigated and were fooled. Then on August 31 a rival newspaper unmasked the author, *Sun* reporter Richard Adams Locke. He said he meant to satirize "overheated scientific prose,"[7] but another obvious motive was to drum up business. James Gordon Bennett of the *New York Herald* attacked the fraud without much hurting *The Sun*—controversy was good for sales—but he did start a discussion of journalistic ethics that bore later fruit.[8]

As of 1835, New York City had more than 270,000 people and 47 newspapers—11 of them dailies and some of them dull. There were "trade papers, abolitionist papers, newspapers affiliated with political parties, a Catholic paper and an anti-Catholic paper, immigrant papers, a labor paper, and business sheets."[9] *The Sun* was one of the new penny papers, and its goal was to be more affordable and more interesting than the six-cent papers. Even with fast new steam-driven printing presses, it took a lot of one-cent sales to make a profit.

Locke's story did boost sales. Before the hoax, circulation had leveled off at about 8,000.[10] By August 29, 1835, the paper had 19,360 buyers for the fourth and most sensational installment; a year later it was publishing 27,000 copies a day. Readers thought twice about believing what *The Sun* printed, but it was bigger than the *Times* of London

Voyages to the Moon Deemed More Plausible Than Microorganisms in a Drop of Water

This image of Hans Pfaall and his balloon illustrated an essay on Edgar Allen Poe by Jules Verne.

Bibliothèque Nationale de France

The Great Moon Hoax had precedents. Godwin's *Man in the Moone* (1638) described "curious, winged, but man-like inhabitants."[14] Cyrano de Bergerac's *The Other World: Comical History of the States and Empires of the Moon* (1657) suggested some imaginative ways to reach space— the hero tried strapping bottles of dew to his person, launching a flying machine from a cliff, and even focusing solar energy through mirrors.[15] But the closest precedent was a June 1835 hoax in *The Southern Literary Messenger*. "The Unparalleled Adventure of One Hans Pfaall" was a story by Edgar Allen Poe, and his hero reached space in a balloon.[16] Poe did not aim at plausibility; he wrote in a satiric vein, and used names like "Professor Rub-a-Dub" and "Sauerkraut Alley." Who could believe these things?

Locke's hoax upstaged Poe's partly because *The Sun* had a much wider circulation than *The Southern Literary Messenger*, but largely because Locke was more believable—his language sounded more scientific. As science advanced, people were just as likely to disbelieve genuine reports as to believe false ones. *The Sun's* readers didn't believe an earlier 1835 story about "microorganisms living in a drop of water."[17]

A miffed Poe accused Locke of plagiarism and made a long list of scientific errors in the *Sun* report. Years later, however, he said Locke's hoax had helped establish the penny papers—and the penny papers weren't really about science.[18]

(circulation 17,000) and all 11 of New York's six-cent papers put together (combined circulation 21,000).[11]

The Great Moon Hoax gave New Yorkers what they may have wanted even more than reliable news—something pleasant to think about. The city was dirty and crowded. Hogs ran in the cobbled streets and gangs rioted there. Locke's moon was clean, lovely, and peaceful.

The story circulated around the world, and poor Herschel was more consulted than ever. He told his Aunt Caroline he'd been "pestered from all quarters with that ridiculous hoax about the Moon—in English French Italian & German!!"[12] But his wife Margaret was charmed by Locke's "very clever piece of imagination," and added, "It is only a great pity that it is not true, but if grandsons ride on as grandfathers have done, as wonderful things may yet be accomplished."[13]

April Fools

Contemporary news media still run stories as far-fetched as the Great Moon Hoax, but they usually do it on April 1. In 1977, *The Guardian* ran a seven-page special on the archipelago of San Serriffe, an Indian Ocean paradise where the main islands (Upper Caisse and Lower Caisse), the capital (Bodoni), and even the president for life (General Pica) were named after printers' terms. The section carried ads; one for a "Reader in Lunar Spectroscopy" for the local university drew many inquiries. (Job seekers may have been attracted by the inclusion of "free housing and use of outrigger.")

The fun is not limited to print. On April 1, 2005, National Public Radio reported that New England's maple trees were exploding in the forests because they had been left untapped. On April 1, 2000, Google launched a new search tool called MentalPlex, because "Typing in queries is so 1999." But there were bugs in the mind-reading system, and users who tried it got error messages such as "Brainwaves received in analog. Please re-think in digital" or "Insufficient conviction. Please clap hands 3 times, while chanting 'I believe' and try again."[19]

Part of the entertainment is finding the clues—one of which, of course, is the date. How else does a reader come to realize that a story is not genuine new information, but a joke? Prior knowledge may help us distinguish facts from absurdities, but it isn't always easy. Newly discovered facts often sound stranger than fiction.

The *Walam Olum*: 90 Generations of Oral History or a Hoax?

Sometimes a hoax is benevolent. Take the *Walam Olum*, or "Red Record," that followed 90 generations (3,600 years) of Lenni Lenape history. It traced their epic migration from Asia across the Bering Sea to the Delaware River.[1] The *Walam Olum* could be seen as evidence that Native Americans deserved better treatment from whites. It showed that the Lenni Lenape had their own civilization before Europeans arrived. They were literate people—not savages.

In 1836, when it was published, the Lenni Lenape and other Native Americans were being forcibly moved from their traditional lands in eastern states to new territories west of the Mississippi. President Andrew Jackson had signed the 1830 Indian Removal Act into law.[2] The *Walam Olum* was a well-meant hoax, but it could not stop the process.

The author was probably Constantine Samuel Rafinesque (1783–1840), a European immigrant who was outraged by policies that compelled Indians "to remove, to emigrate, disperse, sell their lands and homes, at one tenth of the value."[3] He produced a manuscript version of the *Walam Olum* in 1833 and then published it in the first volume of *The American Nations*. He said the work had been handed down in two forms: a set of 183 pictographs etched on a bundle of cedar sticks, and an accompanying chant. The Indians had given the original sticks to the "late Dr. Ward of Indiana" in 1820, and Ward gave them to Rafinesque, who copied them. Somebody else recited the chant; Rafinesque transcribed it, studied Lenape, and produced an English translation.

Skeptics doubted the work was genuine. Nobody could identify Rafinesque's informants; nobody saw the actual sticks. Rafinesque was the only source. He had a spotty education and seemed too obsessively interested in everything to be reliable. He claimed he knew forty languages and had cured himself of tuberculosis.[4] He published at least 939 items—ranging from poems to a book on Ohio River fish—and left more than 250 manuscripts. He has been called both "an arrant lunatic" and the "greatest field biologist of his time."[5] He named thousands of species. Always fascinated by prehistoric America, he tried to decipher Mayan script and explored sites of the Mound Builders who lived in the Mississippi and Ohio River valleys before Columbus; he catalogued 148 ancient earthworks in Kentucky.[6]

Constantine Samuel Rafinesque said he translated the Walam Olum ("Red Record") from Lenape into English. Did he?

Yet the *Walam Olum* appealed to Native American sympathizers, who explained away any signs of fraud. If it was written in nonstandard Lenape, they said, it must be a lost dialect. If there was no reference to it in the oral traditions of the people, those traditions must have been disrupted by European interference.[7] To prove the document authentic, they searched endlessly for traces of Dr. Ward.[8] One philanthropist, ranking the *Walam Olum* with Homer for historic value, financed a twenty–year study by the Indiana Historical Society.[9] While the document may not have achieved its author's ambition, it was widely believed for over a century.

But in 1994, David Oestricher showed that it was a fabrication. The content was a mixture of world mythology and Lenape traditions published by a missionary; the pictographs were a mixture of Chinese, Egyptian, Mexican, and Native American symbols that Rafinesque could have found in books; and the language seemed to have been translated from English to Lenape, not Lenape to English.[10]

There's a faint possibility that Rafinesque was merely a dupe, but that's unlikely. The *Walam Olum* reflects his skills and his beliefs. He did believe that Native Americans came to America across the Bering Strait (as in fact they did, much earlier than he thought). He believed they shared a heritage

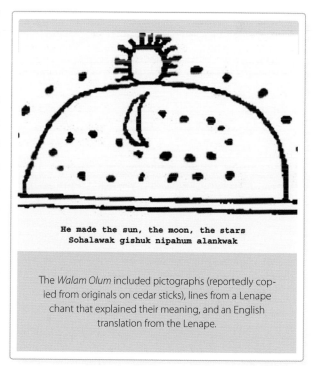

He made the sun, the moon, the stars
Sohalawak gishuk nipahum alankwak

The *Walam Olum* included pictographs (reportedly copied from originals on cedar sticks), lines from a Lenape chant that explained their meaning, and an English translation from the Lenape.

with Eurasians (as in fact they do). In the 1830s, he hoped this would be a political argument against the Indian Removal, but it wasn't strong enough.[11] Rafinesque may have created an epic hoax in hopes of pushing reality a little closer to his ideals.

Slanting History

It's said that "history is written by the winners." The winners and their pet historians can be counted on to make themselves look good and the losers look bad. Cleopatra was a gifted ruler, struggling to keep Egypt independent of Rome—but she lost to Octavian, so she's remembered as a woman of loose morals who clung

From around 3500 BC to AD 1500, Native Americans around the Great Lakes and flood-prone North American river valleys built impressive earthworks to support religious ceremonies, cemeteries, and towns.

to power by seducing Roman generals. The history that's come down to us justifies Octavian and demonizes Cleopatra.

The same thing happens when nations and cultures clash. The winning group becomes dominant, and schoolbooks teach a version of history that supports the dominant culture and makes the losing group look inferior or evil.[12] So U.S. history books have usually told the triumphant story of settlers who came from Europe, bringing civilization with them, and created a great democracy.[13] Less has been said about the great cities and vibrant civilizations that existed before the colonists arrived. It is more comfortable for white Americans to imagine that only about 1,000,000 people lived primitive, nomadic lives in North America, and even the "empires" farther south had barely 7,000,000 inhabitants. But the real number is probably much higher. Settlers brought smallpox and other diseases that by one estimate killed 80 to 100 million of the indigenous population—leaving traumatized survivors to defend themselves against an alien civilization.[14]

If the history schoolbooks give a biased account, maybe it's because they don't pay enough attention to primary sources.[15] Rafinesque tried to correct the political bias against Native Americans, and his ideas about their origins were closer to truth than some at the time—but since he forged his own primary source, his version is the hoax.

Was the Fejee Mermaid a Genuine Fake?

Successful hoaxes show people what they want, and who wouldn't want to see a mermaid? The mermaids of European legend were beautiful creatures. Fishermen fell in love with them, and their voices lured sailors onto the rocks. Hans Christian Andersen's 1837 story of a little mermaid won enduring popularity.

In 1842, P.T. Barnum introduced a mummified mermaid to America, and gentlemen in Charleston, South Carolina, nearly fought a duel over her.[1] It wasn't because of her beauty. She was a shriveled, blackened thing, about three feet long, and looked as if she had "died in great agony."[2] Nobody was in love with her, but they disagreed passionately about whether she was real. A Charleston newspaper editor swore she was genuine, but a local naturalist insisted she was a fraud, "a clumsy affair" smoked up by "our Yankee neighbors."[3]

Barnum (1810–1891) was a Yankee showman, an entertainer who knew that controversy sells tickets. His career took off in 1835 when he bought a slave and exhibited her for seven months as a natural wonder (161 years old!) with national significance (nurse to the infant George Washington!). Natural wonders and patriotic displays were popular. In 1841, Barnum acquired Scudder's American Museum—a wild and seedy jumble where you could see almost anything, from a two-headed lamb to a historic American flag.[4] Or a mermaid.

The mermaid belonged to Barnum's friend, Boston museum operator Moses Kimball. A sea captain had once paid Japanese sailors $6,000 for it, planning to show it profitably in Europe. But Europeans had seen such things before,[5] and the poor man's 1822 London exhibit was a financial disaster.[6] When Kimball bought it, he got Barnum to exhibit it and split the profits. If anybody could make a profit on the thing, it would be Barnum.

Barnum had his ways. He dubbed the creature a "Fejee Mermaid" and paid a man to tour the country with her, lecturing audiences about "scientific theories" of how such a creature could exist. He sent letters to newspapers. He printed up brochures and advertisements. (The mermaid looked much prettier in the ads.)

The notorious mermaid was protected by a glass bell jar, so nineteenth-century museum-goers could not feel any seam between the "human" top and the fishy tail.

And when faced with indignation and near-riot, Barnum tweaked his PR. Instead of claiming that the mermaid was real beyond all doubt, he said there was controversy, and people should see for themselves. "Who is to decide," his new advertisement

How Do You Make a Mermaid?

The Buxton Museum has a mermaid who looks rather like Barnum's, although jollier, and recently a team at the University of Lincoln ran tests to find out just what she was made of. Her hair was human, it turned out, and her teeth were filed-down bits of bone. Her eyes were probably made from mollusk shells. Her body was built around a framework of wood, and an X-ray showed her wire ribs.[11]

The Horniman museum tried DNA testing to find out if the fish part of their merman was really Japanese, but his DNA had deteriorated too much for testing. They did learn that his toothy jaw, fins, and the skin of his tail

The Buxton Museum mermaid.

came from some kind of fish. He has no monkey ancestry, but wood, clay, wire, fabric packing, and paper-maché all went into his construction.[12]

The Horniman Museum merman.

asked, "when *doctors* disagree?"[7] This was an inspired gambit. Kimball and Barnum made money on the Fejee Mermaid's road trips, and she drew yet more crowds into their museums.

Later, Barnum learned that many such "mermaids" were made in Japan; he thought their craftsmanship was "well calculated to deceive."[8]

Nowadays you can find them online, and sometimes they are still presented as real creatures, tossed ashore by hurricanes or tsunamis.[9]

But they were not originally "calculated to deceive" foreigners. Their Japanese name is *ningyo*, and they have had a place in Japanese temples for hundreds of years. The mermaid mummy at one Shinto temple may be 1,400 years old.[10] The Japanese sailors who charged $6,000 may have enjoyed defrauding that sea captain, but the *ningyo* did not really become hoaxes until they were embedded in a European and American pop culture that mixed entertainment and scientific inquiry, lectures and sideshows. Barnum gave his audience what they wanted: a genuine fake.

The Fox Sisters Invent Spiritual Telegraphy

One night in 1848, John D. Fox and his wife Margaret were kept awake by odd raps and thuds in their Hydesville, New York, farmhouse. Was somebody in the pantry? Was an intruder climbing the stairs? Having moved into the house recently, they didn't yet know its normal creaks. The parents, worried for their young daughters, took candles and searched high and low. Nothing. Mr. Fox suggested natural explanations; Mrs. Fox "concluded that the house must be haunted by some unhappy, restless spirit."[1]

Forty years later, Maggie confessed that she and Kate had made the noises—mostly by cracking their toe joints. Nobody suspected them because they were "innocent little children," she said.[2] They were hoaxing their parents for fun.

The next night the noises began as soon as the family lay down. When the girls snapped their fingers and clapped, the noises echoed. Communication was possible! Mrs. Fox challenged the "spirit" to rap out the ages of her children in order. Success. She called in neighbors, and excitement mounted. By getting the spirit to rap for "yes," the group pieced together a story: Mr. Bell, a previous tenant, had murdered a peddler and buried him in the cellar.

Some neighbors dug for the body; others protested the false accusations against Bell. By then it would have been terrifying for the girls to confess their trickery.

Thirty miles away and several weeks later, their older sister learned about the situation from a printed pamphlet. She rushed home. Leah Fox Fish was a single mother teaching music in Rochester; she knew how to cross-examine adolescents. She quickly learned the girls' secret and practiced making the noises herself. Soon she took her mother and sisters back to Rochester. The rappings, no longer confined to the haunted house, followed the girls.

Did Leah exploit her sisters as "an unworked mine of wonder and superstition,"[3] or was she sincere when she said her family had been chosen as mediums "of a new truth, which was destined to revolutionize this world, and establish a communication between the here and the hereafter"?[4] Her advertisement of a public demonstration in 1849 sounded like a P.T. Barnum promotion (Chapter 18).

Foremost among Leah's friends and supporters were Isaac and Amy Post, high-minded abolitionists and Hicksite Quakers. Open to the idea of communications from transcendent powers, they were also open to the idea of reasonable proofs; committees were set up to examine the sisters before, during, and after performances. Women even searched

Currier & Ives/Library of Congress

M.ᴿ FISH AND THE MISSES FOX,

People flocked to see if the Fox sisters—Margaret (1833–93), Catherine (1837–92), and Leah (1814–90)—could really communicate with the spirits of the dead.

Was There Really a Murdered Peddler?

Bones were found beneath the Hydesville house in 1848 and again in 1904, but there's doubt as to whether they added up to an entire human skeleton. There probably never was a murdered ped-

Neighbors dug up the basement of this house, searching for the peddler's bones.

dler. But neighbors believed the story because peddlers led dangerous lives.

According to the raps, the man was murdered for his money: $500, the equivalent of about $15,150 in 2014,[10] which seems like too much to carry around. Peddlers were often immigrants. They began on foot, carrying watches, eye glasses, cloth, and sewing supplies (needles, thread, thimbles, lace, ribbons, and patterns) in their backpacks. They sent money to their families overseas, and they saved; once they could afford horses and wagons, they dealt in heavier goods—even stoves. This was home shopping before the internet. Peddlers served a need, but they were occasionally robbed and murdered, and the papers reported it.[11] Whether you wanted to commit an undetected murder or invent a story about one, it made sense in 1848 for the victim to be a peddler.

their clothes. But the examiners reached no definite conclusions, and audiences believed what they wanted to believe. Many felt the raps were "evidence that a new era of history was about to begin through the agency of reform-minded Christians,"[5] and soon a new religion was born: Spiritualism, which has been defined as "the Science, Philosophy and Religion of continuous life, based upon the demonstrated fact of communication, by means of mediumship, with those who live in the Spirit World."[6]

In 1888, when Maggie explained the toe cracking, her publisher thought it would spell the death of Spiritualism. "The creators of Spiritualism abjure its infamy," he wrote.[7] Kate said it was "all humbuggery."[8] But Spiritualism did not die. What the Fox sisters actually contributed to the new religion was not so much its belief system as a ritual apparatus—rules and conventions for asking questions and interpreting answers.[9] Believers looking for truth through that apparatus managed to find something more convincing than Maggie's book. In the end, Maggie withdrew her confession.

Spiritual Telegraphy and Benjamin Franklin

Library of Congress

In John Gast's 1872 painting, the great spirit of "American Progress" presides over a westward migration, looping telegraph wires across the prairie.

Since at least the 1750s, inventors had been working on schemes to transmit messages electronically. Samuel F.B. Morse invented a code of dots and dashes—short raps and long ones—to represent the alphabet, and in 1844 he telegraphed a message from Washington to Baltimore: WHAT HATH GOD WROUGHT.[12] Would the Foxes and their neighbors have thought raps could be a kind of communication if they hadn't known about the telegraph?[13] Leah, the oldest sister, claimed spirit communication involved "Electricity and Magnetism," so it was "not surprising" that it was initiated by Benjamin Franklin (Chapter 13), still inventive "on the other side."[14]

Faking a Trip to Gold Rush Territory

There's more than one way to make money in a gold rush. Mining is the most obvious, and in 1848, when gold was discovered at Captain Sutter's mill, prospectors hurried to San Francisco to stake their claims. Others hurried after them. California had been a backwater where a healthy Native American population contended with only a scattering of Mexican and American ranchers, traders, and rebels. Suddenly it needed a workforce to provide miners with everything from roads and work clothes to buckets, saloons, and banks. And suddenly the rest of the world needed news of California.

Henry Vizetelly (1820–1894) was just the man to inform the world. A publisher and writer with a keen nose for popular interest, he knew that timing was everything—he had to give readers an authoritative account of California before they lost interest. But Vizetelly was in London. Sailing from London to New York in those days could take six weeks, and passengers risked not only shipwreck but shipboard epidemics of cholera or typhoid. Traveling from New York to San Francisco by ship or covered wagon took months, and news didn't travel much faster than people and cargo.

So Vizetelly faked a trip to California. By early 1849 he'd published a dandy guide under the pseudonym J. Tyrwhitt Brooks, M.D.—"quite the kind of name likely to disarm suspicion," he said.[1] He called it *Four*

A "forty-niner" panning for gold.

Months among the Gold-Finders in California: Being the Diary of an Expedition from San Francisco to the Gold Districts. He advertised it as "The Result of Actual Experience,"[2] but any actual experience was borrowed from other people's writing.

London reviewers liked *Four Months among the Gold-Finders*, and so did the public. It was widely translated and read throughout Europe. The German translator hurried off to California himself, and showed a copy of his translation to Captain Sutter. Sutter was surprised to discover that he and his "lovely daughter" had extended their hospitality to the mythical Brooks at a time when they were in Switzerland. The translator found other indications that the book was faked. For instance:

> Mr. Brooks also introduces a dreadful tale of a sailor-boy whom the Indians scalped, and though it is very well related, I am sorry to say the Indians in California do not scalp at all. If Mr. Brooks ever should invent another story—and it was rather a frivolous thing to do it at that time with California, for I have not the least doubt the book enticed thousands to go over—he ought to be a little more careful how he mentions names or facts, for it is disagreeable to be caught out in such things.[3]

Flakes of gold found near John Sutter's sawmill triggered the California Gold Rush.

1850 daguerreotype by R. H. Vance

Vizetelly was a legitimate "pioneer in the publication of inexpensive illustrated books and magazines"—and a hoax journalist.[4] His pretended diary was a clever blend of fact and imagination. He took geographical and historical background from the western explorations of John Frémont, and he surely drew on other newspaper reports as well. To fill any gaps, "he did not hesitate to invent names and scenes," but he got most of it right. Even after Vizetelly confessed the hoax in his 1893 memoir, scholars considered *Four Months among the Gold-finders* a useful source.[5]

There must have been many California Gold Rush hoaxes in 1849. The hills swarmed with prospectors eager to make their fortunes. Unscrupulous hustlers jumped claims or salted their own worthless claims with gold from elsewhere and sold them to unwary would-be miners at inflated rates. The general chaos provided rich opportunities for skullduggery, but Henry Vizetelly stayed clear of the hurly-burly and still made a tidy profit on the Gold Rush.

Getting to San Francisco

San Francisco harbor at Yerba Buena Cove in 1850 or 1851 —
with Yerba Buena Island, and Berkeley Hills, in the background.
Daguerrotype, from during the California Gold Rush.

News really did travel slowly in 1848. The gold was discovered on January 24—more than a week before the February 2 treaty that finally ended the Mexican-American War, giving California and other Mexican territories to the U.S.[6] When news of the gold reached Mexico, it must have made those losses seem all the more bitter.

The Gold Rush was a disaster for California's Native Americans. The territory's non-Indian population was less than 8,000 in 1846, but rose to about 93,000 in 1850—enough to qualify for statehood. By 1860 it stood at 380,000. Meanwhile, the Native American population plummeted from 150,000 in 1846 to 30,000 in 1860.[7]

The new economic importance of California drove developments in transportation: a railway crossed Panama by 1855, and one crossed the U.S. by 1869. The Panama Canal, begun in 1881, finally opened for business in 1914.

At the height of the Gold Rush, with no quick route, conditions could change by the time you got to California. Who knew if your cargo would be what the market was calling for? But one lucky Maine captain figured the miners would need buckets. After a voyage of 164 days he arrived in San Francisco at last, and on May 4, 1851, when a great fire broke out on the waterfront, there he was, with a deck-load of buckets ready to unload. He and his wife formed a bucket brigade, saving their ship and helping others as well.[8] Sometimes a good bucket is more useful than gold.

When Giants Roamed the Earth

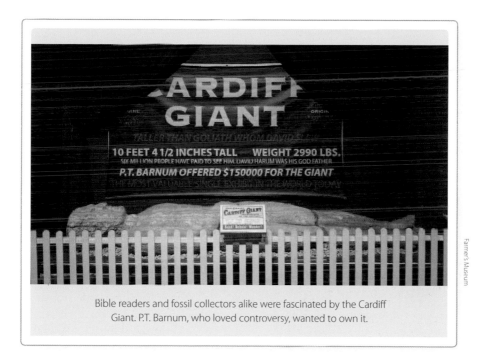

Bible readers and fossil collectors alike were fascinated by the Cardiff Giant. P.T. Barnum, who loved controversy, wanted to own it.

I declare, some old Indian has been buried here!" said the well-digger when he hit the stone foot.[1] It was October 16, 1869, just east of Stub Newell's barn in Cardiff, New York.[2] And there it was, a foot connected to a petrified man more than 10 feet tall. They dug out a trench that day instead of a well, and you could see how the giant had been writhing a little before he turned to stone. The next day was Sunday, so people got a free look. By Monday Newell had set up a tent, and soon he was charging 50 cents for a 15-minute gawk.

The tent was crowded—hundreds came to look every day. Some stood in awe; they believed the giant was "a great and superior being."[3] Scientists were not impressed. Othniel Marsh (later famous as a dinosaur hunter) told the Rochester *Daily Union* that the giant was a mere statue, and not a very old one. If it had been buried longer, the chisel marks and polishing would have eroded and "the unmistakable evidence against its antiquity" would have been less obvious.[4]

The hoaxster—George Hull, a relative of Newell's—had taken great pains to make his giant believable. He had even given it pores by putting "hundreds of large darning needles into a block of wood" and then hammering it all over.[5] But Marsh was right; the thing was a statue.

Hull, a free-thinker and skeptic, cooked up his hoax after losing an argument with a minister who claimed that "giants had once roamed the earth and that eventually the physical evidence to prove their existence would come to light."[6] Darwin's *Origin of Species* had come out in 1859, and people were debating what it meant. Could natural science disprove religion, or prove it? The public craved news of natural wonders, and newspaper men—not to mention showmen like P.T. Barnum (Chapter 18)—catered to that appetite.

So Hull had a block of gypsum quarried in Iowa and sent to a Chicago marble cutter. He had the statue carved secretly. He aged it. (When ink didn't work, he used sulfuric acid to give it "the dark, dingy hue that he wanted."[7]) He shipped it to Cardiff and had it buried. Then, after waiting almost a year, he arranged for a well to be dug. He paid an estimated $2,600 for all this. It was a huge sum in 1870, when an unskilled laborer was paid less than $10 for a 60-hour week,[8] but the investment paid off. Exhibiting the giant at Cardiff brought in $12,000, and on October 23, Hull sold a three-quarter interest to a group of businessmen for $30,000, netting a tidy profit.[9]

P.T. Barnum offered $50,000 for the giant.[10] When the businessmen refused to sell, Barnum made a plaster replica and displayed it two

Mark Twain's Petrified Man

Nineteenth-century journalists were expected to invent hoax stories. Mark Twain, describing his work at the Virginia City (Nevada) Territorial Enterprise, put it this way:

> To find a petrified man, or break a stranger's leg, or cave an imaginary mine, or discover some dead Indians in a Gold Hill tunnel, or massacre a family at Dutch Nick's, were feats and calamities that we never hesitated about devising when the public needed matters of thrilling interest for breakfast. The seemingly tranquil Enterprise office was a ghastly factory of slaughter, mutilation and general destruction in those days.[14]

Imagine this man sitting still long enough for a slow limestone drip to turn him to stone, all the while thumbing his nose at future viewers.

Stories about petrified men had gone viral, and Twain made fun of them in a hoax of his own. He reported that a century-old corpse had been found sitting on a rock, mummified and glued in place by dripping limestone. He was perfectly preserved—even his peg leg and the way he was holding his thumb to his nose, fanning out the fingers. (To Twain's disappointment, readers didn't notice that the petrified man was literally thumbing his nose at them.) A local judge rushed to the scene and conducted a hasty inquest, concluding that the man had died from "protracted exposure."[15]

blocks away. Barnum's fake earned more than the original fake, and the businessmen sued to close down his exhibit—but the judge refused to rule against Barnum unless the businessmen "could guarantee the authenticity of the original Cardiff giant."[11] They dropped their suit and moved their giant to Boston.[12]

Even after the details of his hoax were laid bare, Hull enjoyed the results. He profited financially, and he also felt he had raised doubts about uncritical faith in the Bible. But maybe his "dupes," the viewers who shelled out their quarters to gaze at the giant, gained something valuable as well. They stood at "the unstable boundaries of science, religion, and empirical investigation"[13] and witnessed something strange and interesting. They made up their own minds. Doubt and all, it was a democratic process.

The Keely Motor Company Promises Efficient World Travel

John Ernst Worrell Keely (1837–1898) broke civil laws against fraud, pretended to break the laws of nature, and broke the confidence of his friends and the bank accounts of investors. And he got away with it almost scot-free.

Keely was a Philadelphia carpenter with a taste for music, and he claimed a tuning fork led him to discover a "new motive power" in 1872.[1] It wasn't perpetual motion—he didn't claim he could make an engine run forever without fuel—but it was almost as good. He said he could "liberate" enough power from one quart of water to move a train from Philadelphia to San Francisco. A gallon could fuel a ship from New York to Liverpool and back.[2] His first investors (including some engineers) subscribed $10,000 (nearly $200,000 in 2015 dollars)[3] to launch the Keely Motor Company.

How would the motor work? It would be a "hydro-pneumatic-pulsating-vacu-engine." Nobody really understood what he meant by that, or by terms such as *sympathetic equilibrium*, *etheric disintegration*, or *quadruple negative harmonics*, but it sounded impressive. Modern inventions—like the 1874 light bulb or the 1876 telephone—were amazing and potentially useful, but people didn't expect to understand them. While skeptics pooh-poohed Keely's blather, many found his language all the more convincing because it was baffling.

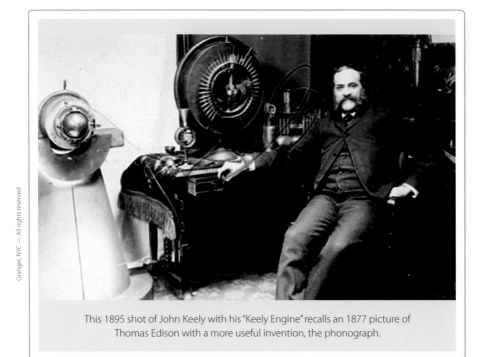

This 1895 shot of John Keely with his "Keely Engine" recalls an 1877 picture of Thomas Edison with a more useful invention, the phonograph.

Keely's apparatus looked impressive. He poured water into a cylinder, and suddenly a pressure gauge measured 50,000 pounds per square inch. His motor tore great ropes apart, broke iron bars, and shot bullets through 12-inch planks.[4] Clerks and widows—people with very small incomes—invested in the Keely Motor Company, dreaming it would help them achieve financial independence.[5]

It helped John Keely. He spent money, gave to charity, and invested in diamonds. But the Keely Motor was never ready to go into production. For years, it was just three weeks short of being ready.[6] Investors lost patience, newspapers labeled Keely a fraud, and the Keely Motor Company disowned him. Then Clara Jessup Moore stepped in to rescue him. She was a writer and an expert on manners, with influential contacts on both sides of the Atlantic. Better yet, from Keely's point of view, she was the widow of a wealthy businessman. She gave him more than $100,000 up front and a monthly salary of $2,500.[7]

Newly funded, Keely invented something new. The Motor Company claimed it, and Keely was thrown in jail. But after a good look at the new apparatus, an examiner reported "whatever Keely believed that he had invented" now was "different from whatever he thought he had invented earlier," and thus it did not belong to the company. The court let him go.[8]

Mrs. Moore, meanwhile, was in danger of losing control of her finances; her children feared she was wasting money on Keely. To prove her competence, she asked scientists to review his work and testify that her investment was sound. But they found at least one of the inventions was bogus. Mrs. Moore cut Keely's stipend to $250 per month. (This was still worth more than $7,000 in 2015 dollars.)

When Keely died in 1898, a Massachusetts electrician bought his equipment, moved it to Boston, and

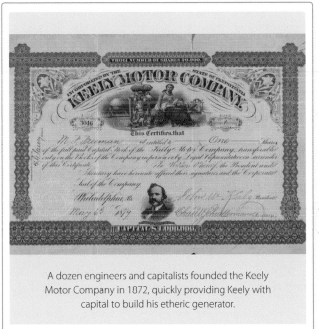

A dozen engineers and capitalists founded the Keely Motor Company in 1872, quickly providing Keely with capital to build his etheric generator.

couldn't get it to work. And no wonder! Keely's Philadelphia laboratory had a false ceiling and a false floor. Motors in the attic and cellar were connected by a drive shaft behind the wall.[9] The Keely motor was not a very portable hoax.

To this day, some people believe it was never a hoax at all. The SVPwiki community maintains that technology based on Sympathetic Vibratory Physics will yet "provide humanity with abundant, cheap and clean energy."[10] Keely's vision lives on.

Scientific Progress and Perpetual Motion

Clara Jessup Moore saw Keely's motor as a force for world peace and harmony; she supported him generously.

"Truth emerges more readily from error than from confusion," said Francis Bacon (1561–1626).[11] A given scientific theory or hypothesis may be wrong; scientists who guide their experiments by it may be in error. But because they are testing a hypothesis, scientists design their experiments in a systematic way. They are more likely to learn something useful using a false theory than using no theory at all.

New evidence forces scientists to throw out pet theories and research projects that once looked promising. For hundreds of years, it seemed possible that someone could invent a "perpetual motion" machine—a device that could generate its own power, running indefinitely without fuel. Between 1617 and 1903, British inventors filed over 600 applications to patent such machines.[12]

But by around 1850, other scientists established the law of conservation of energy, which states that energy can neither be created nor destroyed—only converted from one form to another. This means that a real perpetual motion machine is impossible. Any working machine needs a supply of energy to keep going.[13]

So why did anybody pay attention to Keely? For one thing, people didn't stop believing in perpetual motion as soon as the law of conservation of energy was formulated; disbelief took time. (Most of those perpetual motion patent applications were filed after 1854.) For another thing, new science hinted at possibilities that nobody yet understood. What was radiation, for instance? Was light an element? Scientific understanding of the universe was changing fast, and to non-scientists Keely's ideas sounded plausible, if confusing.

On the cover of a 1920 science magazine, Norman Rockwell's inventor tries to work out a glitch in his design for a perpetual motion machine.

For Mrs. Moore, the spiritual implications of Keely's ideas outweighed the scientific. She belittled the skeptics who wanted him to spell out hypotheses, and she quoted as many clergymen as scientists. "Let us not deny what we are unable to explain," she urged. She kept faith with Keely because she saw his project as part of a divine "dispensation of harmony and peace."[14]

The Case of the Lying Encyclopedia

When you look things up in an encyclopedia, you think you're getting correct information. But you might want a second opinion, because even reference books make mistakes. In 1936, the *New Yorker* reported goofs in a new encyclopedia: a great baseball player's name misspelled and a novelist listed among the Civil War dead 18 years before publishing a famous book that must have been "ghost-written with a vengeance." Errors cropped up in more famous encyclopedias too, and even the *World Almanac*—the "infallible authority" used to settle thousands of bets daily—made mistakes.[1]

"It is not pleasant to have to go after encyclopedias this way," the writer complained, but he sounded like a man who was having fun. A few weeks later Frank O'Brien jumped into the game. He pointed out a mistake in *Bartlett's Quotations* and 14 biographies of imaginary botanists in *Appleton's Cyclopædia of American Biography* (1887–1889).[2]

Fourteen biographies of botanists who never existed? That wasn't just a mistake—it was a crime. The six-volume *Appleton's* was widely respected. School children relied on it, and so did scholars. Yet a previous whistle-blower had gone unheard. In 1919, John Hendley Barnhart reported those 14 fake biographies in *The Journal of the New York Botanical Garden*, but not many people read it; news didn't reach the schoolteachers. The *New Yorker* had more impact.

It turned out that the 14 botanists were not the only imaginary characters in *Appleton's*. They were just the ones Barnhart—a botanist himself—had checked on. He discovered problems when he looked for the books they reportedly wrote and couldn't find any. After all, if an encyclopedia tells you a book "caused a sensation in scientific circles" or was "considered an authority" in its field, you would expect to find copies of that book in research libraries.[3]

Once the news got out, systematic investigations turned up dozens more imaginary scientists in *Appleton's*. Margaret Schindler looked hard for 34 "important" titles by 11 scientists listed in the "H" section alone, and had to conclude that those books (and the scientists who wrote them) probably never existed. But not finding something doesn't *prove*

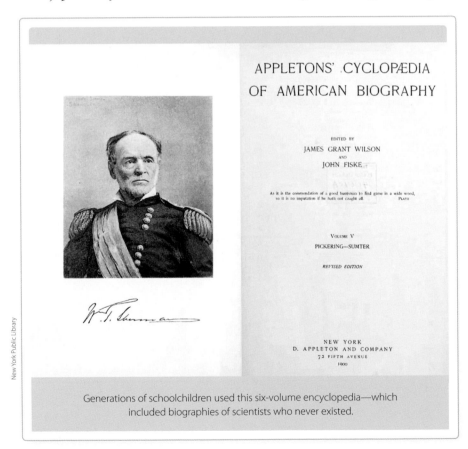

APPLETONS' CYCLOPÆDIA
OF AMERICAN BIOGRAPHY

EDITED BY
JAMES GRANT WILSON
AND
JOHN FISKE

As it is the commendation of a good huntsman to find game in a wide wood,
so it is no imputation if he hath not caught all.   PLATO

VOLUME V
PICKERING—SUMTER

REVISED EDITION

NEW YORK
D. APPLETON AND COMPANY
72 FIFTH AVENUE
1900

Generations of schoolchildren used this six-volume encyclopedia—which included biographies of scientists who never existed.

Wikipedia

Today you're more likely to use Wikipedia than *Appleton's Cyclopædia*. It's quicker, more convenient, and covers more subjects—and if somebody plants a hoax in Wikipedia, it will get caught and corrected in less than 30 years. A French politician once praised an eighteenth-century antislavery activist whose biography appeared in French Wikipedia; the activist never existed, and his Wikipedia biography was a fake. Embarrassing, but Wikipedia itself sets the record straight.[10] Since 2005, when a small study found Wikipedia tied with *Encyclopaedia Britannica* for accuracy, others have also ranked it high.[11]

WIKIPEDIA
The Free Encyclopedia

Wikipedia articles can be written by anybody, anonymously. Librarians used to warn students away from it for just that reason. Anonymous writers could make mistakes; they could lie. Using Wikipedia, you can't judge the reliability of an article by the author's credentials.

But Wikipedia articles can also be corrected by anybody. You can click on "History" and see how many people have corrected an article. Also, Wikipedia editors flag problems with articles they consider less reliable; they often call for better endnotes and bibliographies. So one advantage to starting with Wikipedia is that those endnotes and bibliographies give you additional places to look for information. Go ahead and use Wikipedia—or any other encyclopedia. Just don't stop there!

it's nonexistent, and Schindler checked other "facts" from the suspect articles. One of the imaginary scientists reportedly broke a Spanish monopoly on red dye by smuggling insects in 1755. (False: somebody else really did that, in 1777.) Another helped control a cholera epidemic in Peru in 1783. (False: cholera did not reach Peru until 1868.[4])

Why would anybody salt a major reference source with fake biographies? Probably for the money. The more biographies a writer contributed to *Appleton's*, the more the writer was paid. Experts were recruited to write specific articles for the work, but they could also suggest additional names. Writing imaginary biographies was quicker and easier than writing genuine ones, and the forger wrote quite a few of them; 43 of the 1,140 articles in Volume 3 are "doubtful or spurious."[5]

How did the writer get away with it? Staff in the editorial office revised the articles for form but didn't check content—and the hoaxer chose areas the proofreaders didn't know much about, such as botany and South America, so they were unlikely to notice the fraud.[6] And what if the culprit was actually the subject editor for South America? It's been suspected.[7]

The forger was widely (if secretly) influential. Schindler found *Appleton's* misinformation copied in four bibliographies, one biographical dictionary, and one scientific article published before 1935.[8] *Appleton's* was reprinted without revisions in 1968, giving it a chance to keep infecting new works.[9]

Extracting Gold from Seawater

High tides, swift currents, and a remote location made
Lubec, Maine an ideal place for Jernegan's scam.

Lubec Memorial Library

Farmers, fishermen, and boatbuilders worked hard in Lubec, Maine.
But in 1897, along came Reverend Prescott Jernegan and his friend
Charles Fisher with a fantastic opportunity to get rich quick.[1]

In 1896, Jernegan had been out of work, his wife wanted to leave
him, and he caught typhoid fever.[2] But then he had a vision. He knew
there was gold in seawater, but with about one grain of gold in every ton
of water, scientists said it couldn't be extracted economically.[3] Jernegan

invented a Gold Accumulator to harvest that gold, and he enlisted Fisher to help.

Dishonest miners sometimes salted unpromising mines with good ore before selling. (One salted a mine with melted coins; the new owner found letters engraved on supposedly virgin silver.[4]) Jernegan favored selling shares in a worthless enterprise. Rich, greedy capitalists were fair game, and, like Robin Hood, he could "use the money for good and generous purposes."[5]

Jernegan's Gold Accumulator featured a small battery and a pan of mercury, along with a secret ingredient, in a wooden box with holes.

The respectable-seeming Reverend Prescott Jernegan claimed his secret gold-extraction process was vouchsafed to him in a dream.

The electric current supposedly captured precious metals as tides rushed through the holes.

To lure investors, Jernegan and Fisher honed their demonstration for months, like magicians perfecting a trick. They made it elaborate to draw attention from what was really happening, and they gave the audience an active role. Their first mark was Arthur Ryan, a wealthy acquaintance from Jernegan's preaching days.

Jernegan demonstrated his machine on a pier in Providence, Rhode Island. He explained the apparatus and handed it over to Ryan and a friend, who inserted mercury they'd brought, lowered the box into the water themselves, and retrieved it in the morning. A chemist of their own choice analyzed the mercury and found five grains of gold.[6] How could there be any trickery, when

A prospectus and a sample nugget of gold (supposedly extracted from seawater) lured investors to support Jernegan's bogus scheme.

they were involved at every stage? Together, Ryan and his friend put up more than $10,000 to develop what became the Electrolytic Marine Salts Company.

How was the scam accomplished? Newspapers later reported that Fisher dove underwater to replace the mercury with a sample containing traces of gold and silver.[7] Jernegan said Fisher used sleight of hand, slipping gold into the mercury before it was tested.[8]

In any case, there were soon more than 1,000 stockholders in the new Electrolytic Marine Salts Company, many of them far from rich. By 1897 the company had a plant in Lubec with 240 accumulators and a private laboratory where Fisher pretended to extract gold from mercury. The plant was called Klondike, after the site of an 1896–99 Canadian gold rush. Lubec's boom was smaller than Canada's: 700 laborers filled boarding houses to capacity,[9] and the town's population increased from 2,000 in 1890 to a hair over 3,000 in 1900.

But in 1898, threatened with blackmail, Jernegan and Fisher fled the country. The Lubec accumulators stopped accumulating gold, until an investigator inserted "seven ounces of . . . old tooth fillings."[10] Soon the plant was converted to a sardine factory. Fisher escaped with $100,000; Jernegan took $150,000 and a guilty conscience—he soon returned $144,000 to investors. His wife left him. He spent years writing useful books in the Philippines, and decades later, when he wrote his memoir, it contradicted old accounts of the scandal.[11]

It was "perhaps the most astonishing and picturesque swindle of modern times," according to *Scientific American*.[12] Yet it didn't end all hope of extracting gold from the ocean; between 1904 and 1906, genuine attempts were made both in England and Australia. The English attempt went down in a blaze of lawsuits; the inventor was awarded damages of one quarter of a penny. The Australian enterprise faded from view after 1906.[13] So far it seems Jernegan was right: you can extract more gold from fools than from the sea.

Viking Runes in Minnesota

"8 Goths and 22 Norwegians on a voyage of discovery from Vinland westward. We had our camp . . . one day's journey north of this stone. We were out fishing one day. When we came home we found 10 men red with blood and dead. AVM save us from evil. We have 10 men by the sea to look after our ships, 14 days' journey from their island. Year 1362."[1]

This runic message is carved on a 200-pound slab of stone: the Kensington Rune Stone. Minnesota farmer Olof Ohman unearthed it in 1898, tangled in the roots of an aspen tree he was digging out of his field. Questions arose immediately. Vikings might have reached the shores of North America in 1000, but what were they doing in Minnesota in 1362? Why had they left their ships and hiked deep into the wilderness?[2] If they had time to carve such a long message, why didn't they list the names of their fallen comrades?

In 1899, professors at three different universities called the inscription "probably spurious," "modern," and "a fraud."[3] Neighbors agreed with the experts. They'd heard Ohman say "he wanted to do something that would crack the brains of the learned."[4] He knew some runes; he used to clip them from a Swedish-American newspaper column. His friends—including the prankster John Gran—had the skills to help.

When the authorities sent the stone back to Ohman, he set it as a doorstep in front of his granary, and that might have ended the matter.[5] But in 1907, the stone was rediscovered. Hjalmar Rued Holand was a Norwegian-American journalist and (according to John Gran's son Walter) a "dumb cluck."[6] He was excited by the Kensington runes and spent the rest of his life arguing that they were genuine.

Most experts still argue against the stone. Some of the runes are anachronistic: symbols for "j" and "ö" were not invented until around 1550.[7] Some of the words are modern, too.[8] But Holland was a likeable man, and he wrote well.[9] He caught the imagination of readers; he made people *want* to believe in the stone, and he gave them reasons to do so. If it was a fake, he asked, how did it get buried under a 70-year-old tree? It would have had to be put there before nineteenth-century Norwegians settled Minnesota. ("Well, them kind of trees, they actually get that size in two or three years," said Walter Gran.[10])

Louise Lund Larsen, 1910

The Kensington Rune Stone, unearthed in 1898, tells of a fourteenth-century Viking expedition to North America. Who really carved the runes?

And Holland thought he knew what the Norse were doing in America: spreading Christianity. His last book, published in 1962, was *A Pre-Columbian Crusade to America*. The story has gathered new details since then, and in 2009 the History Channel aired *Holy Grail in America*—a documentary-style show that suggests the Templars might have hidden the Grail in America back in 1362, and evidence may be encoded in the Kensington stone.[11]

Scythian Gold at the Louvre

While Minnesotans debated the Kensington stone, Parisians argued about a golden tiara sold to the Louvre by a Russian art dealer in 1896. It was a fantastic treasure, allegedly a Greek gift to the Scythian king Saitaphernes in the third century BC. The gold weighed about a pound and was decorated with scenes from everyday Scythian life and from *The Iliad*. Saitaphernes had been buried with it, and over the centuries, rocks apparently had fallen in his tomb. They dented the crown, but by some miracle missed the carvings and only hit the smooth bits. Perhaps the king had tossed and turned a bit; dents showed on the back of his head, not just the exposed front.

Or perhaps Louvre authorities should have been more suspicious. The tiara's provenance was murky. Rumor hinted that Crimean peasants had fled

Fabergé Museum

Russia with it; it surely didn't come from a well-monitored archaeological site. Then in 1903, a Russian jeweler said he'd watched his friend, the skilled goldsmith Israel Rouchomovski, make that tiara.[13]

The story came out. Dealers had commissioned Rouchomovski to make the tiara as a gift for an archaeologist. When he heard of the scandal, he went to Paris and claimed credit for his work.[14] The embarrassed Louvre usually hides the tiara out of sight, but another Rouchomovski piece—a 3.5-inch golden skeleton with its own tiny silver sarcophagus—won him a gold medal and went on to fetch $365,000 at a Sotheby's auction in 2013.[15]

This crown, made by a nineteenth-century Russian goldsmith, would have been a worthy gift to a third-century BC king. Instead, it caused a scandal in Paris.

In 1976, the Minnesota Historical Society released a taped inter-view of Walter Gran and his sister, remembering how their father—Olof Ohman's tricky friend—tried to confess the hoax when close to death. The tapes "reinforce the conclusion of the best of scholarship and reveal the stone's rightful place in history as a monument to Scandinavian humor on the American frontier," wrote the editor of *Minnesota History*.[12]

But he also pointed out that the story of what people have believed about that rune stone may really be more interesting than the stone itself. Back in 1898, could Ohman and his friends have been Norwe-gian-Americans who wanted to believe in Viking discoveries? In 2009, were Americans more interested in Templar conspiracies than in sim-ple explorations? How we read the runes may say more about us than about real life in fourteenth-century Minnesota.

A Conspiracy to Justify Murder

The *Protocols of the Elders of Zion* is a forgery and a libel against the Jews.[1] Much of it was plagiarized from *A Dialogue in Hell*, an 1864 satire against French ruler Napoleon III. The *Dialogue*'s liberal author tried to show how a tyrant like Napoleon could use liberalism to bol-ster his power, manipulating people and events to his own advantage. Napoleon (being a tyrant) had the author jailed and most copies of the book destroyed.[2]

Unfortunately, a sur-viving copy found its way decades later to the Okhrana, the Russian secret police. In the late 1890s they repur-posed it to make an attack on the Jews, not Napoleon III.[3] The Okhrana version was a

Viewing the bodies of Jews killed in a 1906 pogrom.

Jewish historical Institute

clumsy piece of work, riddled with bad grammar and spelling,[4] but as a tool for Russian authorities in the 1890s, it was ideal.

For one thing, it diverted public anger from the rulers. Revolution was brewing in Russia; it would break out in 1905 and again in 1917. Peasants could not pay their debts; city workers struggled to survive; and university students were getting radical ideas about democracy, socialism, and liberal reforms.[5] The *Protocols* told people that this national unrest was being stoked by Jewish leaders who were working behind the scenes to topple old aristocracies and institutions. According to the *Protocols*, the Jews were well on their way to world domination.

A successful conspiracy theory gives believers a clear target for blame, and the Jews, even more than other ethnic groups in the sprawling Russian Empire, had always been seen as outsiders. Since 1881, dozens had been killed in pogroms—murderous riots tolerated by the government. In the minds of many readers, the *Protocols* justified a "permanent pogrom against Russian Jews."[6]

At first the *Protocols* circulated in manuscript form. In 1903, a Russian newspaper printed a short version. Then in 1905, Sergei Nilus printed a more complete version in a book warning that the Antichrist was at hand.[7] He claimed his copy had been made by a woman who spent the night with a Jewish leader and found

Alexander Palace

Tsar Nicholas II and his wife, Alexandra, dressed for a 1903 ball. Revolutionary sentiment was building in Russia, but the *Protocols of the Elders of Zion* deflected blame for societal problems from the tsar to hidden Jewish plotters.

these minutes of a 1902 conspiracy meeting in a closet.[8] Nilus printed the work three more times before World War I, and it began to gain traction.

After the war, the *Protocols* were printed in editions around the world. In the U.S., Henry Ford published them in a 1920 newspaper

STOP YOUR CRUEL OPPRESSION OF THE JEWS.

In a 1904 cartoon, U.S. President Theodore Roosevelt urges Tsar Nicholas II to stop the persecution. Jews flee the ruins of Kishinev as Lot and his family fled Sodom.

series and a 1922 book, *The International Jew: The World's Foremost Problem*. (Ford apologized in 1927.)[9] In Germany, young Adolf Hitler found in the *Protocols* support for his own ideas about "Jewish evil." And while the book reinforced his belief in "the Jew" as a powerful enemy, it also taught him strategies for acquiring and keeping power.[10]

In 1933, Swiss Jews sued editors and advocates of the *Protocols* for libel. South Africa held a similar trial in 1934. Both cases required the defendants to authenticate the *Protocols*, and in both cases the defendants failed to do so.[11] But although the book was declared "a forgery" in South Africa and "a fraudulent plagiarism" in Switzerland,[12] anti-Semites continued to believe it. Hitler's Nazi party rose to power in Germany in 1933.

In World War II (1939–1945), Great Britain, the United States, and their allies defeated Germany and its allies, but not before millions of Jews died in concentration camps. They were victims of Hitler's "Final Solution to the Jewish Question," a plan to exterminate the Jewish people. The *Protocols* encouraged some people to engage in anti-Semitic atrocities and other people to let them do it. Even now, although the work was long ago exposed as a forgery, it circulates in print and online and is "still being treated as fact by readers who wish to deny whatever evidence is presented to prove it is a forgery."[13] It is one of the most influential hoaxes in history, and one of the most evil.

Conspiracy Theories and the Damage Done

The *Protocols* is a hoax tailor-made to support a conspiracy theory. A conspiracy theory is a form of delusion that seems to hold out comfort in hard times. When people can't solve complex problems or even agree what's at the root of the trouble, a conspiracy theory explains everything—usually by blaming a group that may appear powerful but can be attacked and overcome more easily than the real problems.

Conspiracy theories routinely sprout after disasters: Romans in AD 64 blamed the Emperor Nero for conspiring to burn Rome; Britons in a nineteenth-century cholera epidemic blamed doctors for making poor people sick so they could use their bodies for medical research. [14]

A conspiracy theory offers a simplified view of life. It is dualistic, dividing the world into "forces of good and evil." The forces of evil—the demonized individuals or groups said to cause all the trouble—are seen as powerful enemies of the common good. Conspiracy theories can lead their believers to discriminate against these perceived "enemies" or even to attack them violently.[15] Six million Jews suffered torture in concentration camps and died because of Hitler's deluded belief that they were a powerful force for evil.

Finding a human enemy to fight may help us feel that we are still in control—even when natural, economic, or political disasters upend our lives—but conspiracy theories are usually wrong. The problems of early twentieth-century Europe had deep, intertwined causes, and a secret conspiracy by Jews was not among them.

A Future Great Novelist Helps Hoax the Royal Navy

Horace de Vere Cole once threw a party and invited only guests whose names included the word *bottom*. He once impersonated a foreman and got a road crew to dig an unauthorized trench in the middle of London. He once bought up selected theater tickets and gave them to bald men; people in the balcony could read what those bald heads spelled out, and it wasn't polite.[1] Cole liked to thumb his nose at authority of all kinds, and he spent money to do it on a grand scale.

With his friend Adrian Stephen and others, Cole nearly got himself expelled from Cambridge University in 1905 by hoaxing town officials. The students spoofed a telegram from the Foreign Office, telling the mayor to expect a visit from the Sultan of Zanzibar's uncle. Arriving in splendid robes and turbans, they enjoyed a royal reception.[2] When the story came out, news reporters had a field day.

So in 1910, when officers on His Majesty's Ship *Hawke* wanted to hoax rivals on HMS *Dreadnought*, one of them remembered Cole. The *Dreadnought* was a grand symbol of authority—a perfect target for Cole. As Virginia (Stephen) Woolf remembered in 1940:

> There were a great many rivalries and intrigues in the navy. The officers liked scoring off each other. And the officers of the *Hawke* and the *Dreadnought* had a feud. . . . And Cole's

friend who was on the *Hawke* had come to Cole, and said to him, "You're a great hand at hoaxing people; couldn't you do something to pull the leg of the *Dreadnought?*"

Cole took five friends—including Adrian and Virginia Stephen—to a well-known costumier. An assistant worked for two weeks to out-fit them: Cole as a gentleman from the Foreign Office, Stephen as an interpreter, and the rest as Prince Makalin of Abyssinia and his retinue. They wore beards, dark make-up, and expensive jewelry.

Again there was a telegram—this time using the name of Foreign Office Under-Secretary Sir Charles Hardinge. Again there was a royal

National Portrait Gallery, London

Six friends dressed for a visit to HMS *Dreadnought*, including Virginia Stephen (Woolf) on the left as Prince Mendax, Horace de Vere Cole in top hat as Foreign Office guide, and tall Adrian Stephen beside him as interpreter.

HMS *Dreadnought* and the Lead-up to World War I

When she was launched in 1906, HMS *Dreadnought* put the United Kingdom ahead in the international race for naval superiority. She was the Admiral's flagship, "technologically innovative, strategically daring, and militarily superior." [9] The sight of her in a 1909 naval pageant on the Thames made the British public feel safer, and her image helped national security as much as her actual strength. Who would attack an island nation defended by such impressive ships?

Enemies were alarmed at how fast and secretly she had been built. Could the U.K. whip up more great ships just as fast? Germany's Kaiser Wilhelm pushed for more and better ships of his own.[10] England and Germany told each other at the time that they were not contemplating war, just trying to stay even. But in 1914, World War I broke out. Although the *Dreadnought* was not involved in any naval battle, she was the only battleship to ram and sink a German submarine.[11] One of the congratulatory telegrams read "BUNGA BUNGA." [12]

A 1909 humor magazine shows France, Great Britain, Japan, Germany, and the U.S. engaged in a "no limit" naval arms race.

welcome. The group's fun was spiced with danger. One of the *Dreadnought* officers was the Stephens's cousin. Virginia, as Prince Mendax, shook his hand with a straight face and spoke as little as possible. According to a news item, she "constantly murmured 'Bunga, bunga,' which the interpreter explained was Abyssinian for 'Isn't it lovely.'"[3] The interpreter of course knew no "Abyssinian"; he recited Latin poetry, breaking up words in odd places to keep any classically educated officers from recognizing them.[4] But even Virginia's fake name, Mendax—Latin for "liar"—did not give the game away, and the Navy missed seeing half of Prince Makalin's mustache fall off.[5]

In the end, one of the group must have told; Stephen believed it was Cole.[6] Like the Mayor of Cambridge, the Royal Admiralty chose not to prosecute because they couldn't control the narrative; the press was having too good a time.[7] The jokers escaped almost unpunished. The Navy squirmed and tightened security.

Reading about it today, we squirm for other reasons. The hoax amused people at the time partly because of shared racist assumptions: superior naval officers bowed to royals who were at the same time Africans, and thus considered inferior. Our society is no longer easy with blackface, let alone racism. But in 1940, with German armed forces again menacing the U.K., Virginia—by then the celebrated author of *Mrs Dalloway, To the Lighthouse,* and other novels, and only a year from her suicide by drowning in 1941—told her version of the story publicly to audiences "helpless with laughter." For them, it wasn't about race. It was about young, inventive Britons outwitting a formidable power—a comforting image as they faced Hitler across the English Channel.[8]

Missing Link Found at Piltdown

I n 1908, British workmen were digging gravel at Piltdown when one brought his pickaxe down hard and shattered what looked like an old coconut. Someone handed a piece of it to a bystander, amateur scientist Charles Dawson. He said it came from "a thick human cranium."[1] Could it be new evidence of human evolution?

Interest in human evolution was high. Scientists had evidence (such as the remains of Neanderthal "cavemen" found in Europe since 1829) and a theory: influential books by Thomas Huxley (1863) and Charles Darwin (1871) argued that humans, like all other animals, developed from earlier ancestors. While the public debated the social and religious implications of this idea, scientists worked to puzzle out humanity's family tree. Amateur fossil hunters could turn up important new clues—maybe even the "missing link," a transitional fossil with characteristics of both apes and humans.

The gravel at Piltdown had been deposited by an ancient river; it was a likely place to find early Ice Age fossils.[2] Dawson dug some more and took his findings to geologist Alfred Smith Woodward at the British Museum (Natural History) in London. In 1912, the two men found "a fragment of ape-like jawbone with two teeth, still more bits of skull, several fossil animal teeth and bones, several flint tools—and later on a remarkable bone implement."[3]

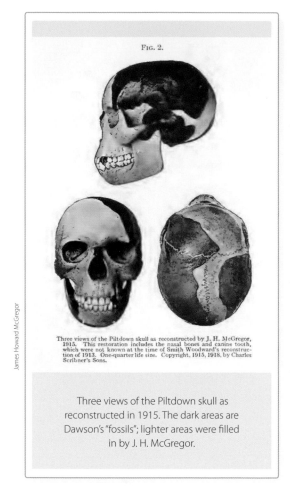

FIG. 2.

Three views of the Piltdown skull as reconstructed by J. H. McGregor, 1915. This restoration includes the nasal bones and canine tooth, which were not known at the time of Smith Woodward's reconstruction of 1913. One-quarter life size. Copyright, 1915, 1918, by Charles Scribner's Sons.

Three views of the Piltdown skull as reconstructed in 1915. The dark areas are Dawson's "fossils"; lighter areas were filled in by J. H. McGregor.

James Howard McGregor

Woodward believed that the skull and jaw came from the same individual—a 500,000-year-old ancestor of humanity. It would be too great a coincidence to find an apelike man and a manlike ape in Piltdown.

One scientist believed Piltdown Man's brain was small; another thought it was large, showing that intelligence drove human evolution.[4] But they all assumed Dawson's find was real. In 1915, he produced more evidence: bits of a second skull, found two miles from the first. For decades, belief in Piltdown Man blocked acceptance of other fossil discoveries.[5] Findings in China, Java, Europe, and Africa made no sense if "the one, true human ancestor" arose in Britain.[6]

Then scientists discovered new methods of dating ancient artifacts. Tests in 1949 showed that Piltdown Man was only about 50,000 years old—too young for a human ancestor. Indeed, the cranium was older than the jaw. In 1953, Piltdown Man was exposed as a deliberate fake. Somebody had paired a human cranium with an orangutan's jaw, stained them with brown oil paint, filed down the ape's teeth to look more human, and carved the "remarkable bone implement" with a metal knife.[7]

Who did it, and why? Suspects range from mystery writer Arthur Conan Doyle to philosopher Pierre Teilhard de Chardin, but the likeliest culprit is Dawson. Living nearby, he had means and opportunity.[8] He may have been motivated partly by a longing for scientific acclaim. Perhaps, too, he had a patriotic desire to see Britain as the cradle of humanity; he certainly wanted to rival the 1907 discovery of *Homo Heidelbergensis* in Germany.[9]

He probably did not mean to stunt the careers of a generation of evolutionary scientists—but he did. The scientists who studied Piltdown Man liked the implications of Dawson's finds, and they had a

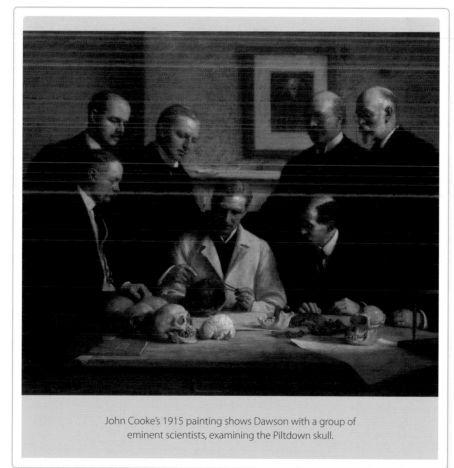

John Cooke's 1915 painting shows Dawson with a group of eminent scientists, examining the Piltdown skull.

John Cooke

The Hornet, 1871

This 1871 cartoon of Charles Darwin as a "venerable orang-outang" satirized his idea that humans are related to the great apes.

tendency "to pressure one another into accepting mainstream (or what they hoped would become mainstream) views."[10] They lacked intellectual caution; they built overly ambitious theories on flimsy evidence,[11] and they rejected evidence that didn't fit their theories.

Once the hoax was discovered, understanding of human origins was clarified. "Darwin is still right," the *Science News Letter* reassured readers, and it became increasingly obvious that Africa, not Britain, was the cradle of the human race.[12]

The Piltdown Chicken

Like the fossils manufactured to fool Dr. Beringer (Chapter 11), this "archaeoraptor" fits suspiciously well on its stone.

In 1999, *National Geographic* announced the discovery of another missing link, a Chinese fossil with the head and upper body of a bird and the long, stiff tail of a dinosaur. Informally dubbed "Archaeoraptor," it turned out to be a forgery and was renamed "Piltdown Chicken."[16] Modern science may have helped create this hoax, but like the clumsy fossils that tricked Dr. Beringer (Chapter 11), it fit suspiciously well on its piece of stone.

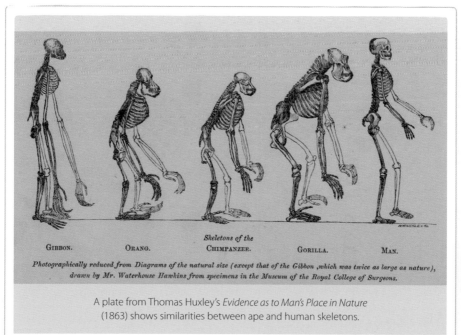

GIBBON.   ORANG.   *Skeletons of the* CHIMPANZEE.   GORILLA.   MAN.

Photographically reduced from Diagrams of the natural size (except that of the Gibbon ,which was twice as large as nature), drawn by Mr. Waterhouse Hawkins from specimens in the Museum of the Royal College of Surgeons.

A plate from Thomas Huxley's *Evidence as to Man's Place in Nature* (1863) shows similarities between ape and human skeletons.

Thomas Huxley

How Do Scientists Decide Which Bones to Trust?

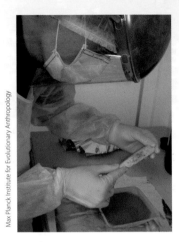

Max Planck Institute for Evolutionary Anthropology

The relationship between Neanderthals and modern humans becomes clearer with DNA analysis.

The Piltdown scandal showed that the fossil record could be faked, but scientists remained confident that other finds were genuine clues to humanity's past. Quantity strengthened some evidence, as did multiple sites. By 1908, hundreds of Neanderthal bones had been found in various European sites.[13] The first skulls found, in 1829, were almost as fragmentary as Dawson's find, but sheer numbers of Neanderthal remains showed they were real. Tests for the age of Neanderthal bones and artifacts are consistent; taken together, they fit into a plausible narrative. And modern DNA testing does not show that Neanderthal skulls and jaws come from different species—instead, it shows that humans today have traces of Neanderthal DNA.[14]

Modern technology can help assess even an isolated find. In 2003, amateur archaeologist Kim Holt found part of a buffalo skull with an embedded projectile point. Whitened with age, the point was in the style of the Calf Creek culture. Researchers had debated whether similar items were used as knives or spear points; this find, if genuine, would help answer the question. But was it a hoax? No. Authenticated by CT

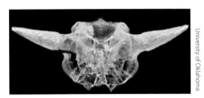

University of Oklahoma

CT imagery was used to authenticate a 5,000-year-old projectile point from the Calf Creek culture.

imagery, biometrics, and radiocarbon assay at the University of Oklahoma, it adds to our knowledge of American life around 3000 BC.[15]

Naked Man Conquers Maine Woods

In August 1913, a naked 44-year-old artist killed a bear. Joe Knowles needed its skin; August nights were chilly in Maine's north woods. So with sharp stones and hard wood he dug a pit four feet deep, baited it with ripe-smelling fish, and hid it with branches. It cost him two or three days' hard work, but he trapped a bear and clubbed it to death. Then he had to do something even harder: skin it. Knowles said proudly it was "the biggest thing" he had "accomplished in the forest."[1] He had once been a Maine guide, but he'd never before left his twentieth-century tools (and clothes) behind.

What was a slightly flabby 204-pound man doing in the woods without so much as a knife or a match? He wanted to show that even in 1913 a person could leave the "artificial life" of cities behind him and "live on what nature intended him to have."[2] He also needed the money. In those days before reality TV, a naked man's wilderness adventure was just the sort of gimmick to sell newspapers and help an underemployed artist earn a living.

The *Boston Post* sponsored the expedition, and readers loved it. Coverage began early, as Knowles explained in the paper what he was going to do. He would eat frogs' legs, he promised. He would build shelters and catch fish barehanded. He would write updates to the *Post* on birch

On August 4, 1913, Joe Knowles stripped to his G-string and said good-bye to supporters. He promised to spend the next two months alone in the woods.

bark using charcoal from his campfires. When doctors checked him afterward, they would find him in the pink of health.[3]

And so they did. On October 4, Knowles emerged in his stinking bearskin, weighing a trim 174 pounds. A *Post* crew took him south by train, stopping for one banquet after another. On October 9, they reached Boston, where tens of thousands of people turned out to greet his motorcade. The *Post* doubled its circulation,[4] and "Nature Man" toured the vaudeville circuit for weeks, showing off his fire-making skills nationwide.

Then on November 30—just when the hoopla was dying down— the *Boston American* published an exposé. Reporter Bert Ford claimed that Knowles hadn't spent his two months alone and naked after all. He'd spent them in a log cabin with an unnamed "manager," provisions, clothes, and a bed. That bearskin had bullet holes in it, according to Ford, and the pit where Knowles claimed he trapped his bear just wasn't deep or bloody enough.[5]

Naked Publicity Gimmicks and Hoaxes

Metropolitan Museum of Art

September Morn, by Paul Chabas (ca. 1912), was just the sort of picture to outrage censor Anthony Comstock.

One of the great hoax artists of the early twentieth century was publicist Harry Reichenbach. In 1920, he booked Mr. Thomas R. Zann into an exclusive New York hotel. Bystanders saw a huge box lifted into the man's window by a crane. What was in it—a piano? The mysterious guest ordered 15 pounds of raw steak delivered to his room, where hotel staff were met with the roar of a huge lion. *The Revenge of Tarzan* opened in theaters just as newspapers were covering T.R. Zann and his terrifying pet. (What a bad pun.) Another time, Reichenbach managed to quadruple the salary of a movie-star client simply by dropping $20 in pennies. Children followed Reichenbach to pick up the pennies, adults followed out of curiosity, and by the time Reichenbach and his client reached the Metro Studios, they had an entourage big enough to make the actor look very, very popular.[8]

But Reichenbach's most famous hoax may be one that he didn't commit. He said he helped an art dealer sell 2,000 prints of a nude painting, *September Morn,* by complaining about it to Anthony Comstock. Comstock, founder of the New York Society for the Suppression of Vice, was famous for censoring things, and people always wanted to see the things he censored. The hoax on Comstock could have worked, so the story was plausible—but false. Reichenbach was hoaxing the public instead.[9]

Knowles said the pit was deep enough, and blood (and other remains) would have disappeared quickly. He bought a bear in Canada and demonstrated his bear-clubbing technique. He told his side of the story in a memoir, *Alone in the Wilderness.* And he went out to California to repeat the experiment in unfamiliar woods, where he had no old friends to serve as possible accomplices.

His second experiment, launched under the auspices of the *San Francisco Examiner* in July 1914, was eclipsed by the outbreak of World War I. A third experiment was supposed to include a beautiful starlet playing

Dawn Woman under Knowles's tutelage, but it fizzled when Dawn Woman realized she would have to kill wild animals.[6]

Knowles *could* have survived naked in the woods, but *did* he? Twenty-five years later, Michael McKeogh told *The New Yorker* that he was the "manager" who had shared a cabin with Knowles, hid him from game wardens, and pushed him through to October 4. Knowles by then was a 68-year-old artist living with his wife in a driftwood beach house at Cape Disappointment, Washington. A sign by his door said, "Welcome, Stranger, pause a while."[7]

Isolated Living in Biosphere 2

Faker or not, Joe Knowles hit on an "experiment" that appealed to people's imagination. He raised a question that mattered: could humans still survive in the wild?

Knowles would have been interested in a very different experiment carried out in the 1990s. Biosphere 2 was an Isolated Confined Environment (ICE) of the kind humans might build on another planet. Could we survive on Mars? Could we re-create the ecologies of

Biosphere 2 is no longer an Isolated Confined Environment, but it still functions as a research facility and is open to the public.

Earth in a three-acre facility? Biosphere 2 has a below-ground infrastructure to support the tiny ecosystems under its domes: a miniature rainforest, an ocean (with its own coral reef), wetlands, grasslands, a fog desert, a farm, and a living area. From 1991 to 1993, eight scientists lived there, cut off from the outside world.[10] Results of the experiment were mixed. Many animal and plant species died off, and the team split into hostile factions. People grew crankier when a cloudy winter cut solar power and oxygen levels fell. Cockroaches flourished.[11] A follow-up experimental mission in 1994 ended early.

The Biosphere 2 experiment was not a hoax, but the team faced problems similar to those that plagued Joe Knowles. "The complete isolation got on my nerves," said Knowles. Loneliness caused him "mental" unease "a hundredfold worse than any physical suffering."[12] The environments we live in are social as well as physical, and to survive we must adapt psychologically as well as physically.

The Spectric Poets Unmasked

On April 26, 1918, a young man challenged a lecturer at Detroit's Twentieth Century Club: "Is it not true, Mr. Bynner, that you are Emanuel Morgan and Arthur Davison Ficke is Anne Knish?" The lecturer said, "Yes."[1] Witter Bynner had just ended his Spectric Poetry Hoax.

The Great Moon Hoax (Chapter 16) succeeded because it sounded like what readers expected to see in newspapers, only more entertaining. The poetry hoaxters played with conventions in a different genre. As poets themselves, Bynner and Ficke had nothing against the conventions of traditional poetry. But they thought modern poetic theories were silly and pretentious. The influential poet Amy Lowell, for instance, had explained what it meant to be a member of the Imagist school:

> 1. To use the language of common speech. . . . 2. To create new rhythms. . . . 3. To allow absolute freedom in the choice of subject. . . . 4. To present an image. . . . 5. To produce poetry that is hard and clear, never blurred nor indefinite. 6. Finally, most of us believe that concentration is of the very essence of poetry."[2]

What did that even mean?

So in 1916, Bynner and Ficke (a.k.a. Emanuel Morgan and Anne Knish) announced a new school: the Spectric. To be Spectric "speaks, to the mind, of that process of diffraction by which are disarticulated the several colored and other rays of which light is composed," wrote Knish. It "connotes the overtones, adumbrations, or spectres which for the poet haunt all objects both of the seen and unseen world. . . ."[3] The Spectrics could be just as hard to understand as the Imagists.

UC Berkeley

Witter Bynner had just seen a ballet, *Le Spectre de la Rose*, when he invented the Spectric school of poetry.

They planned to make fun of the Imagists and others by writing bad poetry that was just stylish and obscure enough to fool critics into thinking it was good. Writing bad poetry proved tricky, however, and recruiting enough members to make the Spectrics a proper school wasn't easy. In the end, they locked their friend Marjorie Allen Seiffert in her bedroom until she "had become Spectric."[4] Under the name of Elijah Hay, she not only wrote Spectric poems but carried on a friendly correspondence with William Carlos Williams—a major poet who thought highly of the new school's work. (Williams liked Morgan's work the best; he thought Knish was too theoretical, as was—in his view—typical of women.)

The friends set up false addresses for correspondence. Rumors circulated about them. Anne Knish was "a devastating beauty,"[5] and Morgan and Hay were rivals for her affection. All three were elusive—people who tried to visit them in one city always found they had just left for another. One editor reassured Bynner "that the school was genuine since friends of his were acquainted with both the founders."[6]

But Ficke, who served with the U.S. Army in France, had the most amusing encounter. A brigadier general asked him if he thought *Spectra* (the 1916 collection of Emanuel Morgan and Anne Knish) was genuine, and Ficke said he suspected it was just a hoax. The general agreed because, as he told Ficke, "I myself am Anne Knish." Ficke ranked this meeting among "the most deliriously happy hours I have ever spent."[7]

After the hoax was revealed, all three poets continued to write and publish, but being Spectric changed them. For Seiffert, whose husband disapproved of her writing, there was something liberating about a pseudonym; after being Elijah Hay, she wrote under the name Angela Cypher as well as her own.[8] Ficke admitted some of his best work was in *Spectra*, and Bynner said he couldn't "get rid of" Morgan: "I don't know where he leaves off and I begin. He's a boomerang!"[9]

Two Spectric Poems

ANNE KNISH

Opus 200

If I should enter to his chamber
And suddenly touch him,
Would he fade to a thin mist,
Or glow into a fire-ball,
Or burst like a punctured light-globe?
It is impossible that he would merely yawn and rub
And say—"What is it?" [10]

EMANUEL MORGAN

These Gulls

These gulls look more
to me like lima-beans.
What difference anyway
Whether a beak and wings
add to the contour
Or a pod and vine?
A round belly can lie
Quietly parallel
To the round edge of the earth.
And yet after all
You whom I love
Look to me like me.
And this becomes you. [11]

Their 1916 book, *Spectra*, alternated poems by "Anne Knish" and "Emanuel Morgan."

The Original Ponzi Scheme

harles Ponzi (1882–1949) was the son of an Italian postman, and stamps fascinated him. So did gambling. His family saved enough money to send him to the University of Rome, but he skipped classes and gambled away his money trying to keep up with rich friends. Even after flunking out, he would not stoop to entry-level jobs or physical labor. So in 1903, his family packed him off to America with $200 to tide him over until he got settled. On the ship, he bought drinks, tipped lavishly, and gambled. He arrived with $2.50, determined to get rich quick.[1]

It didn't happen. He learned English fast enough, but found only the low-level jobs he'd scorned in Italy. In 1907, he moved to Montreal, where he became manager at a new bank serving Italian immigrants. But the owner was using new deposits to pay the interest on existing accounts. (This kind of swindle was then called "robbing Peter to pay Paul" but has since become known as a Ponzi scheme.) When the bank failed, the owner fled to Mexico. Ponzi, trying to organize his own return to the U.S., forged a check and spent three years in a Canadian jail.[2]

In 1911, he allegedly smuggled illegal immigrants across the U.S. border. This time he landed in Atlanta Prison, where he was inspired by Wall Street speculator (and fellow inmate) Charles W. Morse. But although he tried to come up with his own foolproof schemes to get rich, Ponzi's best job after release was with the J.R. Poole Company in

Charles Ponzi (March 3, 1882 – January 18, 1949). Charles Ponzi was a business-man born in Italy who became known as a swindler for his money scheme.

Boston, where his salary rose from $16 per week in 1916 to a supervisor's $50 per week by the end of 1917. It was enough to get married.

Then in September 1918, he quit Poole to join his father-in-law's failing business—which went into bankruptcy in January 1919.[3] Ponzi rented office space and tried to set up an import-export business, but

Pyramid Schemes

A Ponzi scheme can work as long as more and more new investors buy into it. If 16 people invest one month and 32 people invest the next month, the operator can pay the first 16 people back with interest. Charles Ponzi ran short of International Reply Coupons and luck before he ran out of investors, but Boston's population (748,060 in 1920) included many who were too young, too poor, or too wise to take part in his scheme.

Pyramid schemes can be small, like a chain letter that asks you to send a little money to everybody listed in the letter, add your own name to the list, and send copies to everyone you know. Then they (and everyone they know) will supposedly send you money. This type of letter counts as mail fraud.[9]

The schemes can also be large. A gigantic one nearly bankrupted Albania in the 1990s, and in 2008 Bernard Madoff was arrested for a $65 billion Ponzi scheme—called the largest one in history.[10]

without seed capital, he was stymied. He thought of creating a "Trader's Guide" to help other businessmen, but his bank refused him a loan.

At last, being a stamp collector, Ponzi thought of trading International Reply Coupons. The U.S. and 62 other nations had agreed on these coupons in 1906 to help businessmen pay return postage on correspondence across international boundaries. But in the economic turmoil after World War I, some currencies lost value relative to others. By 1919, a dollar would buy 66 coupons in Rome, and those coupons would be worth $3.30 in Boston.[4]

This time Ponzi didn't go to the bank; he advertised to small investors. He promised whatever they put into his new Securities Exchange

Company would be paid back with 50% interest in just 90 days. If they reinvested, they could more than double their initial stake in six months.

Two huge problems made this scheme impossible. First, there weren't enough postal coupons in the world. To pay just his first 18 investors, Ponzi would have needed 53,100 coupons.[5] Second, the post office wasn't set up to redeem coupons for cash.

While he tried to solve these problems, Ponzi smiled charmingly and paid interest to established customers from the deposits of new ones, just as the Montreal bank owner had done. For months he imagined he'd find a way to pay everybody. Meanwhile he lived large, bought the bank that had once denied him a loan, and developed an ulcer. In July 1920, he took in nearly $6.5 million from more than 20,000 investors.[6]

When the *Boston Post* claimed Ponzi was a fraud, even his own publicist agreed.[7] Massachusetts authorities investigated. In August 1920, he was arrested; in November, he pled guilty. His investors lost their money.[8] Ponzi still felt he could have solved the problem, given time. An optimist to the end, he could scam even himself.

Fairies Are Caught on Camera

Sherlock Holmes could see through any villain, but his creator, Sir Arthur Conan Doyle, was fooled in 1920 by two young girls who snapped pictures of fairies.

In 1917, artistic Elsie Wright was 16. She and her parents lived in the peaceful English village of Cottingley, near a small stream. Her 10-year-old cousin lived in South Africa but had been uprooted by World War I. While her soldier father was at the front,[1] Frances and her mother were staying with the Wrights.

Frances was bright, energetic, and clumsy. "Pity anyone with corns who is around when Frances gets excited," said Mrs. Wright.[2] Outdoors, the child kept stumbling into the stream and soaking her clothes. Why? She said she was playing with fairies. The parents scolded, but Elsie backed her up. Fairies did play there, Elsie said, and given a camera, she could prove it.

In Elsie's first picture, Frances looked more interested in the camera than the fairies dancing under her nose. That picture, and a later one of Elsie with a gnome, became family curiosities.

Two years later, Mrs. Wright mentioned them at a meeting of the Theosophical Society. Members were always interested in evidence of the supernatural, and the rumor spread, reaching Doyle in 1920. If not "the most elaborate and ingenious hoax ever played upon the public," he said, an actual photograph of fairies could be an "epoch-making"

Science and Society Picture Library

Frances and the fairies (Elsie Wright's first photograph).

event.[3] He joined forces with Edward Gardner, a Theosophical Society officer, to investigate.

They sought expert opinion. One photographer was skeptical, but Doyle and Gardner listened to the one who said the picture could be genuine. They believed they had an important case, but time was running out—because only the young and innocent could see (and photograph) fairies. Elsie was now 19 and Frances 13. Soon one of them would "'fall in love' and then—hey presto!" said Gardner—they would lose their magic.[4]

Indeed, the girls only captured three pictures with cameras the investigators gave them in 1920. In 1921, a psychic followed the girls around and reported seeing a few fairies, but the girls caught none on film. Elsie said fairies looked more transparent to her as she got older.

Doyle wrote it all up for *The Strand Magazine*, and his article was a sensation. Some readers were outraged that the great Conan Doyle had been taken in by such a silly fraud. Mr. Wright "found it hard to believe that so intelligent a man could be bamboozled 'by our Elsie, and

Alfred Noyes

Elsie's fairy drawings were inspired by this illustration for a fairy-summoning poem, "A Spell for a Fairy," by Alfred Noyes.

her at the bottom of the class!'"[5] Critics pointed out that the fairies looked like modern illustrations; even their hairstyles were modish.

But others sent in accounts of their own experiences with fairies. They liked the idea that humans could make contact with benign intelligences on another plane. World War I had ended by then, and the 1918 flu epidemic was over, but almost everyone in England had lost family and friends. Doyle himself had lost many,[6] and he took comfort in séances, where trusted mediums brought him into touch with his son—not dead, but living in Summerland, a blessed waystation between earthly incarnations.

Many still believed in the Cottingley photographs even after 1982, when the cousins confessed. Elsie had drawn the fairies on cardboard and cut them out with her aunt's sewing shears. Hat pins held them in place. The photos were a hoax meant to be played on their parents, not the public, but Doyle and Gardner were so eager for it to be true, the girls hadn't cared to disillusion them.

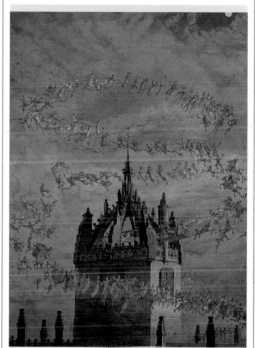

Charles Doyle

This swirl of ghosts about a church tower was painted by Charles Doyle. His son, author of the Sherlock Holmes stories, sought communication with ghosts and other spirits.

Both men profited financially from the affair.[7] Elsie and Frances did not, but they were annoyed by publicity off and on for the rest of their lives.

Why Arthur Conan Doyle Believed in Fairies

New York Times Company, 1914

Sir Arthur Conan Doyle, author of the Sherlock Holmes stories.

Doyle said that he was "a cool observer"[8] and "by nature of a somewhat sceptical turn."[9] He drew on science to explain why we can't always see fairies. They might normally vibrate too fast or too slow for us to see, he speculated.[10] He believed in the Cottingley photographs for several reasons, including:

1. They were consistent with other things he knew and believed about the world, both from science and from spiritualism (he thought young girls were quite likely to have mediumistic powers that would fade with age).

2. He saw the girls as working-class children with no access to the knowledge and skills needed for a successful hoax. (He underestimated them. Elsie had left school at 13, but her greatest talent was drawing, and she had worked for a photographer.)

3. He cherry-picked the reports of photography experts, ignoring the ones likeliest to discredit the girls' pictures.

4. He refused to believe "that because some professional trickster, apt at the game of deception, can produce a somewhat similar effect, therefore the originals were produced in the same way."[11] That is, a thing doesn't *have* to be a hoax just because it *could* be.

But the single most important reason Doyle believed in the fairies must have been desire. He really wanted to believe.

Did Grand Duchess Anastasia Survive the Revolution?

In the chaotic aftermath of World War I, the tragedies of two young women became entangled. Grand Duchess Anastasia Romanov (1901–1918) was a Russian princess; Franziska Schanzkowska (1896–1984) was a Polish factory worker. Both suffered extreme trauma in the war. They never met.

Yet from 1922 on, many people believed that Franziska was really Anastasia. In 1927, a Berlin newspaper exposed her as Miss Schanzkowska and declared the case closed,[1] but in 1967, it was still contested in German courts.[2] Only in the 1990s did DNA evidence show that Franziska was no relation to the Romanovs.

Anastasia grew up in royal palaces, studying hard and doing her chores.[3] When war came, she visited wounded soldiers in hospitals, teaching one of them to read.[4] But revolutionaries took the royal family prisoner in 1917, and in 1918, they were herded into a basement room in the middle of the night and shot to death.

Franziska grew up in a family of Polish farm workers; her alcoholic father died when she was a child. She hid in a wagon, reading, while others harvested the fields.[5]

In her late teens she went to Berlin and worked in a factory that made grenades. But in 1916, her fiancé was killed in the war, and soon afterward she dropped a grenade at work. The explosion injured

"Fräulein Unbekannt" in 1922: "Miss Unknown" had been at the Dalldorf Asylum for two years when a fellow psychiatric patient said she looked like Grand Duchess Tatiana.

Franziska badly and killed the foreman standing next to her.

In 1920, Franziska nearly drowned in a Berlin canal. She had no ID and refused to say who she was. (Maybe she didn't know.) The police sent her to an asylum, where she was called "Miss Unknown." But another patient decided she looked like Anastasia's sister, Tatiana. On release, the other patient told friends about the princess in the asylum. Germany was full of Russian refugees, and soon people who had known the Romanovs began to visit.

"She's too short to be Tatiana," pronounced a baroness. "I did not say I was Tatiana," said Miss Unknown. Her new friends concluded she was Anastasia, and for the rest of her life, she was a claimant to the Romanov legacy—an impostor.

She called herself Anna Anderson. She said a young soldier had rescued her from the basement where her family was killed. They were married, but her husband was shot in the streets of Bucharest in 1919. Anna had traveled to Berlin seeking her relatives, without success. Had she despaired and jumped into the canal, or had she been pushed? She never said.[6]

Anna had an amazing memory for the details of life at the Romanov court. She remembered pets, nicknames, and her father's favorite pipe;

Princess Caraboo

Portrait by Edward Bird, 1817

Franziska Schanzkowska was not the first poor girl to pass herself off as a princess. In 1817, an exotically dressed young woman was found wandering near Bristol, England. She spoke and wrote an unknown language, communicated with the English by signs, and finally established herself as the princess of Javasu—a land as imaginary as her language. Like the false Anastasia, Princess Caraboo reacted with great emotion to things that reminded her of home. (In Anastasia's case, it might be a pipe; in Caraboo's, a pineapple.) Again like the false Anastasia, Caraboo spent time as the privileged guest of wealthy people.

But Caraboo was an independent character, and she had more fun than Anastasia. As an exotic foreigner, she could enjoy activities that were off-limits to most English girls at the time, such as fencing, climbing trees, and "swimming naked in the lake...."[9] She offered a romantic story people wanted to believe, but she confessed her true identity to one hostess: Mary Baker, a servant and the daughter of a cobbler. Her hostess forgave her and bankrolled a trip to America, where Mary found work and supported herself independently.

stray memories would make her weep with emotion. If she was not Anastasia, how did she know these things? Had she learned them from books, magazine articles, and the reminiscences of the first people who accepted her as the Grand Duchess? Her memory, along with her looks and manners, convinced skeptics.

On the other hand, there were astonishing gaps. She seemed to understand Russian, but she would never speak it. Head injuries, tragedy, and a near fatal case of tuberculosis must have left her with partial amnesia, supporters thought.[7]

Some Romanov survivors believed she was Anastasia; others said she was lying, hoping to claim a share of the Tsar's assets. Franziska may have believed her own story, or her real motive may have been a simple need for shelter and protection. She spent the next years, between hospital stays, as the difficult guest of one noble family after another. Finally she married an eccentric Virginia professor and settled down as a hoarder. One writer thought the imposture "happened by accident" and swept her along.[8] In the end, she remembered herself only as Anastasia.

Houdini Debunks a Medium

I t was 1924, and Harry Houdini was on the warpath. Psychic mediums were frauds, he said, exploiting people's grief. They must be exposed, and Houdini—the handcuff king, the magician who could make elephants vanish—would expose them.

He joined four learned doctors on a panel vetting psychics for the *Scientific American*. The magazine had issued a challenge in 1922: a $2,500 reward to a medium who produced a visible psychic manifestation to the satisfaction of the judges.[1] Early candidates had been quickly unmasked, but Houdini's fellow judges thought Mina "Margery" Crandon, a Boston doctor's wife, could be the real thing. Were they in love with her? Houdini, who had picked up his education in dime museums and on the vaudeville circuit, thought he could see through a hoax faster than these experts.

Communications with the dead had evolved from the spirit telegraphy of the Fox sisters (Chapter 19). Table-rapping was still an option, but spirits could also speak out loud—or whisper. Special trumpets amplified their voices. Alternatively they could write, a letter at a time through Ouija boards[2] or by automatic writing.[3] Sir Arthur Conan Doyle's wife channeled Houdini's mother in 1922. Houdini believed in the afterlife, but Lady Doyle's fifteen-page message (in English, headed with a cross) didn't sound like his German immigrant mother, a rabbi's wife.[4] The Doyles' friendship with Houdini was doomed.

Magician Harry Houdini was determined to expose medium Mina "Margery" Crandon as a fraud.

Spiritualists and stage magicians used many of the same techniques. Houdini might have wanted to believe in messages from beyond the grave, but knowing how to fake them made that hard for him.

Margery was a new medium; she began doing séances for her husband and his friends in 1923. Her spirit control was her late brother Walter, a railroad man with an irreverent sense of humor, and her early physical effects ranged from a runaway table to "an ethereal rendition of 'Taps.'"[5] She did automatic writing in at least eight languages (including poor German and obscene Latin), and Walter could stop all the Crandons' clocks at the same moment.

How did these things happen? To make sure Margery wasn't faking, her husband and friends held her hands and feet—and yet the spirit trumpet flew through the air, and electric devices went dead. Later, investigators from the *Scientific American* and the American Society for Psychical Research (ASPR) devised new equipment to test her powers. Could she (or Walter) affect a tamper-proof scale or ring a special bell? She was enclosed in a spirit cabinet—a portable closet from which she couldn't reach these tools.[6]

Or could she? Houdini trusted none of Margery's restraints. Sitting beside her in the dark, he could feel her foot move to ring the bell. He thought she tossed the trumpet with her head. So he had a special box constructed to hold her, allowing only her head and hands to poke out. Still a ruler turned up inside the box. Did Houdini put it there to discredit her, as Margery said, or was Margery planning to move things with it, as Houdini said?[7]

Houdini demonstrates a box designed to keep Margery from using her feet to create "psychic" effects in the dark.

Houdini's quarrels with his fellow judges sold newspapers; his demonstrations of séance cheats sold tickets. Nobody won the *Scientific American* prize, but Margery continued to create amazing séance phenomena. Her dentist showed her how to capture a ghost's fingerprint—and when Walter's thumbprint turned out to match her dentist's, the scientists considered her chicanery obvious.

Houdini died in 1926, promising his wife that he'd come back if possible and deliver a secret message. She held Halloween séances for the next ten years, but never heard the message: "Rosabelle believe."[8]

Other Ways of Knowing: Science and New Religions

The *Scientific American* challenge to psychics highlighted conflicting ways of looking at the world. Believers found religious truth or personal comfort in communicating with the dead; skeptics might hope to be convinced. Many at least regarded psychic phenomena as worthy of respectful study; the American Society for Psychical Research, founded in 1884, included some of America's leading psychologists.

(Continued on next page)

(Continued from previous page)

After all, nineteenth-century science had discovered radiation. If we are sur-rounded by invisible waves of light, sound, and radioactivity, why could there not also be fairies and spirits vibrating at rates we cannot perceive (Chapter 32)? Pseudosci-ence, occultism, and new religions all gained ground as science forced Victorians to question traditional certainties. "The remarkable revival of occult arts in this age of ours

Madame Blavatsky and Henry Steel Olcot.

is a source of wonder to scientific men," said one scholar in 1904; it is "a reaction against the rampant materialism of the times."[9]

Religious ways of knowing generally involve revelation and authority—sometimes reinforced by miraculous phenomena. For instance, Joseph Smith, led by the Angel Moroni to a buried book of gold plates, translated it into Eng-lish and published it as *The Book of Mormon* in 1830[10] ; since nobody else saw the plates, this must be taken on faith. Helena Petrovna Blavatsky, co-founder with Henry Steel Olcott and others of the Theosophical Society, was guided by the teaching of Mahatmas Koot Hoomi and Morya; since she zealously protected their true identi-ties,[11] this too must be taken on faith. She was characterized as a charlatan: "This nineteenth century being the age of woman's rights, it is only natural that the great-est charlatan should be a woman."[12] She was a magnetic character who seemed to cause showers of roses and other wonders, but her reputation suffered from reports of fraud in 1884 and 1885.[13]

By 1886, Olcott was arguing for a "total abandonment of sensationalism,"[14] and the Society was torn. The debate raged over who had access to rooms where won-ders had occurred—who could have, or would have, drilled holes and faked appear-ances. But was this relevant to the Society's objectives, from forming "the nucleus of a Universal Brotherhood of Humanity without distinction of race, creed, or color" to investigating "the hidden mysteries of nature and the psychical powers latent in man"? Were miracles, in an age of scientific skepticism, just too much of a distraction?

If You Believe That, I Have a Tower to Sell You

At noon a man stepped out of a third-floor jail window overlooking New York's West Street. A watchman noticed him; so did lunch customers across the street. The man stood on a narrow ledge, pulled out a long white cloth, and began cleaning the window. Then suddenly his cleaning rag became a rope of bedsheets, he shinnied down to the street and ran away. A stunned onlooker knocked on the jail door. "Mister," he asked the guard, "did you know that somebody just escaped from the third floor?"[1] The escapee, "Count Victor Lustig," was scheduled for trial the next day.

Lustig usually performed his hoaxes for a select few; he liked to research his marks in advance. He usually performed in elegant clothing, not prison-issue blue jeans and slippers. But even with limited resources, Lustig could set up a hoax. He knew how to give people something they could easily believe, and how to act as if their belief was never in doubt.

Legally he was Robert Miller, born in Czechoslovakia in 1890, a dropout from the University of Paris.[2] He excelled at languages, gambling, and flirting—all skills that involved paying attention to people. As a young man he enjoyed ocean liners. While crossing the Atlantic, he could get to know the wealthy passengers and decide which ones to scam.

© Bettmann/CORBIS

Counterfeiter Victor Lustig.

One of his favorite con games was the "money box" scheme. He was an aristocrat in name only, he would tell a mark. (That part was true.) He maintained a good lifestyle because he had a Romanian money box that could duplicate a $100 bill. Put one bill in, and after six hours, two bills would come out. He would agree to sell it for a high enough price (usually over $10,000).[3] Leaving the machine primed with two $100 bills, he had a good 12 hours to escape before the hoax was discovered.

During the war, German torpedoes ruined his ocean liner trade. Lustig managed on land, scamming people in the U.S. and Europe under one alias after another. He scammed crooks (including Al Capone) and lawmen (including a Texas sheriff who paid $123,000 for a money box).[4]

In 1925, a Paris newspaper gave him the idea that made him famous. The Eiffel Tower needed expensive maintenance, the paper said.[5] Lustig quickly assumed a new role: Deputy Director of the Ministry of Posts and Telegraphs. He had fake stationery printed up and invited five contractors to meet with him privately on a matter that called for discretion. He was selling the Eiffel Tower for scrap, he told them; the contractor with the winning bid could demolish it and sell tons of metal.

One of them, Andre Poisson, was new in town. He didn't know Paris well, but he knew a corrupt official when he saw one. When Lustig hinted that the ministry didn't pay much, Poisson quickly gave him a $70,000 bribe. Almost as quickly, Lustig left France, but Poisson was too embarrassed to report the crime. Having sold the Eiffel Tower once, Lustig tried again— and was nearly caught. He ran away to the U.S.

Selling public monuments was an old game in America. The "chief failing" of a conman known as "I.O.U. O'Brien" was selling "property

The Romanian money box?

he did not own"; he sold the Brooklyn Bridge in 1901.[6] Another crook, George C. Parker, sold it several times. American comics started using phrases like "If you believe that, I have a bridge to sell you."[7]

But Lustig turned to another moneymaker: forgery, a federal crime. In 1935, a jealous girlfriend told federal agents where to find him, and they caught him in New York with $51,000 in counterfeit bills. After his lunch-hour jail break, they caught up with him again in Pittsburgh. He spent the rest of his life in Alcatraz, a maximum security federal prison where Capone also did time. Both men died in 1947.

Unloading the Eiffel Tower

Library of Congress

Eiffel Tower, looking toward the Trocadero, Exposition Universal, 1900, Paris, France.

When the Eiffel Tower opened in 1889, it was the tallest structure on earth—but it wasn't meant to stay in place forever. It was just part of the Paris Exposition, a great fair held to mark the hundredth anniversary of the French Revolution and to show off French scientific and industrial power. It was supposed to be removed in 1909.[8] Some Parisians could hardly wait for it to disappear. But the builder, Gustave Eiffel, really wanted it to stay, so he worked from the beginning to make it an indispensable platform for scientific experiments. (Father Theodor Wulf discovered cosmic rays at the Eiffel Tower in 1910.)[9] In the end, it was height that kept the tower in place. It proved useful for radio and telegraph transmissions, and in World War I it was used to jam German military communications. By 1925, many Parisians admired the tower, but others still considered it an eyesore. Lustig's hoax was plausible.

The Loch Ness Monster

Sam Fentress

Loch Ness with Urquhart Castle in the foreground.

Mention Loch Ness and most people don't think of its natural beauty or its role in generating hydroelectric power. They don't think of it as part of the 60-mile Caledonian Canal that cuts from the east coast to the west coast of Scotland.[1] They think of its legendary monster, Nessie.

"Loch" means "lake," and Loch Ness is a big one: 22½ miles long, nearly a mile wide on average, and more than 750 feet deep at its deepest. Its surface is some 50 feet above sea level.[2] Salmon swim up to it from the sea; porpoises and seals (which could more easily be mistaken for monsters) do not.

In April 1933, a local couple reported seeing a creature like a whale, rolling and plunging less than a mile from them. When it submerged, it left a wave as big as a steamboat's.[3] Their friend Alex Campbell soon publicized the "monster." Campbell, the lake's water bailiff (law enforcement officer), also wrote for the *Inverness Courier*.[4]

The Loch Ness monster was national news. The *Daily Mail* even hired big-game hunter Marmaduke Wetherell, who made casts of the monster's footprint—but experts at the British Museum found the print had been made by the rear left foot of a hippopotamus. (Such feet were sadly available; people kept them by the front door to hold wet umbrellas.) The monster "became a national joke."[5]

Interest was renewed in April 1934 when the *Mail* published a photograph of a sea serpent's head, allegedly taken by a "surgeon." This

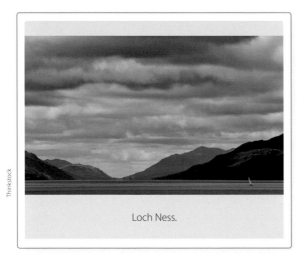

Loch Ness.

Thinkstock

convinced many people, but doubters noticed that identifying scenery had been cropped. Did the photo show something large in Loch Ness or something small in a duck pond? It turned out to be something small in Loch Ness: a toy submarine with a model head on top. Wetherell's stepson confessed in 1994 that he made it for Wetherell to photograph; the surgeon fronted for them.[6] Unlike the hippo foot, Wetherell's second hoax was debated for decades.

Sightings increased, along with occasional photographs. Frogmen dove into the loch. (One magazine called it a "gross invasion" of the monster's privacy.)[7] In 1971, a whiskey manufacturer offered one million pounds for the monster's capture, and took out an insurance policy in case they had to pay up.[8] In 1972, strobe-lit underwater cameras caught what looked like (maybe) a huge flipper.[9] Also in 1972, the monster's dead body was found floating in the loch—but it turned out to be the corpse of an elephant seal, dumped as an April Fool's prank by a 23-year-old zoo worker.[10]

In an age of special effects, it's easy to make a Loch Ness Monster.

Museum of Nessie

Some think the monster is a surviving plesiosaur. One team of scientists argued tongue in cheek that to survive in the loch from prehistoric times, a long-lived species would need a breeding population of at least ten; the biomass of fish in the loch might support up to twenty.[11]

Photographs of Nessie are hard to make out. Some are known fakes; others could be logs, cormorants, or otters. Mirage effects could look like a monster; waves made by motorboats or earthquakes could look like waves made by a submerged monster.

Sightings of Nessie are still frequent and still inconclusive. The Official Loch Ness Sightings Register lists 1,074 sightings from 565 to 2015.[12] An Apple satellite has caught an image that looks a bit like a plesiosaur just beneath the surface.[13] Google sent its street-view cameras to the loch, teaming up with Catlin Seaview Survey for underwater shots, and captured what looks like an undulating serpent until you zoom in on it.[14] And Google Maps allows you, too, to search for the Loch Ness monster from your own computer.[15]

Standards of Evidence and Scientific Names

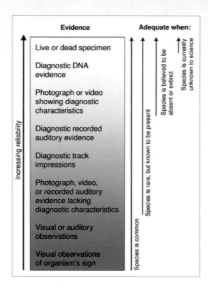

In this proposed ranking of evidence for the occurrence of a rare species, an actual specimen is the most reliable proof.

James St. John

An ivory-billed woodpecker specimen preserved in the Carnegie Museum of Natural History at Pittsburgh.

It's difficult to prove that something doesn't exist. But to prove that rare and endangered species *do* still exist, scientists need more than anecdotal evidence—unverifiable observations of the animals or traces of them. If a single person sees an ivory-billed woodpecker in Arkansas, can we be sure it was there? The last verifiable sighting was in 1944; the bird was believed extinct before 2004, when it was caught in a "blurred and pixilated" video. An acoustic recording *could* be the woodpecker, but it *could* be a blue jay. To be sure that ivory-billed woodpeckers still exist, scientists want photographs or videos that clearly show identifying characteristics; or, better, DNA evidence; or, best of all, an actual specimen, living or dead. To be sure of a creature currently unknown to science, such as the Loch Ness monster, they need the specimen.[16]

If the monster does exist, it should be protected under Britain's endangered species law. For that it needs a scientific name, so in 1975, Sir Peter Scott and Dr. Robert Rines proposed "Nessiteras rhombopteryx," which means "Ness monster with diamond-shaped flipper." British news quickly reported that the scientific name is an anagram for "monster hoax by Sir Peter S."[17]

Martians Attack

On the evening of October 30, 1938, fog shrouded New Jersey.[1] Or was it poison gas? Special bulletins interrupted dance music on the radio to say that a metal cylinder had just hit the town of Grover's Mill with earthquake-like force. Martians were invading Earth! A reporter assured listeners that the army had everything under control. Then he choked, evidently overcome by fumes, and went silent.

Some Grover's Mill residents snatched up guns and hurried out into the night. They opened fire on a huge blurry structure. Truth dawned the next morning: they had shot the local water tower full of holes.[2] The Martians and their poison gas were just the Mercury Theatre's Halloween special, directed by young Orson Welles (1915–1985). But people were frightened around the nation, not just at ground zero.

The Mercury Theatre had broadcast *Dracula* back in July.[3] Their October 30 selection was less traditional Halloween fare, and all the more terrifying for that. People might have laughed off a story of ghosts or witches, but an estimated 28% believed in Martians.[4] Families in Newark fled home, wrapping their faces in wet cloth as a protection from that poison gas. New Yorkers headed for parks. Police and radio stations were inundated with calls. Traffic and telephones were tied up; bus schedules were changed.[5]

Did Welles mean to panic his audience? No, he told reporters; the reaction took him by surprise. After all, the show's introduction

Today a monument pinpoints the Martians' famous
landing point at Grover's Mill, New Jersey.

identified it as fiction: "The Columbia Broadcasting System and its
affiliated stations present Orson Welles and the Mercury Theatre on
the Air in *The War of the Worlds* by H.G. Wells."[6] There were three other
disclaimers during and after the show. Listeners who paid attention
would have known that Martians were not really invading.[7]

But many people tuned in late, after their favorite comedy skit on
the *Edgar Bergen and Charlie McCarthy Show*.[8] They missed the first dis-
claimer, and they didn't wait around for the next one, which came some
40 minutes into the broadcast. They didn't check the CBS radio sched-
ule in their newspapers. They heard "poison gas," saw the fog thickening
outside their windows, and thought the worst.

The world was jittery that fall. Nazi Germany had annexed Austria in the spring, then seized part of Czechoslovakia. Britain and France hoped to avoid war by appeasement—letting Hitler get his way. But the war scare meant that news bulletins often interrupted regular broadcasts,[9] and the *War of the Worlds* sounded just like real crisis reporting. Listeners heard that a Martian machine had wiped out 7,000 U.S. troops, leaving only 120 survivors. They heard a message to "citizens of the nation" from "the Secretary of the Interior" in Washington.[10] "It was the worst thing I ever heard over the air," said one New Jersey man.[11]

The broadcast was not a hoax, but it was crafted like one. It eased listeners in gently; it invited belief by using the rhetoric and conventions of real news broadcasts. And all too many people believed it.

The Federal Communications Commission (FCC) launched an investigation, and Congress debated new legislation. In the end, after Orson Welles apologized and CBS promised to ensure that no such

Orson Welles after the broadcast, telling reporters that no one expected the show to cause panic.

Acme News Photos

thing would ever happen again, the investigation was dropped. Nowadays, regulations forbid the airing of false content "where it is foreseeable that the broadcast will tie up the resources of first responders. . . ."[12] Hoax or not, a broadcast that affected people like the *War of the Worlds* would be heavily fined today.

The BBC Panics Britain

National Portrait Gallery

Portrait of Father Ronald Knox.

Twelve years before Orson Welles announced the Martian landing in New Jersey, Father Ronald Knox announced a riot in London's Trafalgar Square. Like the *War of the Worlds* skit, *Broadcasting the Barricades* interrupted normal-sounding material—cricket scores and other announcements—with special announcements about an emergency in progress. The riot was supposedly led by Mr. Poppleberry of the National Movement for the Abolishment of Theatre Queues. (Could anybody who heard that have taken it seriously?) The mob knocked over Big Ben (Greenwich Mean Time would have to be "given from Edinburgh on Uncle Leslie's Repeating Watch"). Decades later, the British would laugh at the *Goon Show* and *Monty Python's Flying Circus*, but in 1926, they weren't used to that type of humor on air. Some may have laughed, but at least one woman fainted and at least one man called the Admiralty. Father Knox was astonished.[13]

Operation Mincemeat Deludes Hitler

The dead man's life vest had kept his body afloat. He was hauled ashore on the Atlantic coast of Spain, northwest of Gibraltar, before dawn on April 30, 1943, and identified by his uniform and papers as Major William Martin, a British marine. World War II was in progress, and enemy fire knocked planes into the Atlantic on a regular basis. Downed soldiers died of wounds, shock, hypothermia, or drowning. Here was another.

The Spanish did an autopsy. Then, since Spain was officially neutral in World War II, they turned the remains over to the British vice-consul at Huelva. Major Martin was buried with military honors, a wreath from his fiancée, and a marble tombstone.[1]

Meanwhile, a British attaché at Madrid asked for Martin's briefcase. It was "retained for judicial purposes," said the Spanish. Officially neutral, they really favored Hitler and the Axis powers. They copied all Martin's papers for the Germans before returning them.[2]

The briefcase had been chained to Martin's wrist.[3] Some of the papers had only personal value: a letter from Martin's father and two from his sweetheart, a bill for an engagement ring, and an overdraft warning from his bank. But Martin also carried top secret documents, including a letter from a British general to an American one—a letter about the Allies' plans to invade Sardinia and Greece.[4]

National Archives UK

Along with his forged top-secret documents, the dead man carried letters from his imaginary fiancée: "Don't please let them send you off into the blue the horrible way they do nowadays."

But all the papers were forgeries. The man himself was a forgery; Major William Martin never existed. The British and Americans planned to invade Sicily, which would be easier if Hitler was waiting for them somewhere else. This was Operation Mincemeat, one of many hoaxes organized by the Twenty Committee. In Roman numerals, "twenty" is XX; the "Double Cross" committee ran counterespionage and deception operations.

The Germans expected Allied hoaxes, of course. Hitler's spymasters constantly sifted through intelligence, trying to separate truth from fiction. The success of Operation Mincemeat depended on how convincing the Allies could make it look.

The corpse reportedly belonged to a homeless suicide who took two days to die of rat poison in January 1943; his body had been refrigerated for three months.[5] He was dressed as an officer, but did he look like one?[6] One theory: a more suitable corpse was taken from a navy ship that blew up in March.[7] Another problem: the corpse was too

The Classic Haversack Operation: 1917

Famous 1917 photo of dismounted General Sir Edmund Allenby entering the Holy City of Jerusalem on foot.

Mincemeat was a "haversack operation"—it planted false information in a way that was intended to look accidental. In World War I, a British colonel named Robert Meinertzhagen dropped an actual haversack (a small pack with a single shoulder strap) to fool the Germans and Turks. The British had been stalemated in the Sinai desert for too long. The Turks and Germans held Gaza, and all British attacks had failed. In 1917, Sir Edmund Allenby was put in charge of the army at Sinai, and he decided to try something everyone else had ruled out because it was deemed impossible: a cavalry sweep through Beersheba.

The approach to Beersheba was so difficult for horses that the Turks and Germans didn't guard it carefully. To make them even more careless, Colonel Meinertzhagen dropped his famous haversack, carefully bloodstained in advance. Inside, false documents told a story the enemy could easily believe: The British were going to *pretend* they were moving on Beersheba in late November, but they really planned to attack from the usual direction at a later date. A secret code made the haversack's contents appear doubly valuable. Also included were money and letters: the imaginary officer's wife said he was a new father, and a fellow officer griped about their new general's rudeness and ambition. Meinertzhagen rode out into the desert until a Turkish patrol began shooting at him. Then he fled, dropping his binoculars, water bottle, and rifle. He did a wonderful imitation of a wounded man, escaping with his life. Later, he fed the enemy more misinformation by radio, using the secret code he'd arranged for them to find. Allenby took Gaza, and Meinertzhagen's disinformation campaign helped.[16]

decomposed to have been dead for less than a week.[8] In a Spanish post-mortem, would he pass for a man who had fallen into the ocean days earlier?[9] A Spanish doctor did wonder why there were no fish and crab bites on his ears.[10]

What about the papers? Women in the British Security Service contributed the photograph and letters from Major Martin's fiancée, Pam. General Nye helped forge his own letter to General Alexander. The briefcase was needed in case the Spanish were too religious to take papers from a dead man's pockets.[11]

The corpse was rushed from cold storage to a waiting submarine by a racecar driver who needed glasses but wouldn't wear them. He nearly ran into a tram and did run straight over a roundabout, but he arrived safely.[12] Two weeks later the submarine's commander sent his crew below, gave his officers a cover story, and tipped Major Martin into the Atlantic.[13]

The rest depended on Hitler. By May 12, intercepted communications showed that the Germans had read Nye's letter and believed it. They were strengthening defenses on the Mediterranean—especially Sardinia and southern Greece. On May 14, Hitler disputed Mussolini's view "that Sicily was the most likely invasion point." Papers "found on the body of a British courier washed up on the southern coast of Spain" proved Mussolini wrong.[14] In July, when the Allies attacked Sicily, they faced Italian troops reinforced by only two German divisions.[15] Two months later, Italy surrendered.

Dutch Artist Arrested for Selling a Vermeer to Hermann Göring

Van Meegeren painted *Christ in the Temple* to prove he was merely an art forger, not guilty of selling a genuine Vermeer to Nazi Hermann Göring.

Nationaal Archief NL

The Netherlands declared neutrality in World War II, but still Nazi Germany occupied them for five years, forcing citizens to work in German factories. Some resisted; some hid Jews; and in the last winter of the war, 30,000 starved to death. Those who survived by collaborating with the enemy faced harsh punishments after the war.[1]

One accused collaborator was a painter named Han van Meegeren (1889–1947). He faced a death sentence for selling a national treasure—a painting by seventeenth-century master Jan Vermeer—to

Hermann Göring. Göring was Hitler's second in command, founder of the Gestapo and one of the most hated men in Europe. How could van Meegeren have let Göring, of all people, buy a Vermeer?

He hadn't. The artist's defense surprised the art world and made him one of the most popular men in the Netherlands. He was not a collaborator, but a swindler. He had painted *Christ and the Adulteress* himself, and Göring had agreed to pay 1.6 million guilders for a fake Vermeer.[2]

As a student, Van Meegeren had won a gold medal that helped launch his artistic career.[3] He sold out exhibits in 1916 and 1922; he succeeded as a portraitist; he gave art lessons. His nine-minute sketch of Princess Juliana's deer was seen on greeting cards and calendars everywhere.

U.S. troops unpack van Meegeren's *Christ and the Adulteress* in 1945 after recovering it from Göring's collection.

But van Meegeren felt he got too little respect from critics, and he was always short of money. In 1923, he and a partner sold two portraits as the work of Frans Hals: the *Laughing Cavalier* and the *Satisfied Smoker*. Van Meegeren did the painting; his partner did chemistry and psychology. Chemistry helped keep new oil paints from dissolving in alcohol, which made a forgery harder to detect. Psychology helped the men figure out just how to make a famous expert believe in the forgeries, by including details that bore out his pet theories. The expert pronounced them genuine, and the *Laughing Cavalier* sold for 50,000 florins. After chemical tests proved it was a fake—it used a cobalt blue not available in Hals's lifetime—the expert still bought it for his own collection.[4]

Later van Meegeren broke with his partner and handled his own chemistry and psychology. He experimented for years, eventually discovering a formula for paints that would keep their bright colors even when hardened in the oven to mimic age. (The formula included lilac oil. His studio smelled of flowers.) Once he'd perfected the formula, van Meegeren carefully scraped existing paint from an old canvas and prepared to create his masterpiece, the 1937 *Supper at Emmaus*, by Vermeer.

Vermeer died poor; his seventeenth-century contemporaries apparently underrated him. Van Meegeren's contemporaries ranked Vermeer with Hals and Rembrandt, the best of the best—and they hoped more examples of his work would surface. Van Meegeren helped fill in a gap between Vermeer's early work (when he did large pictures on religious themes) and his later work (when he did smaller pictures of domestic life). *The Supper at Emmaus* showed the risen Christ blessing bread for his disciples, and the bread was painted in Vermeer's

Van Meegeren on trial with paintings hanging around the courtroom.

Nat o'aal Archief NL

later manner. The critics loved it. One claimed it was "*the* masterpiece of Johannes Vermeer of Delft," with its "luminous" colors and its "nobly human" sentiment.[5]

If van Meegeren only wanted to prove he was a great painter, why didn't he confess in 1937? Forgery was lucrative; he sold his false Vermeers for millions in today's currency. In the end he confessed only to save his life. The court gave him a one-year sentence, but he died of a heart attack before he could serve time. He's still remembered fondly, not as a great artist, but as the man who swindled Göring.

Detecting Art Forgeries

The field of art history developed in nineteenth-century Europe and North America, and professional connoisseurs arose—experts who specialized in judging the value of art. They would base a work's price on the importance of its artist compared with other artists, and the quality of the work itself in comparison with the artist's other work.[6] Some believe that the discerning eye of a connoisseur remains the best way to identify forgeries.[7] According to this view, Van Meegeren's fakes would have been detected after the war even without his confession.[8] During the war, confusion reigned; it was hard for experts to examine a questionable work, and anybody could understand why a work's provenance (record of previous ownership) might be missing. Van Meegeren said *The Supper at Emmaeus* belonged to an old Dutch family living in Italy, but their name had to be protected because smuggling art out of Fascist territory was so risky.[9]

Others argue that science is more reliable than a connoisseur's eye. If a forger in need of old canvas paints over an older work, X-rays will show the underpainting. One such underpainting was made two centuries after the death of the artist whose work was forged on top of it.[10] (To avoid that kind of dead giveaway, van Meegeren scraped away the underpainting.) If a medieval illumination uses a green pigment that wasn't available before 1814, chemistry will reveal the forgery. (Van Meegeren knew a great deal about how paints were formulated in different centuries, but he did like that anachronistic cobalt blue.)[11]

A 1946 investigation discredited van Meegeren's false Vermeers by the cobalt blue and other physical evidence.[12] Connoisseurs would have noticed that some of the hands are poorly drawn and the faces, with their downcast eyes, look too much alike. One American investigator noticed that "a thumb-piece on the pewter lid of a seventeenth-century tankard or jug, used as an accessory in several of the 'Vermeers,' was a nineteenth-century restoration."[13] In the end, even van Meegeren's carefully chosen props gave him away.

The Cursed Tomb of the Last Aztec Emperor

On September 26, 1949, bells rang in the poor Mexican village of Ixcateopan. Men left the fields, women left tortillas to burn. Archaeologist Eulalia Guzmán's team had dug through the church altar and tons of nineteenth-century masonry, and everyone had to see what they'd found. There were bones and treasure. The bones were scattered fragments; the treasure consisted of a few rings and beads—metal, jade, and amber. But a copper plaque displayed a name and dates.[1] This was surely the tomb of Cuauhtémoc, just where recently discovered documents said he'd been buried in 1529.

Cuauhtémoc was the last Aztec emperor. His cousin Moctezuma II had played host to the Spanish, and ended up as a prisoner and then a corpse in the imperial city of Tenochtitlán. Cuauhtémoc led the last resistance, defending the city through a desperate siege until the Spanish captured him, too, in 1521. They executed him in 1525 (nowhere near Ixcateopan) for his alleged role in an alleged plot against Cortès. His burial place had been unknown for 400 years, but he was a folk hero. His tomb could bring tourists and new prosperity to Ixcateopan, and here was the evidence.

Not everybody believed the evidence, but rumor said disbelievers were cursed. By 1951, it was said that four people had died for their disbelief in the emperor.[2]

Bust of Cuauhtémoc by Jesus F Contreras
(1866–1902) at the Museo Regional Tuxtepec
in Santiago Tuxtla, Veracruz, Mexico.

Disbelief was justified, however. Those recently discovered documents had been recently created—in the 1890s, not the 1520s. Experts at Mexico's National Institute of Anthropology and History (INAH) dismissed them as crude forgeries. The "treasures" had also been made in the nineteenth century, and the bones belonged to five different people—"an adolescent, a young man, a young woman and two small children."[3]

Who had perpetrated such a hoax? Probably Florentino Juárez, a *mestizo* laborer who rose to wealth and influence, acquiring not only lands and offices, but more than 300 books. He had means: literacy and information to forge documents. He had a motive, too. The neighboring village of Ixcapuzalco wanted to secede from the municipality, which would cost Ixcateopan—and Juárez—dearly. A buried emperor would restore Ixcateopan's importance. As for opportunity, it struck in 1891, when lightning hit the dome of the local church. The repairs gave him a chance to create the false tomb and bury it under new masonry.

Unfortunately for Juárez, getting the bones and treasure discovered was harder than getting them buried. He told the priest where to look; he told merchants and *jefes*. He showed a forged document that told where to look. He claimed to be a "living letter"—the latest link in a chain of oral transmission, bringing ancestral knowledge into the present. But the false tomb stayed hidden.

So it was his grandson, Salvador Rodríguez Juárez, who slipped Florentino's document to the priest in 1949. Cuauhtémoc was in fashion again.[4] The governor of Guerrero, General Baltasar Leyva Mancilla, leapt at news of the tomb and hurried the archaeologists along. Threatened with political overthrow, he needed a great nationalist symbol in 1949 as much as Florentino Juárez had needed it in 1891.

This time the bones came to light, followed by inconvenient facts and controversy. (The emperor had two right kneecaps? Really?) A "carefully done and lavishly illustrated" 1950 debunking "should serve to put an end to a great deal of gossip," claimed a note in the *Catholic Historical Review*, but gossip continued.[5] The villagers of Ixcateopan became grassroots nation-builders, invoking the tomb in petitions for state-funded roads, drinking water, and other needs. Rodríguez Juárez failed to persuade scholars, but he did benefit from the family hoax

A mural by Siqueiros shows the Spaniards torturing Cuauhtémoc, the last Aztec emperor.

Alejandro Linares Garcia

both economically and in influence. The story had power because the romance of the last Aztec emperor, courageously resisting Spanish colonizers, was part of Mexico's identity.

Tombs of Heroes

Tom Ordelman

Was the legendary King Arthur really buried at Glastonbury Abbey? Visitors who believed the story surely boosted the abbey's revenues.

Nationalism has motivated more than one faked archaeological discovery. In 1278, England's King Edward I presided over the opening of a tomb at Glastonbury Abbey. Was it really the resting place of King Arthur and Queen Guinevere? By identifying himself with the storied Arthur, Edward probably hoped to legitimize his rule of Wales.[6] He certainly heightened interest in Glastonbury, where a steady stream of pilgrims—like medieval tourists— boosted the local economy.

In 1850, Spanish workers found a buried marble sarcophagus at Tarragona. It was covered with carvings and inscriptions that told a romantic story of Spain's past: in the days when Hercules broke a mountain to make the Straits of Gibraltar, the peninsula had been colonized by ancient Egyptians! Sadly for the dreams of Spanish nationalists, this story was not believed. A French critic pooh-poohed the sarcophagus as a "childish parody" of ancient Egyptian art.[7]

Donald Crowhurst
Vanishes at Sea

In the late 1960s, while the U.S. and Russia raced to put men into moon orbit, British and European sportsmen raced around the world in sailboats. In 1967, Francis Chichester circled the globe single-handed in a 54-foot sailboat in 274 days, a small-vessel speed record. Braving the stormy seas south of the Cape of Good Hope and Cape Horn, he stopped only once, in Australia.[1] Britain cheered his return, and he was knighted by the queen.

So London's *Sunday Times* announced the Golden Globe Race: who could sail around the world single-handed and *nonstop*? Contestants would have to set out between June 1 and October 31, 1968. There would be two prizes, one for the first to finish and one for the speediest voyage.

Nine men set out, but soon only four were left in a race of attrition: Robin Knox-Johnston, Bernard Moitessier, Nigel Tetley, and Donald Crowhurst. Crowhurst hoped the race would save his failing company, Electron Utilisation, which sold marine electronics. His business backer, Stanley Best, was about to withdraw funds, but Crowhurst convinced Best that the race would sell their products—including new inventions of his such as a computer-triggered buoyancy bag for righting a capsized trimaran.[2]

Teignmouth Electron (named for Crowhurst's sponsor town of Teignmouth) wasn't ready by October 31: Crowhurst's visionary computer

Crowhurst struck a confident pose just before setting out in 1968.

was a mass of unconnected wires and transistors. Hatch covers weren't watertight, the boat pump was missing hose, and the masthead buoyancy bag was inoperable. He said good-bye to his wife and children and set sail anyway.

By November 15, hampered by boat and equipment problems, his progress was intolerably slow. If he withdrew from the race, he would go bankrupt. On the other hand, victory seemed impossible, and his boat was proving vulnerable even in temperate latitudes. In the stormy Southern Ocean, where prevailing westerly gales circle the globe unimpeded, Crowhurst reckoned his chances of survival at 50/50 or less. Should he attempt the Cape of Good Hope or give up?[3]

In the end, he did neither. Instead he sailed circles in the South Atlantic for months, staying out of the shipping lanes to avoid detection and keeping two logbooks: one that showed where he really was each day, and one that showed where he might plausibly have been if he'd sailed into the Indian Ocean and then the Pacific. To fake his logbook, Crowhurst had to plot a believable course and then reverse-calculate sextant sights that would show each day's position as if he'd really been there. His forgery was a masterpiece of imagination and mathematics, and his months at sea in a leaky boat constituted a notable piece of seamanship.

He pretended to be off the Cape of Good Hope on January 19 (when in fact he was 20 miles off Brazil and just a few hundred miles south of the equator) and told the world he was experiencing generator problems that would put him out of radio contact—something that was believable then but would be implausible now, on a globe circled with communications satel-

lites.[1] He put ashore in Argentina in March. Pretending to be nearing Cape Horn after crossing the Pacific, he resumed radio contact on April 10. Knox-Johnston completed the race on April 22, 1969, but the English media thought Crowhurst would do it

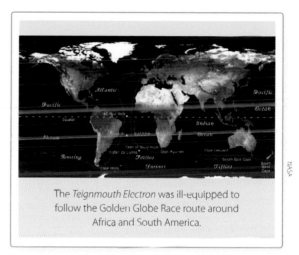

The *Teignmouth Electron* was ill-equipped to follow the Golden Globe Race route around Africa and South America.

faster. Moitessier dropped out; Tetley's boat (a Victress-class plywood trimaran like Crowhurst's) sank a thousand miles from England—after a voyage of 29,000 miles—because Tetley, fearing he would lose to Crowhurst, pushed it too hard.

On June 25, when Crowhurst received word that the BBC was sending a crew to record his triumphant return, he knew that his apparent victory would be followed by scandal. The race committee would examine his logbooks carefully, and Chichester, the chief judge, would not be fooled.

On July 10, *Teignmouth Electron* was found drifting in mid-Atlantic. The lifeboat was still there, and a half-drunk mug of tea sat on the dinette table. Crowhurst's logs (true and false), his calculations on brown wrapping paper, and his poems and essays recorded three voyages—the real one, the fake one, and his desperate inner voyage.

But Crowhurst was gone. He had imagined an alternative life, but he could not face real life after his hoax was discovered. Investigators concluded that he must have jumped into the ocean and watched his boat sail away.

Yachting Technology

National Museum of American History

The first successful minicomputer, the PDP-8 (1965) could fit aboard a yacht. Computerized navigational equipment was within reach.

Donald Crowhurst had radical ideas about yachting technology. The first computers could barely squeeze into a house (the 1946 ENIAC took 1,000 square feet of floor space), but by 1968, a minicomputer might have fit into a sail locker.[5] Crowhurst imagined programming a computer to respond if *Teignmouth Electron* capsized, triggering a buoyancy bag on her masthead. Once inflated, the bag would prevent the capsized trimaran from turning upside down, and the next wave would jolt it back upright. It was an ambitious idea, but not crazy.

Today's great luxury yachts can have rotating masts and computerized sail controls. Competitors for the America's Cup can sail faster than the wind, thanks to aerodynamically designed hulls and sails that mimic airplane wings.[6] Crowhurst would have loved the way modern catamarans skim above the sea on foils.

Competitors in the 2013 America's Cup race used technology Crowhurst couldn't dream of.

Doran Raven

But for ordinary sailors, the most dramatic change in yachting technology is the system of communications satellites now circling Earth. The Global Positioning System (GPS) lets sailors check their locations anywhere on earth, whether they can see the sun and stars or not. E-mail keeps them in touch with family, friends, and offices. It is harder to vanish at sea today than it was in 1969.

The Tasaday: A Stone-Age Tribe or a Hoax?

In 1971, a Stone-Age tribe walked out of the Philippine rainforest and captured the world's imagination.[1] They were the Tasaday (pronounced Taw-*saw*-dai), and they had no words for war and aggression. Yet there was conflict all around their shrinking forest on the island of Mindanao.

Could an entire tribe be a hoax?

Before World War II, large parts of the Mindanao interior were still unexplored. But elsewhere in the Philippines, demand for sugar and other cash crops was changing land use, squeezing out traditional farmers.[2] In 1936, the government moved to resettle a million citizens on Mindanao.[3] The island was already home to at least a dozen minorities with differing languages and religions. Newcomers competed for tribal land, and indigenous farmers were pushed out of their fertile valley homes. Loggers, miners, and ranchers followed them uphill, closer to the Tasadays' forest. In May 1971, a T'boli tribal leader was accused of murder after fighting back against gunmen who killed his daughter.[4]

Manuel Elizalde, Jr. rushed to the defense. A Harvard-educated playboy, Elizalde had founded PANAMIN, the Private Association for National Minorities, and he had governmental authority as well: he was President Marcos's advisor on minority affairs.[5] He met with

John Nance

Tasaday men greet Manuel Elizalde, Jr., in July 1971. They called him "Momo Dakel Diwata Tasaday," loosely translated as "big man-god of the Tasaday."

the T'boli, and through them he learned of the Tasaday, an even more endangered group.

There were only six adult male Tasaday, five adult females, twelve boys, and two girls.[6] They lived in caves, dressed in leaves, and ate "roots, wild bananas, grubs, berries, and crabs and frogs fished by hand from small streams."[7] They improvised stone tools and made fire with sticks, living as their ancestors had lived since prehistoric times.

Or did they? Elizalde stage-managed their introduction to the world. He asked the Tasaday "to dress like they used to,"[8] and he took journalists and scholars by helicopter to a picturesque glade. Visitors photographed children swinging on vines and parents splashing in streams with their babies. But anthropologists were not allowed to do thorough field research; they had to be content with short visits. What if the Tasaday were actors from other tribes, hired by Elizalde to pose as innocent primitives?

President Marcos created a "Tasaday Reserve" on ancestral tribal land,[9] and access to the Tasaday was cut off in 1974. But Marcos was ousted in 1986. A Swiss journalist hiked into the reserve and found the Tasaday wearing clothes and living in houses. The next week, German reporters photographed a Tasaday man wearing leaves over modern underwear.[10]

The Tasaday were labeled "the most elaborate hoax perpetrated on the anthropological world since Piltdown Man."[11] If they were genuine, where were their middens (garbage heaps)? What had happened to their discarded stone tools? How could they have survived on their reported diet? Why hadn't they ever walked the three hours to a farming village and met other people? One of the men told the Swiss journalist that before 1971, they used to wear shabby clothes and do some farming, but "Elizalde forced us to live in the caves so that we'd be better cavemen."[12]

Some thought Elizalde had political or financial motives for fraud.[13] Marcos, too, had a possible motive: by using the Tasaday as a national symbol, he might have hoped to unify the Philippines.

Tasaday people in 2012, with rainforest in the background. Intermarriage with surrounding groups raised the Tasaday population to 216 by 2008.

Suzanne Haerpfer

We know now that the Tasaday had not lived in total isolation since the Stone Age. They shared words with nearby tribes and could almost understand their languages. But differences showed they'd lived apart for more than a century.[14] Unlike nearby tribes, the Tasaday had no borrowed words from Chinese, Sanskrit, or Spanish.[15] The Tasaday are a real tribe—but was the story Elizalde told about them a hoax?

Survivals from the Dawn of Humanity

Indian Coast Guard

After the 2004 tsunami, a Sentinelese hunter aimed his arrows at a helicopter.

How did our ancestors live before civilization? For those of us who live in modern cities, it's hard to imagine. Archaeologists and anthropologists piece together clues found at ancient sites, but like forensic artists reconstructing faces from skeletal remains, they can only approximate reality.

There are also living clues—and that was what made the Tasaday so fascinating in 1971. Scattered around the world, groups of indigenous people still live much as their ancestors did. For instance, Bolivia's Tsimane hunt and grow crops; the Hadza in Tanzania and the San in Namibia are hunter-gatherers. All live without electricity, so sleep researchers turned to them for answers: how much would we sleep if we didn't have electronic lights and screens? The answer: probably not more than seven hours a night on average. The San and Tsimane had no word for insomnia and thought the study was comical, but were happy to participate.[16]

By contrast the Sentinelese may be the world's most isolated tribe. They migrated from Africa to the Andaman Islands, in the Bay of Bengal, as long as 60,000 years ago, and even after a 2004 tsunami devastated the coasts and islands of the Indian Ocean, they wanted no help of any kind from the outside.[17] They attempt to kill any visitors, so little is known of them.[18]

Even where contacts between indigenous and modern populations are less fierce, they are usually uneasy. The World Health Organization estimates that indigenous populations of 370 million survive in seventy countries,[19] but, like the Tasaday, they survive in environments that shrink as dominant groups exploit more of their natural resources. In the Amazon, for instance, when "nakeds" emerge from the forest to scavenge near village settlements, violence can erupt in either direction.[20] Indigenous tribes may give us windows into humanity's shared past, but their own future is uncertain.

A Faked Autobiography
of Howard Hughes

Clifford Irving (b. 1930) is a novelist, but his 1969 best seller was nonfiction—or was it? A biography of his friend and neighbor Elmyr de Hory (1906–1976), it was proudly titled *Fake!* De Hory's claim to fame was art forgery: he sold fake Picassos and Renoirs. His arrest in 1968 was international news, so when he told his story to Irving, both of them stood to profit. Did it matter if de Hory faked his life as well as his paintings?

Irving didn't think so. "I believe that the past is fiction, the future is fantasy, and the present for the most part is an ongoing hoax," he wrote in 2006.[1] He'd enjoyed writing a biography, and he had the perfect subject for another: Howard Hughes.[2]

An authorized biography of Hughes would be a hot property. Producer of classic movies, inventor, engineer, aviator, airline owner, and billionaire, Hughes had been a glamorous presence in the 1930s. He escorted movie stars; he flew around the world in under four days. But after a near-fatal plane crash in 1946, he withdrew from public life and began living in a hotel penthouse. When management asked him to move, he bought the hotel. When a neighboring hotel's lights bothered him at night, he bought that one, too.[3]

By 1970, Hughes was an invisible celebrity. He hadn't been interviewed in 15 years; he had employees who'd never seen him.[4] Of course,

The Briscoe Center / University of Texas

Controversial author and investigative journalist Clifford Irving. A highly regarded writer, Irving may be best known for his 1972 conviction for fraud after elaborately faking an autobiography of Howard Hughes.

he wouldn't authorize Irving to write his biography—but if Irving wrote it, Hughes might never come out of hiding to challenge him in court. Irving thought he could get away with it. He enlisted his friend Richard Suskind as a collaborator and talked his publisher, McGraw-Hill, into giving him a contract.

The project involved forgery at every step of the way. To land the contract, Irving forged letters from Hughes; a handwriting expert pronounced them genuine. McGraw-Hill would write huge checks to

Hughes as well as Irving. To cash these checks, Irving got his terrified wife to deposit them in a Swiss bank account under the name "H.R. Hughes."

Armed with a $100,000 initial advance, Irving and Suskind did genuine research. Suskind combed through every publication on Hughes. Irving turned up documents at the Pentagon and the Library of Congress—where he nearly got caught as he smuggled a 300-page subcommittee transcript out of the building in his pants.[5] By sheer luck, the conspirators acquired an unpublished autobiography of Noah Dietrich, Hughes's right-hand man for 32 years.[6]

Irving and Suskind immersed themselves in the material until they could imitate the way Hughes spoke. The friends took turns playing Hughes for taped interviews. Gradually the book became an autobiography, and the interviews produced anecdotes about things that never happened, such as Hughes's imaginary trip to India and his friendship with Ernest Hemingway. "The wilder the story," Irving told Suskind, the more people would want to believe it. "And, of course, it's less checkable."[7] They invented a story about a 1920 Peerless automobile, and the fact-checkers verified it—except the car was a 1902 model. Irving assured them it was "just a typing error."[8] McGraw-Hill loved the transcripts.

Eventually management at Hughes Tool heard about the upcoming publication and announced, "There is no such book."[9] Even then, it seemed as if Irving's version of the story might prevail. Hughes called journalist Frank McCulloch to denounce the book, and McCulloch concluded that the call was from a Hughes impersonator. Noah Dietrich, unaware that Irving and Suskind had cribbed his own material, said insider knowledge proved the work genuine.[10]

But the hoax unraveled when investigators followed the money. Irving and Suskind spent months in jail; Irving's wife spent time in a Swiss jail as well, and the two divorced. Irving was left bankrupt. "Maybe," he admitted later, it was "amoral—or immoral—but we didn't grasp that."[11]

A Memoir of Life with Wolves

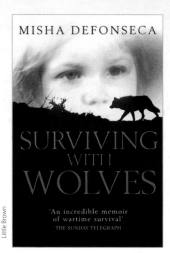

MISHA DEFONSECA

SURVIVING
WITH
WOLVES

'An incredible memoir
of wartime survival'
THE SUNDAY TELEGRAPH

Little Brown

In this "incredible memoir,"
Monique de Wael imagined
herself as a fleeing Jewish
child, nurtured by wolves.

Irving and Suskind faked a living celebrity's autobiography without permission. It is safer to fake the autobiography (or diary) of somebody who is no longer around to dispute the facts.

Other autobiographers have written contested versions of their own lives. Augusten Burroughs was sued over his 2002 memoir, *Running with Scissors;* James Frey's 2003 *A Million Little Pieces* erupted into televised controversy. Burroughs may not have fictionalized his story enough: he changed names, but people who could still be recognized claimed defamation of character and invasion of privacy. Frey may have fictionalized too much: his survival of drug addiction was inspiring to Oprah Winfrey and her viewers, but only if true. Neither man could tell his story without betraying acquaintances or readers. Similarly, Misha Defonseca's readers felt betrayed by her 1997 bestseller, *Misha: A Mémoire of the Holocaust Years*. She really was a child in Europe during the Holocaust, but she did not have to walk 1,900 miles, kill a German soldier, or take shelter with wolves. She was born Monique de Wael and her family was Catholic, not Jewish.[12] Still, she says, "The book is a story, it's my story." Do writers' feelings represent deeper truths than the facts of their lives?

Similar questions arise in the case of Rachel Dolezal, who self-identifies as black and was an NAACP leader until 2015, when her parents publicly identified her as white.[13] Was she misrepresenting herself? Why? If an autobiography represents a life, what are the important truths?

Moon Landing Conspiracy Theory

Sometimes an alleged hoax is a genuine event, and people just don't believe it. In 1969, 125 million Americans watched two Apollo 11 astronauts step out from a landing vehicle onto the moon.[1] After centuries of moon hoaxes, here was the real thing: Neil Armstrong and Buzz Aldrin on live TV.

But seeing was not necessarily believing. Photographs could be doctored; nobody believed in the Cottingley fairies (Chapter 32) anymore. Slick modern advertisements and movies made old hoaxes look clumsy. At the same time, conspiracy theories were gaining traction. Growing numbers of people believed the U.S. government was hiding the truth about UFOs and the Kennedy assassination.[2]

NASA (the National Aeronautics and Space Administration) landed a total of six expeditions on the moon; twelve astronauts walked there. Though Russians sent the first man into space, Americans went farther.[3]

But the last moon landing was in 1972. The Watergate scandal broke that year, forcing President Nixon to resign in 1974—and stoking American distrust of national leaders. In 1976, Bill Kaysing published *We Never Went to the Moon.* Kaysing, a writer who had worked for a NASA contractor, said the landings were staged to make the world believe the U.S. had won the Space Race. The 1978 movie *Capricorn One,* a thriller in which the U.S. government faked a Mars landing, helped

NASA

Astronaut David R. Scott salutes the U.S. flag during the Apollo 15 moon landing in 1971. Conspiracy theorists believe that this and other NASA photographs were taken on movie sets, not the surface of the moon.

people envision just how the hoax could have been staged, assassinated astronauts and all.

Conspiracists (believers in the conspiracy theory) lined up evidence that NASA television footage and photographs were fake. In 2001, Fox News ran a special that made the conspiracy sound plausible.[4] By 2002, at least one conspiracist was ambushing Apollo astronauts, asking them to swear on a Bible that the landings took place.

NASA and independent scientists contested the conspiracists' supposed evidence. Some rebuttals, from BadAstronomy.com[5]:

* *Photographs show the American flag rippling in what looks like a good breeze, but there is no air on the moon. Why didn't the flag just dangle on its pole?* Because it hung from a horizontal rod along the top. *Then why wasn't it totally flat?* Because the mechanism for that rod was slightly bent when the astronauts deployed it.

* *Why are no stars visible in the pictures?* Because the moon's surface is bright. To get clear images of the astronauts in their shining white suits, cameras needed shutter settings too fast to catch the relatively faint stars.

* *Why didn't the landing vehicle make a big crater on the moon? Why didn't it blow away all the dust, so astronauts couldn't leave footprints?* Because they throttled down to about 3,000 pounds of thrust—only 1.5 pounds per square inch.

The arguments are fiercely technical. Conspiracists look for "flaws in what the other side is saying."[6] Scientists may refute each alleged flaw, but scientific rebuttals are harder to follow than accusations. As one astronomer puts it, "You've got to do the work; you've got to put the elbow grease to it."[7]

The moon landings were real; the arguments against them amount to a hoax. In general, people who distrust authority are more likely to believe conspiracy theories, and people who believe one conspiracy theory are likely to believe others.[8] But do conspiracists gain anything by disbelief in moon landings?

The moon as photographed from Earth.

NASA

Unlike some hoaxes, this one doesn't offer its believers hope of fame or riches. Maybe buying into it brings psychological rewards.[9]

Or maybe it's just easier to pooh-pooh moon landings than to think about what they meant—and why they ended. In 1969, America greeted NASA's achievement with hope and awe. A new age of exploration was dawning, and wonderful things seemed possible.[10] Would conspiracists rather forget that disappointed hope?

Scientific Literacy

In nineteenth-century America, teen-aged teachers in one-room school-houses introduced their pupils to the "3 R's": Reading, Writing, and 'Rithmetic. Basic literacy was served.

American educators today call for more advanced literacy, and more kinds of literacy—including scientific literacy. As consumers, U.S. citizens select everything from automobiles to medications based on evidence drawn from scientific experiments. As voters, we participate in setting policies that guide scientific exploration and technological developments.

So the National Science Foundation conducts a survey on American knowledge and attitudes toward science and technology. One question in 2012: "Does the earth go around the sun, or does the sun go around the earth?" Americans are comparable to Europeans and more knowledgeable about science than people in most other parts of the world, but one in four said the sun orbits the earth.[11] Answers showed that some people knew what scientists would say, but did not believe it. For instance, 48% said they thought it was true that "human beings, as we know them today, developed from earlier species of animals," but 72% said this was true "according to the theory of evolution."[12]

Science is a cumulative project. Discoveries build on each other; findings are tested again and again; old beliefs are challenged, and abandoned if new tests prove them wrong. But we are not all scientists, and we cannot test all scientific knowledge for ourselves. Even if we learned some experimental techniques in school, we learn most of our scientific knowledge from teachers, the media, and the internet. We accept it on authority—or we reject it, because we accept a different authority. Does having to choose between conflicting authorities make us easier to hoax?

Genuine Fake Hitler Diaries

It was 1999, and Konrad Kujau was up before the Stuttgart court. Again. Previously, he'd been caught with a supply of fake drivers' licenses; this time it was unregistered weapons.[1] In the 1980s, he'd served time for creating a highly illegal set of diaries. The judge at that trial, too, expressed "disbelief and disgust"[2] as Kujau and his co-conspirator Gerd Heidemann blamed each other for their crime against history.

Heidemann was an ace reporter for the weekly news magazine *Stern*. He collected Nazi keepsakes, and he had black market contacts. When he heard that 27 volumes of Hitler's diaries had been salvaged from a 1945 plane crash, Heidemann had to have them. He couldn't afford them, but they would be a journalistic bombshell. He tracked down the source—Kujau, under a fake name—and went over his editor's head. Without authorization, he made promises to Kujau on behalf of *Stern*: complete anonymity and lavish payment.[3]

Kujau specialized in faking Nazi memorabilia for wealthy collectors. He faked so much that when handwriting experts compared the diaries to known samples of Hitler's penmanship, some of those known samples were also Kujau's work. He worked carelessly, but making the Hitler diaries would take time. He would research content, write it in school notebooks, and age the volumes by sloshing tea over them. To buy time, he told Heidemann that his brother had to smuggle the diaries out of East Germany one at a time; it would take months.

Stern Magazin

"Hitler's Diaries Discovered," boasted Germany's *Stern Magazin* in 1983. The forger mistakenly pasted the wrong initials on the cover—not "AH" for Adolf Hitler, but "FH." Editors guessed they stood for "Fuhrer's Headquarters."

The work went faster than he expected, and soon he could copy out a whole notebook in four and a half hours.[4] He plagiarized most of his content from *Hitler's Speeches and Proclamations, 1932–45*, by Max Domarus. It was unbelievably dull—lists of appointments and official announcements—but that made it more believable. Kujau livened it up with an occasional complaint about health; a June 1941 entry said new pills gave Hitler "violent flatulence" and "bad breath."[5]Kujau's writing materials were no more authentic than his content. Chemical analysis showed the notebooks were from the 1950s. Paper, binding, glue, and thread had all been manufactured after 1945, when Hitler died. As for the initials on the diary covers—not only was "FH" the wrong monogram, the letters were made in Hong Kong.

Whipping up fake diaries and selling them to *Stern* was easy money, so Kujau "found" more than the 27 originally promised. In the end, he sold 60, netting more than 2 million marks, or $1.1 million.[6] He was happy with the profit until he found out that *Stern* had given Heidemann 9 million marks to buy the diaries.

In April 1983, the magazine held a press conference to announce the discovery and publication of the diaries. Scholars would have to rewrite history. The diaries showed Hitler as a sensitive guy who didn't even know about the Holocaust.

Two weeks later, *Stern* had to announce that the diaries were fakes. Heidemann was arrested. Kujau escaped to Austria—but returned and gave himself up when he heard how much Heidemann had skimmed off his payments. In court, Heide-

Konrad Kujau, the likeable forger, gave himself up when he realized his partner in crime hadn't been paying him a fair share of their ill-gotten gains.

Achim Necker

mann claimed he never knew Kujau forged the diaries. Kujau claimed Heidemann knew all along. Kujau's defense attorney argued that the owners of *Stern* were the true guilty ones: "they subconsciously wanted to be defrauded so as to expand circulation, make profits from republication rights, and even humanize the image of Hitler."[7]

Top editors resigned from *Stern*. Heidemann emerged from prison embittered and burdened with debt.[8] But Kujau bounced back. He took to forging art as well as drivers' licenses. He sold copies of masterpieces by Gauguin, Magritte, da Vinci, and Monet as "original Kujau forgeries" for as much as $4,000 each. Years after his death, a woman who claimed to be his niece was convicted

Gerd Heidemann, reporter of the German magazine 'Stern', presents the alleged Hitler diaries at a press conference in Hamburg, 25 April 1983.

Alamy

of forging Kujau forgeries.[9] Konrad Kujau would have laughed.

Why 1983?

Patriotic members of Hitler Youth in 1938; Heidemann and Kujau were too young to join.

In 1983, the fiftieth anniversary of Hitler's rise to power, there was a great upwelling of interest in the Nazis.[10] Hitler had gained control of the German government in 1933, before Gerd Heidemann turned two. World War II began in 1939, when Konrad Kujau was a baby, and when Germany surrendered, Heidemann was still a few months too young to join the Hitler Youth. So Kujau and Heidemann were members of a generation that started out believing in the invincible power of the Third Reich and then had to live through defeat. In middle age, they were still fascinated by images of what their nation had lost, and many collected Nazi keepsakes. If there was ever a forgery designed to attract more readers than the autobiography of Howard Hughes in 1971, it was the diary of Adolf Hitler in 1983, just in time to help the children of the Reich reassess what it all meant.

More Lying Stones: Moroccan Fossils in the Himalayas

"There were no particularly dire consequences, just a few death threats," Australian professor John Talent told a radio interviewer in 2005,[1] describing the aftermath of a presentation he'd made at a 1987 geology conference in Canada. On one screen, he showed two fossils: an ammonoid that Dr. V.J. Gupta said he'd found in the Himalayas, and an almost identical ammonoid that a French rock shop said was from Morocco. Gupta, sitting in the front row, "obviously wanted to punch me out," Talent remembered 18 years later.[2]

Gupta was a fellow scientist, a professor at India's Panjab University. He had published hundreds of scientific papers—averaging at least one a month over 20 years—and his co-authors included top paleontologists from the U.S., Australia, and Europe, as well as India. "He invites an expert in some particular fossil type to join him in a scientific paper," Talent explained in 1989. The co-author would describe "fossils provided by Gupta," and Gupta would describe "the locality from which the fossil is said to have been recovered."[3]

Gupta's co-authors had little reason not to trust him, but Talent had been suspicious of him for years. In the 1970s, Talent worked in areas of the Himalayas that Gupta had described in 1966, and "nothing matched up."[4] Talent's group found none of the delicate fossils Gupta had reported there, and they disagreed with Gupta about the age of the rocks.

Luca Galluzzi

Mount Everest is the tallest peak in the Himalayas, formed millions of years ago when a major landmass (now known as India) moved north through the ocean and collided with Asia. By pinpointing the exact locations of fossil species, paleontologists help us understand this ancient event.

Talent did not take immediate action, but he sifted through Gupta's articles and compiled evidence, and in 1987, he published his findings. Gupta had "recycled" his fossils, said Talent. He had reported finding them at many "phantom localities"; he had failed to give "appropriate stratigraphy" (descriptions of the rock layers in which specimens were found); and he had reported "incredible associations" of fossils that lived 15 to 30 million years apart.[5]

Gupta did not create artificial fossils, like the hoaxsters who plagued Dr. Beringer (Chapter 11); he simply reported finding genuine fossils in places they couldn't have been. He falsified the fossil record.

Why the Scientific Record Needs Setting Straight

Science is a cumulative effort, and each generation's scientists build on the work of their predecessors. They have to be able to trust what they find. But even without deliberate fraud, it's easy to get things wrong. In 2005, John P.A. Ioannidis published a famous paper on "Why Most Published Research Findings Are False."[13] Most of his reasons have to do with statistics, because studies in his field (medicine) typically use statistics to test their hypotheses. For instance, small sample sizes can give unreliable results—when studies don't have enough subjects to represent the general population, researchers can get the wrong answers just by chance. Small effects can also cause errors—when an outcome (such as lung cancer) has multiple contributing causes (such as genetics, smoking, and exposure to environmental hazards), some of the causes may have real effects that are too small to measure reliably. But Ioannidis also found that financial interests, the prejudices of researchers, and competition for achievement in "hot" scientific fields could increase the risk of biased results.

The vast majority of scientists are honest; they intend to contribute high-quality data to the pool of human knowledge. But they are human, too. Like the rest of us, they are quicker to see what they expect to see—or what they want to see.

The fossil record is a clue to geological history, and scientists want to understand the geological history of the Himalayas for several reasons. The region contains Earth's highest mountains, pushed up when the landmass now called India rammed into what's now Tibet. It made a high plateau that may have helped drive "global climate change over the past 50–60 million years." It may affect annual monsoons—the seasonal winds that drive Asia's patterns of flood and drought.[6]

But such hypotheses can't be properly tested without good data. Geologists record what fossils they find and where; they look for patterns that "make sense in terms of the history of the continents."[7] Much as the faked remains of Piltdown Man (Chapter 28) distorted scientific ideas about human evolution, Gupta's false reports distorted geological history. What was known about the area from Kashmir to Bhutan became a confused "quagmire," Talent said in 1989. "Not only does the record include a menagerie of fossil species that probably never inhabited the region, but the pattern inferred from the fossils for the rock strata is a knotty tangle rather than a neat gradation from old to young."[8]

The Geological Survey of India and the Society for Scientific Values concluded that Gupta's fossils did not come from the Himalayas, and he was suspended from his position as director of the Institute of Paleontology at Panjab.[9] He held onto his professorship, not retiring until 2004.[10] But Talent and other colleagues began a systematic review of Gupta's publications, identifying errors and setting the record straight.[11] And in India, Gupta's technician was killed in a hit-and-run accident just a day after promising to tell the whole story.[12]

Crop Circle Artists Confess

A 1966 incident in Australia caught Doug Bower's attention: could a "nest" of flattened grass really be evidence that a UFO had landed? Bower discussed it with Dave Chorley back in England, and the two friends decided to copy the nest in a local field and see what happened. Their first efforts, starting in 1978, got little attention. In 1981, they found a more visible location on a hillside, and the publicity began.[1] Soon people were giving lectures and writing books about the mysterious phenomena. The study of crop circles even had a name: cerealogy.[2]

Some "experts" thought the circles were natural phenomena. Perhaps they were made by animals—love-crazed hedgehogs (in England)[3] or wallabies high on opium poppies (in Australia).[4] Or perhaps weather caused them. British physicist Terence Meaden believed a sea breeze hitting a low hill might "throw long, unstable eddies far downwind," occasionally giving rise to "spinning vortices" even in calm weather.[5] Americans investigated tornadoes, and in Japan—where odd circles were imprinted in the dust beside Tokyo subway tracks—one researcher thought electricity must be involved.

But many circles were too elaborate to be the work of hedgehogs or gusts of wind. Some said they were coded messages from nonhuman intelligences (extraterrestrials, or nature spirits, or some other spiritual energy).[6] Scientists were reluctant to enter such debates.

thinkstock

Flattened grass in a simple crop circle. Could it have been caused by a tornado or a UFO?

They didn't want "a reputation among fellow scientists as working on weird and off-beat things."[7]

Hoaxsters can make basic crop circles with simple equipment: a length of rope and a plank. They walk in existing tractor ruts to the middle of a field and anchor the rope. (One member of the team can hold it, being careful not to leave evidence.) Holding the other end of the rope, another team member makes the circle's perimeter by stomping on the plank over and over. The result is a circle of squashed grain with no footprints.

Bower and Chorley, still in good shape in their sixties, laughed at the cerealogists and made fancier circles to mystify them. For the two friends it was art, driven by "a wicked sense of the comic and absurd."[8] They didn't confess until 1991, when they heard there might be a government inquiry—a waste of taxpayer money.

They weren't the only crop circle makers to confess that year. The Wiltshire Skeptics even made circles on film to show how it was done.[9] But confessions didn't stop either the cerealogists or a new generation of artists. Until 1991, crop circles were mostly an English phenomenon; after the new flurry of publicity they became common in the U.S.[10]

In Britain, artists made complex designs with fancy names such as the "DNA Double Helix," the "Koch Snowflake," and the "Julia-set Fractal."[11] Simple string and wooden planks were no longer enough; crop circle artists began to use "computing power to generate fractal designs, lasers, microwaves and global positioning systems (GPS)."[12] Crowds of mystics and cerealogists still flocked to examine each new crop circle, but so did art lovers; when a critic complained in Britain's *Daily Mail* that the 2013 crop was poor, he was talking about the art, not the grain.[13]

Decoders found heavenly messages in this 2013 California crop circle. It turned out to be a marketing stunt for Nvidia's new Tegra K1 processing chip.

Objecting to the ever-larger circles and crowds that destroy their fields, many farmers quickly mow down the designs to discourage repeat performances. A Crop Circle Access Centre solicits donations to reimburse agricultural losses,[14] but British law now forbids trespass and destruction of crops.

The art of crop circles is declining, and people who believe the *real* circles are made by nonhuman intelligences may be even happier about this than the farmers. After all, with so many hoax circles on view, how can we pick out the genuine messages?

The Will to Believe

Hoaxes succeed because people want to believe them. Being a skeptic by nature, the American journalist H.L. Mencken found this both sad and funny. He thought Socialists and Marxists—people who believed in political theories—were the same kinds of people who believed in fad diets and miracle cures. They had "believing minds," and if they couldn't be Socialists they would be prohibitionists or chiropractors, he said. They would go in for mental telepathy, "Texas oil stocks, numerology, the poetry of T.S. Eliot, the music of Eric Satie, or the [O]uija board." Some of them even believed in Dr. Albert

Newspaperman H.L. Mencken was tough-minded; he required proof before he would believe anything.

Abrams, who claimed he could diagnose and cure almost any disease with electronic vibrations. They suffered from "an overwhelming compulsion to believe what is not true," Mencken said, especially if it "seems to be pleasant."[15] Mencken himself wrote an entertaining history of the bathtub that was widely believed although any facts in it were purely accidental. Did true believers really want to believe it, or did they just see no reason not to?

Physicist Alan Sokal Spoofs Postmodern Scholarship

Alan Sokal's 1996 hoax was a blow in the "Science Wars" of the 1990s.[1] His Trojan Horse was an article in *Social Text*, a leading journal in the field of cultural studies. Sokal, a physicist, thought intellectual standards in the humanities were declining. He decided to test that suspicion by writing "an article liberally salted with nonsense." Would *Social Text* publish it "if (a) it sounded good and (b) it flattered the editors' ideological preconceptions?"[2] They did.

Meanwhile, Sokal debunked it in a very different magazine. *Lingua Franca* reported on academic life—the more controversy, the better. In Sokal's attack on his own article, he said that he "wrote the article so that any competent physicist or mathematician" would see it as a spoof. "Evidently the editors of *Social Text* felt comfortable publishing an article on quantum physics without bothering to consult anyone knowledgeable in the subject."[3] By publishing and then exposing a parody, Sokal meant to embarrass humanities scholars—especially postmodernists.

What kind of war pits physicists against postmodernists? As twentieth-century university disciplines grew more specialized, the humanities and social sciences had less and less contact with the natural sciences. Nobody had time to learn everything. In 1959, British scientist C.P. Snow said there were two cultures, with a gulf between "literary intellectuals" and scientists. The literary types couldn't explain the Second

Law of Thermodynamics, he said; they couldn't define mass or acceleration. They were scientific illiterates.[4]

The gulf has widened since then. Subdisciplines have proliferated on both sides of the gulf, and scholars in different fields don't just know different things, they study them differently. They hold different ideas about epistemology (that is, how we can know what we know); they use different kinds of evidence and different standards for sorting truth from error. Sokal, as a physicist, tried to be rigorously objective in his work. Post-

Physicist Alan Sokal debunked his own hoax to prove academic journals should review submissions more carefully.

modernists said that no one—not even scientists—can be completely objective and logical; we see what we expect to see. Our habits of mind and even our scientific theories are "social constructs"—ideas shaped by social experiences.

Sokal thought postmodernists used too many fashionable buzzwords, so he used as many as he could in his *Social Text* article, beginning with the title: "Transgressing the Boundaries: Toward a Transformative Hermeneutics of Quantum Gravity." He believed some postmodernists committed "science abuse," basing ideas on scientific concepts they didn't fully understand,[5] so in the article he connected postmodern ideas to quantum gravity, which physicists are still struggling to understand.[6] He believed postmodernists relied on too little logic and too much quoting of sources, so he filled his article with deliberately nonsensical quotations from leading postmodernists.

What really outraged Sokal, though, was postmodernist epistemology. In his article, he pretended to make fun of scientific realists—old-fashioned thinkers who held that "there exists an external world, whose properties are independent" of human beings and "are encoded in 'eternal' physical laws."[7] He pretended to believe that "physical 'reality'" was a social construct.[8] He suggested that even π (*pi*, the ratio of a circle's circumference to its diameter) and Newton's G (the universal gravitational constant) were not unchanging facts. He discussed the need for a "liberatory science" that would free humans "from the tyranny of 'absolute truth' and 'objective reality.'"[9] This was about as ridiculous as a physicist could get. Many readers found it hilarious.[10] The editors of *Social Text* were naturally distressed.[11] One said it was "blatantly dishonest" to equate postmodernist approaches with "disbelief in the physical world."[12]

Arguments raged in *Lingua Franca* and the *New York Times*, but participants couldn't even agree on what they were arguing about. Objective truth versus relativism? The possibility that women and minorities might observe scientific realities through different lenses from white men? The need to equip ordinary citizens with scientific knowledge? Looking back, one anthropologist said the affair "contributed to . . . a growing consensus even among social scientists and anthropologists that postmodernism had gone too far." Not everything was a social construct.[13] Sokal's hoax served its purpose.

Legislating Pi

Two years after Sokal's hoax, another physicist resorted to humor in defense of science. Writing under the pseudonym "April Holiday," Mark Boslough broke some astonishing news: the Alabama legislature was moving to bring *pi* closer to its "biblical value" by redefining it as 3.0 instead of 3.14159. The article was published in the April 1 edition of *New Mexicans for Science and Reason*, but word got back to Alabama; angry callers told legislators to reconsider.[14]

Scholarly Journals and the Peer Review Process

Journals play an important role in evaluating new scholarship. Scientists, social scientists, and humanists use different research methods and strategies, but scholars in almost every field want to publish in peer-reviewed journals. Here's how it works:

1. The scholar submits an article to a journal, following guidelines at the journal's website. Author information does not appear on the article itself.

2. The journal editor sends the article to referees—experts who will evaluate the article without knowing who wrote it.

3. The referees send back their recommendations: accept the article as is, ask the author to revise it, or reject it.

4. If the article is accepted, the editor negotiates revisions with the author.

Articles in peer-reviewed journals are considered more reliable than articles in magazines, but unreliable papers do get through the process; consider V.J. Gupta's misplaced fossils (Chapter 46). A blog called Retraction Watch keeps track of papers that have been found false or fraudulent after publication—and occasionally reports the good news when researchers are cleared of misconduct.[15]

Social Text did not use the peer-review process. Instead, it was produced by an editorial collective—a group of editors who discussed articles face to face. The editors didn't see it as a strictly academic publication, but as a "little magazine" in the "tradition of the independent Left." They included political opinion, fiction, interviews, and essays, and their criteria were flexible. They found Sokal's article "a little hokey" and were annoyed when he refused to revise it, but they printed it because their readers might be interested in a physicist's thoughts about postmodernism.[16]

Would a peer-reviewed journal in culture studies have accepted Sokal's parody? If it had slipped through the peer-review process at a more conventional scholarly journal, he might have had better proof of his hypothesis that intellectual standards in the humanities lacked rigor.

Joining the Campaign to Ban DHMO

Quantities of dihydrogen monoxide have been found in almost every stream, lake, and reservoir in America today," warns the Coalition to Ban DHMO. "But the pollution is global, and DHMO contamination has even been found in Antarctic ice, *all the world's oceans* and even in mother's milk in developing nations."[1] The coalition was formed by students at UC Santa Cruz in the 1980s, after a Michigan newspaper reported that DHMO, found in city water pipes, could be "fatal if inhaled" and was known to "produce blistering vapors."[2]

The Dihydrogen Monoxide Research Division reports that DHMO "is a known causative component in many thousands of deaths" and contributes to "millions upon millions of dollars in damage to property and the environment" every year.[3] Known health risks include not only accidental inhalation but tissue damage from exposure to solid DHMO and severe burns from gaseous DHMO. Worse yet, the substance is addictive. For "those who have become dependent, DHMO withdrawal means certain death."[4]

On the environmental side, DHMO is:

* A major component of acid rain.

* A factor in soil erosion.

* A cause of corrosion and oxidation of many metals.

* A cause of short-circuits in electrical systems.

* A factor in automobile brake failure.

* Associated with killer cyclones, hurricanes, and the El Niño weather effect.

The scary rhetoric sounds familiar. Since World War II, American worries about invisible dangers in air and water have increased. Congress passed a clean water act in 1948 and a clean air act in 1955,[5] but unseen threats persisted. From 1951 to 1992, nuclear weapons tests released fallout into Nevada air and aquifers. Downwind, in Utah, cancer rates climbed[6]; as far away as Maine, children were told not to catch snowflakes on their tongues for fear of radiation. Meanwhile, the insecticide DDT was killing butterflies in New Jersey, and in 1962 Rachel Carson's best seller, *Silent Spring*, alerted the world.[7] DDT is colorless, odorless, and almost tasteless; it can save human lives by eliminating insects that carry disease, but while killing lice and mosquitoes, it also harms birds and causes cancer in humans.[8]

What is the lethal substance issuing from this tap?

The U.S. banned agricultural use of DDT in 1972, but since then many other useful chemicals have turned out to have dire side effects. As dangers become known, citizen groups rise up to combat them; petitions to ban hazardous substances are now common. So when 14-year-old Nathan Zohner circulated a petition to ban DHMO, he had no trouble gathering signatures. Of the 50 ninth-graders he asked, 43 signed the petition and only one refused flat out. That was the one who realized what DHMO is.[9]

Zohner called his 1997 science fair project "How Gullible Are We?"[10] DHMO.org reports Zohner's results this way: "Research conducted by award-winning U.S. scientist Nathan Zohner concluded that roughly 86 percent of the population supports a ban on dihydrogen monoxide. Although his results are preliminary, Zohner believes people need to pay closer attention to the information presented to them regarding Dihydrogen Monoxide."[11] The DHMO.org website sticks to the literal truth. For instance, DMHO (otherwise known as water) is fatal when inhaled; on average, ten Americans die of accidental drowning every day.[12] And Zohner was indeed an "award-winning U.S. scientist"—he won first prize in the Greater Idaho Falls Science Fair.[13] The site doesn't quite lie to you; it just tricks you into believing that water is dangerous. Is that a hoax?

An editorialist in a teachers' journal was optimistic. Nathan Zohner's science fair experiment proved that at least *some* Idaho Falls students were learning science, he wrote. But he concluded that "we often pay too little attention to the statistics that directly concern our lives."[14] Maybe we should discount the polls and research the issues ourselves before signing.

Getting Both Sides of the Story

The anti-DHMO websites use what magician Penn Jillette calls "the vocabulary and tone of environmental hysteria."[15] It would be kinder to call it the language of political engagement—but can we be politically engaged without putting our minds in gear? As critical readers, we might ask about the DHMO. org site's authority. (Is it really published by the United States Environmental Assessment Center? Is that a government agency? Why doesn't the domain name end in ".gov"?) The Coalition to Ban DHMO site is a more obvious political spoof, with quotations from Secretary of State Jim Kerry and President Barack Obema (not the real John Kerry and Barack Obama) and even Pope Jon XXXVII ("un papa immaginario").[16] The bibliography lists imaginary books—more clues that the site is unreliable.

(Continued on next page)

(Continued from previous page)

At either site, we might ask what information is missing, aside from the fact that DHMO is water. Those bulleted assertions look overwhelming—but where is the proof? And we might ask to hear the other side of the argument.

You can find the other side at "DHMO: Your All-Natural Friend." Here, the mystery substance is called "hydrogen hydroxide" and described as beneficial, environmentally safe, benign, and natural.[17] The pro-DHMO rallying cry sounds familiar, too—it uses the vocabulary and tone of political hysteria. "Don't let an uneducated and terror-stricken mob of fanatics railroad you into giving up your right to choose! Support the use and distribution of hydrogen hydroxide in your neighborhood, city, state, and country!"

Arguments based on the "right to choose" have been used in debates on issues from tobacco smoking to global warming. So have *ad hominem* arguments (also known as name-calling); obviously, uneducated and terror-stricken fanatics are the last people we'd trust to make our decisions. But where's the evidence that DHMO opponents are uneducated and terror-stricken?

Americans are often asked to vote on issues, and voter education often means giving equal air time to each side of the debate and then surveying the audience. But does this really help us understand the issues? If the Idaho Falls ninth-graders had seen the pro-DHMO website, maybe 86% of them would not have signed Zohner's petition.

But if they still didn't know DHMO was water, their opinion poll would still have been based on ignorance of the facts. "You can't poll a scientific fact," writes *Time* columnist Jeffrey Kluger. "The speed of light is the speed of light (186,282.4 miles per second) whether 90% of people believe it or 25% believe it."[18] This may be a good thing. If our mistaken beliefs had any effect on the speed of light or the organization of the solar system, life might be even more confusing than it already is.

Microsoft Technical Support

In the mid-1980s, computer users were a small minority. By the mid-1990s, more and more people had home computers, and friends were telling each other, "You have to get on e-mail." Like other novelties before it, the internet had quickly become a necessity.

With computers and online access came a new way to fool a mass audience, and pranksters were quick to take advantage of it. In 1994, a bogus press release went the rounds.[1] Microsoft was acquiring the Roman Catholic Church! Pope John Paul II would become senior vice-president of the company's new Religious Software Division, and two Microsoft vice-presidents would become cardinals. Believers could take communion, confess their sins, and receive absolution without leaving home.

Most people realized this was a joke, but many took it seriously. Microsoft published a denial and an apology. The joker's identity remains unknown.[2]

Since 2008, bogus Microsoft agents are going after money, not just laughs. Pretending to be agents from the company's technical support division, they make "cold calls"—unsolicited calls—to random consumers. The fake agents often have an exotic accent. Western consumers expect such an accent, because technical support is often outsourced to countries where educated workers speak English and work for lower wages than Americans. The agent might say, "Hello, we are calling from

Windows and your computer looks like it is infected. Our Microsoft Certified Technician can fix it for you."[3] But real technical support agents do not make cold calls; they help only when asked. A consumer who trusts the caller is an ideal "mark," a victim to be fooled.

Some scammers trick victims into calling *them*, by taking out internet ads that pop up on the browser when users search for tech support phone numbers. In this variation, the customer sees the fake ad, dials an apparently legitimate number, and is connected to a fraudulent help desk instead.[4]

The U.S. Federal Trade Commission combats tech support scammers, many of them based in India.

thinkstock

Once the con artists establish telephone contact, they get marks to open the PC's Event Viewer and count the "Error" and "Warning" messages—which are normal, but do look scary. "These errors and warnings are very much harmful for your computer," one false agent said. "These are major problems and it doesn't matter if you have one or two errors or more than that. Each one has already started corrupting your whole computer system."[5]

People have legitimate worries about computer viruses and spyware, and good marks believe the con artist who says their computer is about to crash. To avoid disaster, the mark allows the fake technician to control the computer through a remote access program. The hoaxster then reports more evidence of danger to the computer, and asks the mark to pay online for program upgrades or other measures to solve the imaginary problem; this might cost $300 or $400. Worse, while in control of the computer, the hoaxster may install password-snatching malware and gain access to the victim's personal and financial information.[6,7]

By 2012, at least 2,400 people worldwide had lost "tens of millions of dollars"[8] to fake tech support scams, and the U.S. Federal Trade Commission (FTC) was prosecuting 14 corporate defendants and 17 individuals for "unfair and deceptive commercial practices."[9] In 2014, British authorities clamped down on one operation, the "Smart Support Guys,"[10] and Microsoft itself sued Omnitech Support and other firms for "unfair and deceptive business practices and trademark infringement."[11]

Legal measures can slow the false tech support business, freezing assets in the U.S. and blocking fraudulent ads in search engines. But can they stop it? For centuries, confidence tricksters have played on their victims' fears to sell expensive solutions to imaginary problems. Skepticism may be the first line of defense.

Scam artists impersonating tech support representatives get victims to look at system logs, and tell them the "Error" and "Warning" flags need immediate attention.

Curses and Crashing Computers: Frightening the Marks

Some people believe all fortune-telling is a scam. That would be difficult to prove. But there is a classic fortune-telling fraud, and it goes something like this. A troubled person visits a fortune-teller, who sees a dark cloud. The client's past is full of loss, the present is difficult, and the future is shadowed by evil. What can be done about this? First, the fortune-teller will make a full diagnosis—which costs money. Then comes the cure—which costs more. The fortune-teller will burn special candles in her church (if the first candles cost $100 apiece, the platinum ones that come later will cost $1,000).[12] Or maybe the client will have to send the fortune-teller to the Middle East to get a special root for the potion that will lift the curse.[13]

John Stephen Dwyer

A storefront fortune-teller's shop doesn't look much like a computer help desk, but curse-lifting scams and tech support scams work the same way.

The curse is always harder to combat than the fortune-teller realized at first, and the client will have to pay ever-increasing sums in hopes of achieving spiritual health. (One woman paid over $55,000 and was forced to sell her Long Island house before she discovered the whole thing was a scam.[14]) When the client's resources are exhausted, the fortune-teller will disappear. Some are caught. (In 2013, a New York psychic who conned more than $130,000 from two women was ordered to pay them back in full—and sentenced to five to 15 years in prison.[15]) But even if the fortune-teller makes full restitution, the client is worse off than before; being swindled is a depressing experience.

The tech support scam and the fortune-telling fraud are alike, though they look and sound different. Tech support involves modern technology and geeky vocabulary, while people expect a fortune-teller to use a crystal ball and use words like "aura" and "negative presence" and "spiritual cleansing." But tech support and fortune-telling scams both rely on fear. Computer hackers and curses are unseen threats that can take over a life; they frighten people. Con artists produce evidence—a row of warning symbols in the event log, or an egg with a mysterious dark taint in its yolk—and say it means trouble. They offer expensive solutions that grow more expensive as marks are pulled deeper into the hoax. Both frauds work because people are afraid of dangers they don't understand, and eager to trust experts who promise them safety.

Conclusion

*For what a man had rather were true he more readily believes. Therefore he
rejects difficult things from impatience of research; sober things, because they
narrow hope; the deeper things of nature, from superstition; the light of experience, from arrogance and pride; things not commonly believed, out of deference
to the opinion of the vulgar. Numberless in short are the ways, and sometimes
imperceptible, in which the affections color and infect the understanding.*

— Francis Bacon, *Novum Organum*, 1620

Hoaxes manipulate our beliefs—our sense of what is real and what is
not—and in the process they change reality itself. Sometimes we think
of reality as just physical facts, or "what's out there." The earth under
our feet, the sky above us, the apple falling from a tree—all these things
are real, whether we believe in them or not. They're "out there."

But our beliefs affect the way we experience what's out there. The
earth revolves around the sun, but to believe this we have to imagine the
universe without ourselves at the center of it. One in four Americans
may still believe the sun revolves around the earth, and all of us experience sunrise every morning. It feels as if we are at the center and the sun
goes around us.

And what's out there is not our only reality. We live in a world of
other people—ambitious people who build cities and nations, indus-
tries, financial empires, newspapers and internets, entertainment
careers, moon rockets, and new technologies. Ambition, powered by
energy and imagination, has created a world that depends partly on
what's out there, but also on what we *believe* is out there.

Hoaxsters know that we act according to our beliefs, and by manipulating our beliefs they try to get us to act in certain ways. Benjamin Franklin tried to get a friend to be more tolerant by making her think the Bible called for tolerance. William-Henry Ireland tried to get his father to love him by forging documents with Shakespeare's signature. In wartime, spies plant false clues to make enemies mass their troops far away from a planned attack. In times of rapid change, when people are awed and confused by new technologies, entrepreneurs peddle devices that just might be true, like Keely's motor or Jernegan's gold accumulator.

Hoaxsters get us to believe what they want us to believe by dressing it up as what we ourselves want to believe. Francis Bacon understood this. We don't like to believe things that are too difficult to understand, or too frightening, or too different from what our friends and neighbors believe. But if we are in the mood for entertainment, we like to believe in things like the Fejee mermaid. If life is drab, we like to believe that a lost prince or princess is still alive in the world. If we need to get rich quick, we like to believe that it's possible, thanks to Mr. Ponzi's foolproof investment or to an unexpected inheritance we can access simply by sending a check for a few thousand dollars to an offshore address. If we are worried about curses or computer malware, we like to believe that a fortune-teller or help desk technician can protect us from the threat.

So to guard ourselves against being taken in, we need to think critically. As we open our minds to learn new things, we need to think about how they stack up with our existing sense of reality: given what we already know, is new information likely to be true? Sometimes new information seems unlikely, but turns out to be so compelling that we have to revise our whole idea of the world to fit it in. The earth goes around the sun? Humans evolved from other creatures? Since the dawn of the Scientific Revolution, these and other big new ideas have forced us to rearrange our worldviews. But often, if new information doesn't gibe with what we already know, there's a hoax involved. (One convenient place to begin checking out the truth of interesting claims is snopes.com, where you can also find a list of current top scams: http://www.snopes.com/fraud/topscams.asp.)

We also need to think honestly about human motives. Why would somebody be telling us this new thing? If it is not true, would somebody benefit from our belief that it *is* true? And what about our own motives? Do we *want* it to be true? Why?

In the end, hoaxes and ambition come from the same human capacity to imagine things that haven't happened—yet. Things that could make life better, both for perpetrators of a hoax and (if only it were true) for its victims. "It is only a great pity that it is not true," said Margaret Hershel of the 1835 Moon Hoax, "but . . . as wonderful things may yet be accomplished." What a hoaxster can imagine, an inventor may yet turn into reality. And reality—what's out there, threaded with human imagination—is truly a wonderful thing.

Glossary

Anecdotal evidence: Evidence based on isolated incidents. A person who noticed a black cat before one or two bad experiences might conclude that black cats are bad luck—but the conclusion would be based on anecdotal evidence. A scientist would want to know what percentage of black cat sightings are actually followed by bad luck, and what percentage of bad-luck events happened with no previous sightings of black cats. To establish a correlation between black cats and bad luck, the scientist would need a statistically significant number of incidents, not just anecdotal evidence.

Anthropology: The scientific study of human origins and development.

Appeasement: Conciliating or placating someone. In the 1930s, the British and French adopted a policy of appeasement, making concessions to Hitler and Mussolini in hopes of avoiding war.

Chapterhouse: A building or room set aside for meetings within a cathedral or monastery.

Connoisseur: An expert in matters of taste.

Conspiracist: A person who supports a conspiracy theory.

Data: Given facts; individual bits of information formatted or arranged for analysis.

Epistemology: The philosophical study of knowledge, epistemology can help distinguish valid knowledge from unsupported opinion.

Gestapo: Hitler's secret police, tasked with intelligence and quelling dissent.

Haversack: A small backpack or shoulder bag used by soldiers or hikers.

Hypothesis (*plural* hypotheses): A supposition or explanation made on the basis of limited observations, and proposed for investigation. A hypothesis may be based on anecdotal evidence (see above), but scientists will test it systematically before accepting it as a theory.

Humbug: A kind of hoax; a deceptive person (like the Wizard of Oz) or fraudulent thing (like Christmas, according to Scrooge). Humbug may be a useful element in advertising and public display.

Impostor: A person who pretends to be somebody else, often for financial gain.

Indigenous: Native to a particular place. Indigenous populations have historic ties to their home territories, predating the arrival of other groups.

Leprosy: Now known as Hansen's disease and curable with multidrug therapy, leprosy was greatly dreaded in the Middle Ages. It was fatal, but disfigured its victims long before killing them. People with leprosy were called "lepers" and cut off from their communities for fear of contagion.

Mark: In a confidence game or scam, the mark is the intended victim. Also, a denomination of German currency.

Medium: A person who is believed to mediate communication between the living and spirits of the dead.

Minerva: Roman goddess of wisdom and strategic warfare.

Pogrom: A massacre, usually carried out by a rioting mob with public approval.

Provenance: The history of an object, from its origin onward; records proving authenticity and ownership.

Reformation: In sixteenth-century Europe, a religious and intellectual upheaval that divided Christendom into Catholic and Protestant factions.

Renaissance: Beginning in fourteenth-century Italy, a cultural movement that revived and extended the humanistic arts, sciences, and philosophies of ancient Greece and Rome.

Rhetoric: The art of using language, spoken or written, to achieve planned effects on an audience.

Sample size: The number of observations in a statistical sample. To minimize error, a sample size must be large enough to represent the population from which it is drawn.

Sapphire: A blue gemstone.

Skeptic (British spelling, sceptic): A doubter; a person who questions assertions and seeks evidence before accepting them.

Snake-stones: Animal bones or stones used as folk medicine for snake bite in Africa, South America, and Asia.

Spurious: False or invalid.

Taradiddle: A fabrication, often tongue-in-cheek.

Theory: A supposition or a system of ideas intended to explain something. A theory has been more systematically tested than a hypothesis.

Theosophical Society: Founded by Madame Helena P. Blavatsky and Colonel Henry Steel Olcott in 1875, an international society for the pursuit of divine wisdom and inner enlightenment.

Sources and Additional Resources

A word about the research process:

Original research—"primary" research—is based on direct investigation. Research scientists may devise experiments to test their hypotheses; historians may gather and analyze data from archives.

This book is not a work of original research. Instead, it is based on secondary research—looking things up and making sense of them. To write the book, I had to gather sources on each topic, compare and synthesize them, and summarize each story. You may often have to do secondary research for school reports, and you probably go about it much the way I did. We rely on our "information literacy."

Basic information literacy skills include defining the task; deciding on an information-seeking strategy; locating and accessing sources; reading (or viewing or listening to) the sources and taking from them what you need; synthesizing what you've taken from multiple sources and presenting it; and finally, evaluating and possibly revising your product —whether it's a book or a class presentation. Each time you go through this process, you get a little more efficient, which helps you the next time.

I don't always do the steps in order. Often I go back and forth between them. For instance, I define my task, start searching—and redefine my task. I locate a source, jump forward to read it, and decide not to use it—or find it mentions three other sources I need to locate. Here are my first three steps:

Defining the task: For this book, the task was clear. I had to introduce 50 different hoaxes, in chapters between 500 and 700 words long. Each chapter had to tell what the hoax was and how it affected history. Taken together, the chapters needed to show a wide range of different world-shaping ambitions, and a variety of different hoaxes. Some of the hoaxes affected history (like the Donation of Constantine and the *Protocols of the Elders of Zion*); some reacted against modern trends (like Spectric Poetry or Sokal's hoax on the peer-review process); others just go to show what ambitious people want to believe, or can be made to believe.

Plotting a search strategy: First I looked for lists of hoaxes in general—and found hundreds of them. To limit the search, I used these rules of thumb:

* The hoax had to be more than a simple lie; it had to be a scam that used corroborative evidence (such as a large wooden horse, or a forged letter, or a fake machine) to persuade intended victims that the lie was true.

* The hoax had to be well documented. For instance, Frederick Cook claimed he reached the North Pole in 1908; the claim has been contested ever since, but I wasn't satisfied that Cook was a hoaxster. I left him and his fellow Arctic explorers out of this book with regret.

For a few of the hoaxes, I found entire books by writers who had already located and collated many sources. For others, I sometimes started with Wikipedia. (Wikipedia should be handled carefully, as should any source, but it's constantly being reviewed and corrected, and most of its articles have sources you can follow up. Think of it as a jumping-off point, and keep going.) Another jumping-off point was Alex Boese's book, *The Museum of Hoaxes* (Dutton, 2002), and online Museum of Hoaxes (http://hoaxes.org/). For many of my hoax stories, I pieced together information from scholarly articles that I accessed through my university library, using databases such as Academic Search Complete and JSTOR.

Locating and accessing sources: Physical access was not a problem. School, public, and university libraries have online catalogs of their holdings, and online databases of articles. Before going to the library, I make a list of things I want to look at when I get there.

But not every source is useful. Before leaving the library, I check the index of each book and look at the pages that should be most relevant to my question. Before reading a whole article online, I use "find" the same way. Is the book or article really about my topic? Can I understand it? Do I trust it? If not, I will not borrow it from the library or download it.

How do I know what to trust? I look for documentation—bibliographies, endnotes, and other evidence that the authors have done their homework. I look for balance—if there's a controversy, I want both sides to be explained fairly. On the internet, I tend to trust academic or nonprofit sources more than commercial sources, but that's not a foolproof guide to reliability. The best strategy is to compare multiple sources and see where they agree.

Reading, synthesizing, writing, and rewriting: In the later stages of my secondary research, I go back and forth between steps more and more. Writing makes me notice questions that still need answering. My writing is not a fast or predictable process. But it absorbs me; it is a process of discovery. I hope you can use this book—with its source lists and suggested resources—as a jumping off point for your own voyage of discovery.

1. The Original Trojan Horse

Sources

Cline, Eric H. *1177 B.C.: The Year Civilization Collapsed*. Princeton, NJ: Princeton University Press, 2014.

Gayley, Charles Mills. *The Classic Myths in English Literature and Art*, new ed. New York: John Wiley and Sons, 1939.

Sparkes, B. A. "The Trojan Horse in Classical Art." *Greece & Rome* 18, 1 (1971): 54–70.

Virgil. *The Aeneid of Virgil: A Verse Translation by Allen Mandelbaum*. Berkeley: University of California Press, 1981.

Wikipedia. "Trojan Horse." en.wikipedia.org/wiki/Trojan_Horse (accessed 11/12/2015).

Additional Resources

d'Angour, Armand. "How Many Greek Legends Were Really True?" BBC News (23 July 2014): bbc.com/news/business-27923256 (accessed 11/12/2015).

Lovgren, Stefan. "Is Troy True? The Evidence Behind Movie Myth." *National Geographic News* (May 14, 2004): news.nationalgeographic.com/news/2004/05/0514_040514_troy.html (accessed 11/12/2015).

"Trojan Horse." mlahanas.de/Greeks/Mythology/TrojanHorse.html (accessed 11/12/2015).

"Trojan War." History. history.com/topics/ancient-history/trojan-war (accessed 11/12/2015).

2. The Forgery Underlying the Power of Medieval Popes

Sources

Bowersock, G. W. "Introduction." In Lorenzo Valla, *On the Donation of Constantine*. Cambridge, Massachusetts: Harvard University Press, 2007.

Duff, Eamon. *Saints & Sinners: A History of the Popes*. New Haven: Yale University Press, 2001.

Eusebius, *Church History. Life of Constantine the Great, Oration in Praise of Constantine*. In *Select Library of the Nicene and Post-Nicene Fathers of the Christian Church*, Second Series, Philip Schaff and Henry Wace. New York: Christian Literature Company, 1890–1900. Sage Digital Library (found at archive.org).

Fowden, Garth. "The Last Days of Constantine: Oppositional Versions and Their Influence." *The Journal of Roman Studies* 84 (1994): 146–170.

Johnson, Paul. *A History of Christianity*. New York: Atheneum, 1976.

Liverani, Paolo. "Saint Peter's, Leo the Great and the Leprosy of Constantine." *Papers of the British School at Rome* 76 (2008): 155–172.

O'Malley, John W. *A History of the Popes*. New York: Rowman & Littlefield, 2010.

Prosser, Peter E. "Church History's Biggest Hoax." *Christian History* 20, 4 (2001).

Rosenblum, Joseph. *Practice to Deceive: The Amazing Stories of Literary Forgery's Most Notorious Practitioners*. New Castle, Delaware: Oak Knoll Press, 2000.

Wells, Charles L. *The Age of Charlemagne*. Volume 4, *Ten Epochs of Church History*, ed. John Fulton. New York: The Christian Literature Company, 1898.

Whitford, David M. "The Papal Antichrist: Martin Luther and the Underappreciated Influence of Lorenzo Valla." *Renaissance Quarterly* 61 (2008): 26–52.

Wikipedia. "Languages of the Roman Empire." en.wikipedia.org/wiki/Languages_of_the_Roman_Empire (accessed 12/4/2015).

Wikipedia. "Constantine the Great and Christianity." en.wikipedia.org/wiki/Constantine_the_Great_and_Christianity (accessed 12/4/2015).

Additional Resources

Cohen, Shaye I. D. "Legitimization Under Constantine: From persecuted minority to official imperial religion - what caused this extraordinary reversal for Christianity?" PBS Frontline: pbs.org/wgbh/pages/frontline/shows/religion/why/legitimization.html (accessed 11/12/2015).

"Constantine the Great" [10–minute video, Part 1 of 6]. BBC. youtube.com/watch?v=RnVTf10YUdY (accessed 11/12/2015).

"Ecclesiastical Property Ownership in the Middle Ages." Unam Sanctam Catholicam: unamsanctamcatholicam.com/history/historical-apologetics/79-history/501-church-owned-land-middle-ages.html (accessed 11/12/2015).

"Martin Luther and the 95 Theses." History.Com: history.com/topics/martin-luther-and-the-95-theses (accessed 11/12/2015).

Whaley, Joachim. "The Holy Roman Empire: From Charlemagne to Napoleon." British Museum (October 13, 2014): blog.britishmuseum.org/2014/10/13/the-holy-roman-empire-from-charlemagne-to-napoleon/ (accessed 11/12/2015).

3. A Letter from the Mythical Prester John

Sources

Eisenstein, Elizabeth L. *The Printing Revolution in Early Modern Europe* (New York: Cambridge University Press, 1983), 195–200.

Helleiner, Karl F. "Prester John's Letter: A Mediaeval Utopia." *Phoenix* 13, 2 (Summer 1959): 47–57.

Nowell, Charles E. "The Historical Prester John." *Speculum* 28, 3 (1953): 435–445.

"Prester John," *Catholic Encyclopedia*, New Advent: newadvent.org/cathen/12400b.htm (accessed 11/14/2015).

Salvadore, Matteo. "The Ethiopian Age of Exploration: Prester John's Discovery of Europe, 1306–1458." *Journal of World History* 21, 4 (December 2010): 593–627.

"Tales of Land and Sea: More on Medieval Mappae Mundi." *In Romaunce as We Rede* (April 27, 2012): inromaunce.blogspot.com/2012/04/tales-of-land-and-sea-more-on-medieval.html (accessed 10/21/2015).

Additional Resources

The Crusades. History Learning Site. historylearningsite.co.uk/the_crusades.htm (accessed 11/14/2015).

"The Letter of Prester John." [Taken from a Welsh version.] *Selections from the Hengwrt Mss. Preserved in the Peniarth Library*. Williams, Robert, ed. & trans. London: Thomas Richards, 1892. maryjones.us/ctexts/presterjohn.html (accessed 11/14/2015).

"Letter of Prester John [Unabridged English]." Menagerie of the Unseen. menagerieoftheunseen.tumblr.com/post/89066882999/letter-of-prester-john-unabridged-english (accessed 11/14/2015).

Phillips, Jonathan. "Call of the Crusades." *History Today* 59, 11 (November 2009): historytoday.com/jonathan-phillips/call-crusades (accessed 11/14/2015).

4. Did Marco Polo Really Go to China?

Sources

Fleck, Andrew. "Here, There, and In Between: Representing Difference in the 'Travels' of Sir John Mandeville." *Studies in Philology*, 97, 4 (Autumn 2000): 379–400.

Jackson, Peter. "Marco Polo and His 'Travels.'" *Bulletin of the School of Oriental and African Studies, University of London*, 61, 1 (1998): 82–101.

Kohanski, Tamarah, and Benson, C. David. "The Book of John Mandeville: Introduction." TEAMS Middle English Text Series, Robbins Library Digital Projects, University of Rochester, 2007. d.lib.rochester.edu/teams/text/kohanski-and-benson-the-book-of-john-mandeville-introduction (accessed 11/14/2015).

Mosely, C. W. R. D. "'New Things to Speak of': Money, Memory, and *Mandeville's Travels* in Early Modern England." *The Yearbook of English Studies*, 41, 1 (2011): 5–20.

Wikipedia. "Kublai Khan." en.wikipedia.org/wiki/Kublai_Khan#Emperor_of_the_Yuan_Dynasty (accessed 11/14/2015).

Woods, Frances. *Did Marco Polo Go to China?* Boulder, CO: Westview Press, 1996.

Additional Resources

"Kublai Khan In Battle, 1287." EyeWitness to History (2000): eyewitnesstohistory.com/khan.htm (accessed 11/14/2015). [From Yule, Henry (translator, editor), The Book of Ser Marco Polo (3rd Edition), (1929).]

Mandeville, Sir John. *The Book of John Mandeville*. Ed. Kohanski, Tamarah, and Benson, C. David. TEAMS Middle English Text Series, Robbins Library Digital Projects, University of Rochester, 2007. d.lib.rochester.edu/teams/text/kohanski-and-benson-the-book-of-john-mandeville (accessed 11/14/2015).

———. *The Travels of Sir John Mandeville*. Project Gutenberg. gutenberg.org/ebooks/782 (accessed 11/14/2015).

Marco Polo [resources]. TES Connect. tes.co.uk/teaching-resource/marco-polo-6090913 (accessed 11/14/2015).

Marco Polo [video clip]. Teacher Tube. teachertube.com/video/marco-polo-114089 (accessed 11/14/2015).

Mosely, C. W. R. D. "'New Things to Speak of': Money, Memory, and *Mandeville's Travels* in Early Modern England." *The Yearbook of English Studies*, 41, 1 (2011): 5–20.

"On the Road with Marco Polo." EDSITEment! National Endowment for the Humanities. edsitement.neh.gov/lesson-plan/road-marco-polo-boy-13th-century-venice (accessed 11/14/2015).

Yule, Sir Henry, trans. *The Book of Ser Marco Polo, the Venetian: Concerning the Kingdoms and Marvels of the East*. London: John Murray, 1871. archive.org/details/bookofsermarcopo00polo (accessed 11/14/2015).

5. The World's Most Mysterious Book

Sources

Amancio, Diego R., *et al.* "Probing the statistical properties of unknown texts: application to the Voynich Manuscript." 2013. ia601901.us.archive.org/28/items/arxiv-1303.0347/1303.0347. pdf (accessed 11/14/2015).

Beinecke Rare Book & Manuscript Library. "Linda Sue Park: The 39 Clues." (April 24, 2013): beinecke.library.yale.edu/programs-events/events/Linda_Sue_Park%3A_The_39_Clues (accessed 10/22/2015).

Child, James. "The Voynich Manuscript Revisited," nsa.gov/public_info/_files/tech_journals/ Voynich_Manuscript_Revisited.pdf (accessed 12/4/2015).

D'Agnese, Joseph. "Scientific Method Man." *Wired* 12, 9 (September, 2004). archive.wired. com/wired/archive/12.09/rugg.html (accessed 11/14/2015).

Goldstone, Lawrence and Nancy. *The Friar and the Cipher: Roger Bacon and the Unsolved Mystery of the Most Unusual Manuscript in the World*. New York: Doubleday, 2005.

Grossman, Lisa. "Mexican Plants Could Break Code on Gibberish Manuscript." *New Scientist* (February 7, 2014): newscientist.com/article/dn24987-mexican-plants-could-break-code-on-gibberish-manuscript.html#.VUDMQ5V0zwp (accessed 11/14/2015).

Lutz, Philip. "A Composer Opens Up Her Creative Process, Online." *New York Times* (September 25, 2015): nytimes.com/2015/09/27/nyregion/a-composer-opens-up-her-creative-process-online.html (accessed 10/22/2015).

Manly, John Matthews. "Roger Bacon and the Voynich MS." *Speculum* 6, 3 (July 1931): 345–391.

McCormick, Rich. "Decrypting the Most Mysterious Book in the World." *The Verge* (February 28, 2014): theverge.com/2014/2/28/5453596/voynich-manuscript-decrypting-the-most-mysterious-book-in-the-world (accessed 11/14/2015).

Rigby, Nick. "Breakthrough over 600-Year-Old Mystery Manuscript." BBC News (February 18, 2014): bbc.com/news/uk-england-beds-bucks-herts-26198471 (accessed 11/14/2015).

Schinner, Andreas. "The Voynich Manuscript: Evidence of the Hoax Hypothesis." *Cryptologia* 31, 2 (April 2007): tandfonline.com/doi/abs/10.1080/01611190601133539 (accessed 11/14/2015).

Singh, Sukhwant. "Voynich Manuscript Is Written in Landa Khojki Scripts and Belongs to Sindh Regions Mahajan": voynich-manuscript-landa-khojki-scripts-sindhi-mahajans-book. net/home.html (accessed 11/14/2015).

The Voynich Manuscript (digitized). Archive.com. archive.org/details/TheVoynichManuscript (accessed 11/14/2015).

"The Voynich Manuscript: Evidence of the Hoax Hypothesis," *Cryptologia* 31, 2 (April 2007): tandfonline.com/doi/abs/10.1080/01611190601133539 (accessed 12/4/2015).

Yale University. Beineke Rare Book and Manuscript Library. "Voynich Manuscript." Early Books and Manuscripts (before 1500). beinecke.library.yale.edu/collections/highlights/voynich-manuscript (accessed 11/14/2015).

Wikipedia. "Esperanto." en.wikipedia.org/wiki/Esperanto (accessed 12/4/2015).

Wikipedia. "Romani People." en.wikipedia.org/wiki/Romani_people (accessed 12/4/2015).

Zandbergen, René. "The Voynich Manuscript." (2004–2015): voynich.nu/ (accessed 11/14/2015).

Additional Resources

D'Agnese, Joseph. "How to Create an 'Indecipherable' Manuscript." *Wired* 12, 9 (September, 2004). archive.wired.com/wired/archive/12.09/rugg.html?pg=4 (accessed 11/14/2015).

Graham, Ruth. "Why Scholars Can't Resist the Uncrackable Voynich Manuscript." *Boston Globe* (February 23, 2014). bostonglobe.com/ideas/2014/02/23/why-scholars-can-resist-uncrackable-voynich-manuscript/FWGMJjrqolrQ50L86SpkQP/story.html (accessed 11/14/2015).

6. Was Lambert Simnel a Lost Prince?

Sources

Bennett, Michael. *Lambert Simnel and the Battle of Stoke.* New York: St. Martin's Press, 1987.

Hicks, Michael. "The Second Anonymous Continuation of the Crowland Abbey Chronicle 1459–86 Revisited." *The English Historical Review* 122, 496 (Apr., 2007): 349–370.

The Museum of Hoaxes. "The History of Crowland." hoaxes.org/archive/permalink/the_history_of_crowland (accessed 11/16/2015).

Holmes, Peter. "The Great Council in the Reign of Henry VII." *The English Historical Review* 101, 401 (October 1986): 840–862.

Martin, F. X. "The Crowning of a King at Dublin, 24 May 1487." *Hermathena* 144 (Summer 1988): 7–34.

Roffe, David, "The Historia Croylandensis: A Plea for Reassessment," *The English Historical Review* 110, 435 (February 1995): 93–108.

Wikipedia. "Succession to the British Throne." en.wikipedia.org/wiki/Succession_to_the_British_throne (accessed 11/16/2015).

Additional Resources

Ashdown Hill, John. "Lambert Simnel: Richard III's Heir Who 'Had a Stronger Claim to the Throne than Henry VII.'" History Extra, BBC (February 23, 2015): historyextra.com/feature/tudors/lambert-simnel-richard-iii%E2%80%99s-heir-who-had-stronger-claim-throne-henry-vii (accessed 11/16/2015).

"The Lambert Simnel Rebellion." History Learning Site (2014). historylearningsite.co.uk/lambert_simnel_rebellion.htm (accessed 11/16/2015).

"Mystery People of History – Lambert Simnel." History Times History (January 19, 2013): historytimeshistory.blogspot.com/2013/01/mystery-people-of-history-lambert-simnel.html (accessed 11/16/2015).

Wars of the Roses. History.com. history.com/topics/british-history/wars-of-the-roses (accessed 11/16/2015).

Wikipedia. "Wars of the Roses." en.wikipedia.org/wiki/Wars_of_the_Roses (accessed 11/16/2015).

7. Michelangelo Fakes an Antiquity

Sources

Brown, Mark. "Michelangelo's Bronze Panther Riders Revealed after 'Renaissance whodunnit.'" *The Guardian* (February 1, 2015). theguardian.com/artanddesign/2015/feb/02/michelangelo-bronzes-sculptures-fitzwilliam-museum-cambridge (accessed 11/16/2015).

Italian Renaissance Resources. "The Rise, Fall, and Resurrection of Ancient Rome." italianre-naissanceresources.com/units/unit-7/essays/rise-fall-and-resurrection-of-ancient-rome/ (accessed 11/16/2015).

Koortbojian, Michael. "Pliny's Laocoön?" In *Antiquity and Its Interpreters*, ed. Alina Payne, Ann Kuttner, & Rebekah Smick, 199–216. New York: Cambridge University Press, 2010.

Norton, Paul F. "The Lost Sleeping Cupid of Michelangelo." *The Art Bulletin* 39, 4 (December, 1957): 251–257.

Parker, Deborah. *Michelangelo and the Art of Letter Writing*. New York: Cambridge University Press, 2010.

Rubinstein, Ruth. "Michelangelo's Lost *Sleeping Cupid* and Fetti's *Vertumnus and Pomona*." *Journal of the Warburg and Courtauld Institutes* 49 (1986): 257–259.

Russell, John. "A Michelangelo on 5th Avenue? It Seems So." *New York Times* (January 23, 1996): nytimes.com/1996/01/23/arts/a-michelangelo-on-5th-ave-it-seems-so.html (accessed 11/16/2015).

Unger, Miles J. *Michelangelo: A Life in Six Masterpieces*, New York: Simon & Schuster, 2014.

Wallace, William E. *Michelangelo: The Artist, the Man, and His Times*. New York: Cambridge University Press, 2010.

Wikipedia. "Annio da Viterbo." en.wikipedia.org/wiki/Annio_da_Viterbo.

Additional Resources

Early Modern Europe: Renaissance. Best of History Websites. EdTech Teacher: besthistory-sites.net/early-modern-europe/renaissance/ (accessed 11/16/2015).

Italian Renaissance Resources, in collaboration with the National Gallery of Art: italianrenais-sanceresources.com/ (accessed 11/16/2015).

Katz, Jamie. "The Measure of Genius: Michelangelo's Sistine Chapel at 500." Smithsonian.com (April 9, 2009): smithsonianmag.com/arts-culture/the-measure-of-genius-michelangelos-sistine-chapel-at-500-123313873/?no-ist (accessed 11/16/2015).

8. A Mythical Island Appears on Maps of the North Atlantic

Sources

Eisenstein, Elizabeth L. *The Printing Revolution in Early Modern Europe*. New York: Cambridge University Press, 1983.

Glassie, John. *A Man of Misconceptions: The Life of an Eccentric in an Age of Change*. New York: Riverhead Books, 2012.

Irminger, Admiral [Carl Ludwig Christian]. "Zeno's Frislanda Is Iceland and Not the Faeroes," *Journal of the Royal Geographical Society of London* 49 (1879): 398–412.

Johnson, Donald S. *Phantom Islands of the Atlantic: The Legends of Seven Lands That Never Were*. New York: Walker and Company, 1994. ("III. Frisland." pp. 44–62.)

Lucas, Fred W. *The annals of the voyages of the brothers Nicolò and Antonio Zeno in the North Atlantic about the end of the fourteenth century and the claim founded thereon to a Venetian discovery of America: a criticism and an indictment*. London: H. Stevens Son & Stiles, 1898. [microform digitized at archive.org/details/cihm_29528.]

Major, R. H. "The Site of the Lost Colony of Greenland Determined, and Pre-Columbian Discoveries of America Confirmed." *Proceedings of the Royal Geographical Society of London* 17, 5 (1872–1873): 312–321.

Probasco, Nate. "Cartography as a Tool of Colonization: Sir Humphrey Gilbert's 1583 Voyage to North America." *Renaissance Quarterly* 67, 2 (Summer 2014): 425–472.

Rye, E. C. S. "New Books." *Proceedings of the Royal Geographical Society and Monthly Record of Geography* 5, 11 (Nov., 1883): 676–682.

Smith, Brian. "Earl Henry Sinclair's fictitious trip to America." orig. *New Orkney Antiquarian Journal*, 2 (2002); revised at web.archive.org/web/20080206091002/http://www.users.zetnet.co.uk/ahamilton/sinclair.htm (accessed 11/16/2015).

Wallis, Helen. "England's Search for the Northern Passages in the Sixteenth and Early Seventeenth Centuries." *Arctic* 37, 4 (December 1984): 453–472.

Wikipedia. "Thule." en.wikipedia.org/wiki/Thule.

Additional Resources

"Earl Henry Sinclair." Orkneyjar. www.orkneyjar.com/history/historicalfigures/henrysinclair/index.html (accessed 11/16/2015).

Jacobs, Frank. "62 – Frisland, an Italian Fabrication in the North Atlantic." Strange Maps. bigthink.com/strange-maps/62-frisland-an-italian-fabrication-in-the-north-atlantic (accessed 11/16/2015).

"The Renaissance Rhetoric of Discovery." Osher Map Library. oshermaps.org/exhibitions/map-commentaries/renaissance-rhetoric-of-discovery (accessed 11/16/2015).

"The Zeno Map and Narrative." Temple of Mysteries. templeofmysteries.com/henry-st-clair/the-zeno-map-&-narrative.php (accessed 11/16/2015).

9. Secrets of an Imaginary Alchemist

Sources

Pierce, C. S. "Note on the Age of Basil Valentine." *Science, New Series* 8, 189 (August 12, 1898): 169–176.

Principe, Lawrence M. *The Secrets of Alchemy.* Chicago: University of Chicago Press, 2013.

Stillman, John Maxson. "Basil Valentine: A Seventeenth-Century Hoax." *Popular Science Monthly* 81 (December, 1912): en.wikisource.org/wiki/Popular_Science_Monthly/Volume_81/December_1912/Basil_Valentine:_A_Seventeenth-Century_Hoax (accessed 8/11/2015).

Additional Resources

"Alchemy." *In Our Time*, BBC Radio (February 4, 2005). bbc.co.uk/programmes/p003k9bn (accessed 11/16/2015).

Basil Valentine. Wikipedia. en.wikipedia.org/wiki/Basil_Valentine (accessed 8/11/2015).

Keiger, Dale. "All That Glitters...." *Johns Hopkins Magazine* (February, 1999): pages. jh.edu/~jhumag/0299web/glitter.html (accessed 8/11/2015).

Wikipedia. "Paracelsus." en.wikipedia.org/wiki/Paracelsus (accessed 8/11/2015).

10. The Stagecraft of Athanasius Kircher

Sources

Brauen, Fred. "Athanasius Kircher (1602–1680)." *Journal of the History of Ideas* 43, 1 (January, 1982): 129–134.

British Library. "Cabinet of Curiosities: 1710," *Learning Timelines*. bl.uk/learning/timeline/item107648.html (accessed 10/22/2015).

Eisenstein, Elizabeth L. *The Printing Revolution in Early Modern Europe.* New York: Cambridge University Press, 1983.

Glassie, John. *A Man of Misconceptions: The Life of an Eccentric in an Age of Change.* New York: Riverhead Books, 2012.

Godwin, Joscelyn. *Athanasius Kircher's Theatre of the World: The Life and Work of the Last Man to Search for Universal Knowledge.* Rochester, VT: Inner Traditions, 2009.

Museum of Hoaxes. "Athanasius Kircher, Victim of Pranks." hoaxes.org/archive/permalink/athanasius_kircher (accessed 10/23/2015).

Wikipedia. "Scientific Revolution." en.wikipedia.org/wiki/Scientific_revolution (accessed 10/23/15).

Additional Resources

"Athanasius Kircher." Wikipedia. en.wikipedia.org/wiki/Athanasius_Kircher (accessed 11/16/2015).

"Athanasius Kircher at Stanford." web.stanford.edu/group/kircher/cgi-bin/site/ (accessed 11/16/2015).

Stewart, Jim. "Athanasius Kircher's Museum in Rome." The Zymoglyphic Museum Curator's Web Log. (February 10, 2007): zymoglyphic.blogspot.com/2007/02/athanasius-kirchers-museum-in-rome.html (accessed 11/16/2015).

Stolzenburg, Daniel. "Athanasius Kircher and the Hieroglyphic Sphinx." *Public Domain Review*. publicdomainreview.org/2013/05/16/athanasius-kircher-and-the-hieroglyphic-sphinx/ (accessed 11/16/2015).

Westfall, Richard S., comp. "Kircher, Athanasius." The Galileo Project. galileo.rice.edu/Catalog/NewFiles/kircher.html (accessed 11/16/2015).

11. Dr. Beringer Reads Lying Fossils

Sources

Gould, Stephen Jay. *The Lying Stones of Marrakech*. New York: Harmony Books, 2000.

Jahn, Melvin E., and Woolf, Daniel J., translators and annotators. *The Lying Stones of Dr. Johann Bartholomew Adam Beringer, Being His* Lithographiæ Wirceburgensis. Los Angeles: University of California Press, 1963.

Wikipedia. "Fossils." en.wikipedia.org/wiki/Fossil#History_of_the_study_of_fossils (accessed 12/2/2015).

Additional Resources

Jackson, Brittany, and Rose, Mark. "The Beringer Stones." *Archaeology Archive* (2009). archive.archaeology.org/online/features/hoaxes/beringer.html (accessed 12/2/2015).

Museum of Hoaxes. "The Lying Stones of Dr. Beringer." hoaxes.org/archive/permalink/the_lying_stones_of_dr._beringer/ (accessed 12/2/2015).

Peacay. "Fossil Fakes." BibliOdyssey. (August 15, 2006). bibliodyssey.blogspot.com/2006/08/fossil-fakes.html (accessed 12/2/2015).

Simanek, Donald E. "Beringer's Autographed Stones." lhup.edu/~dsimanek/berstone.htm (accessed 12/2/2015).

Wikipedia. "Beringer's Lying Stones." en.wikipedia.org/wiki/Beringer's_Lying_Stones (accessed 12/2/2015).

12. An Ancient Bard Awes the Literary World

Sources

Murphy, Peter T. "Fool's Gold: The Highland Treasures of MacPherson's Ossian." *ELH* 53, 3 (Autumn 1986): 567–591.

Porter, James. "'Bring Me the Head of James Macpherson': The Execution of Ossian and the Wellsprings of Folkloristic Discourse." *The Journal of American Folklore* 114, 454 (Autumn 2001): 396–435.

Rosenblum, Joseph. "'Ossian' James Macpherson," in *Practice to Deceive: The Amazing Stories of Literary Forgery's Most Notorious Practitioners*, 19–54. New Castle, Delaware: Oak Knoll Press, 1999.

Additional Resources

"Culloden: Past, Present & Future." National Trust for Scotland. nts.org.uk/culloden/ (accessed 12/2/2015).

Macpherson, James, trans. *The Poems of Ossian*, Volume 1. London: J. Mundell & Co., 1796. archive.org/details/poemsofossiantra05macp (accessed 12/2/2015).

"The Samuel Johnson Sound Bite Page." samueljohnson.com/ (accessed 12/2/2015).
Wikipedia. "Ossian." en.wikipedia.org/wiki/Ossian (accessed 12/2/2015).

13. Benjamin Franklin Pretends to Be the King of Prussia

Sources

Aldridge, Alfred Owen. "A Religious Hoax by Benjamin Franklin." *American Literature* 36, 2 (May 1964): 204–209.

Davies, Owen. *America Bewitched: The Story of Witchcraft after Salem.* Oxford: Oxford University Press, 2013.

Franklin, Benjamin. "An Edict by the King of Prussia." *The Public Advertiser* (September 22, 1773). founders.archives.gov/documents/Franklin/01-20-02-0223 (accessed 12/5/2015).

———. "A Witch Trial at Mount Holly." *Pennsylvania Gazette* (October 22, 1730). founders.archives.gov/documents/Franklin/01-01-02-0056#BNFN-01-01-02-0056-fn-0001-ptr (accessed 12/5/2015).

Hall, Max. "An Amateur Detective on the Trail of B. Franklin, Hoaxer." *Proceedings of the Massachusetts Historical Society*, Third Series, 84 (1972): 26–43.

Kulikoff, Allan. "Silence Dogood and the Leather-Apron Men." *The Pennsylvania Magazine of History and Biography* 81, 3 (Summer 2014): 364–374.

Mulford, Carla. "Benjamin Franklin's Savage Eloquence: Hoaxes from the Press at Passy, 1782." *Proceedings of the American Philosophical Society* 152, 4 (December 2008): 490–530.

Steiner, Prudence L. "Benjamin Franklin's Biblical Hoaxes." *Proceedings of the American Philosophical Society* 131, 2 (June 1987): 183–196.

Weinberger, Jerry. "Benjamin Franklin: Philosopher of Progress." *The Good Society* 17, 1 (2008): 20–25.

Additional Resources

"The Electric Ben Franklin." U.S. History.org. ushistory.org/franklin/info/kite.htm (accessed 12/2/2015).

Harrington, Hugh T. "'The Sale of the Hessians' and the Franklin Legend. *Journal of the American Revolution* (February 10, 2015): allthingsliberty.com/2015/02/the-sale-of-the-hessians-and-the-franklin-legend/ (accessed 12/2/2015).

National Archives. Founders Online: Correspondence and Other Writings of Six Major Shapers of the U.S. founders.archives.gov/ (accessed 12/5/2015).

14. The Potemkin Village: More Than Just a Pretty Façade

Sources

Duran, James A. "Catherine II, Potemkin, and Colonization Policy in Southern Russia." *The Russian Review* 28, 1 (January 1969): 23–36.

Griffiths, David M. "Catherine II Discovers the Crimea." *Jahrbücher für Geschichte Osteuropas, Neue Folge* 56, 3 (2008): 339–348.

Montefiore, Sebag. *Prince of Princes: The Life of Potemkin.* New York: Thomas Dunne Books, 2000.

Soloveytchik, George. *Potemkin: Soldier, Statesman, Lover and Consort of Catherine of Russia.* New York: W. W. Norton, 1947.

Wikipedia. "Crimean Khanate." en.wikipedia.org/wiki/Crimean_Khanate (accessed 12/14/2015).

Wikipedia. "Potemkin Village." en.wikipedia.org/wiki/Potemkin_village (accessed 12/14/2015).

Additional Resources

The Columbia Encyclopedia. "Russo-Turkish Wars." encyclopedia.com/topic/Russo-Turkish_Wars.aspx (accessed 12/14/2015).

The Daily Bell. "Potemkin Village." Glossary: thedailybell.com/glossary/28348/Potemkin-Village/ (accessed 12/14/2015).

Valdés, Juan, and Rosemary Wardley. "300 Years of Embattled Crimea History in 6 Maps." *National Geographic* (March 5, 2014): news.nationalgeographic.com/news/2014/03/140305-maps-crimea-history-russia-ukraine/ (accessed 12/14/2015).

15. Newly Discovered Shakespeare Play Jeered by Theater-Goers

Sources

Ireland, William-Henry. *Confessions of William-Henry Ireland, Containing the Particulars of His Fabrication of the Shakespeare Manuscripts.* New York: Burt Franklin, 1969 [reprint of the 1874 edition].

Miles, Robert. "Trouble in the Republic of Letters: The Reception of the Shakespeare Forgeries." *Studies in Romanticism* 44, 3 (Fall 2005): 317–340.

Rosenblum, Joseph. "The Marvelous Thomas Chatterton," in *Practice to Deceive: The Amazing Stories of Literary Forgery's Most Notorious Practitioners,* 57–105. New Castle, Delaware: Oak Knoll Press, 1999.

———. "Shakespearean Forgery 101," in *Practice to Deceive: The Amazing Stories of Literary Forgery's Most Notorious Practitioners,* 107–155. New Castle, Delaware: Oak Knoll Press, 1999.

Wiley, Michael. "Coleridge's 'The Raven' and the Forging of Radicalism." *Studies in English Literature, 1500–1900* 43, 4 (Autumn 2003): 799–813.

Additional Resources

Ireland, William-Henry. *Confessions of William-Henry Ireland, Containing the Particulars of His Fabrication of the Shakespeare Manuscripts.* London: Ellerton & Byworth, for T. Goddard, 1805. archive.org/details/confessionsofwil00irelrich (accessed 12/2/2015).

Stewart, Doug. "To Be...Or Not: The Greatest Shakespeare Forgery." *Smithsonian Magazine* (June 2010): smithsonianmag.com/history/to-beor-not-the-greatest-shakespeare-forgery-136201/?no-ist (accessed 12/2/2015).

———. "William-Henry Ireland's Great Shakespearian Hoax." NPR (June 19, 2010): npr.org/templates/story/story.php?storyId=127931669 (accessed 12/2/2015).

University of Delaware Library, Special Collections. "William Henry Ireland and the Shakespeare Fabrications." Forging a Collection. lib.udel.edu/ud/spec/exhibits/forgery/ireland.htm (accessed 12/2/2015).

Vortigern Studies. vortigernstudies.org.uk/vortigernhomepage.htm (accessed 12/2/2015).

Wolfe, Heather, and Hunt, Arnold. "Shakespeare's Personal Library, As Curated by William Henry Ireland." *The Collation: A Gathering of Scholarship from the Folger Shakespeare Library* (June 17, 2013): collation.folger.edu/2013/06/shakespeares-personal-library-as-curated-by-william-henry-ireland/ (accessed 12/2/2015).

16. An Astronomer Discovers Intelligent Life on the Moon

Sources

Castagnaro, Mario. "Lunar Fancies and Earthly Truths: The Moon Hoax of 1835 and the Penny Press." *Nineteenth-Century Contexts* 34, 3 (July 2012): 253–268.

Curtis, Heber D. "Voyages to the Moon." *Publications of the Astronomical Society of the Pacific* 32, 186 (April 1920): 145–250.

Fernie, J. Donald. "Marginalia: The Great Moon Hoax." *American Scientist* 81, 2 (March 1993): 120–122.

Locke, Richard Adams. *Moon Hoax: Or, A Discovery That the Moon Has a Vast Population of Human Beings* [reprint of the 1835 series]. New York: William Gowans, 1859.

Maliszewski, Paul. "Paper Moon." *The Wilson Quarterly* 29, 1 (Winter 2005): 26–34.

Smith, Moira. "Arbiters of Truth at Play: Media April Fools' Day Hoaxes." *Folklore* 120, 3 (December 2009): 274–290.

Wikipedia. "*Comical History of the States and Empires of the Moon.*" en.wikipedia.org/wiki/Comical_History_of_the_States_and_Empires_of_the_Moon (accessed 12/2/2015).
Wikipedia. "John Herschel." en.wikipedia.org/wiki/John_Herschel (accessed 12/2/2015).
Wikipedia. "The Unparalleled Adventure of One Hans Pfaal." en.wikipedia.org/wiki/The_Unparalleled_Adventure_of_One_Hans_Pfaall (accessed 12/2/2015).

Additional Resources

Dengrove, Richard. "A New Take on the Moon Hoax of 1835." *The Challenger: A Science Fiction Fanzine* (Winter 2004/2005): challzine.net/21/21moonhoax.html (accessed 12/2/2015).
"The Great Moon Hoax of 1835." Victorian Gothic (October 29, 2011): victoriangothic.org/the-great-moon-hoax-of-1835/ (accessed 12/2/2015).
Poe, Edgar Allen. "The Unparalleled Adventure of One Hans Pfall." The Electronic Books Foundation. archive.org/details/TheUnparalleledAdventureOfOneHansPfall/v2 (accessed 12/2/2015).
Pressman, Gabe. "Remembering the Great Moon Hoax of 1835. NBC New York: nbcnewyork.com/news/local/moon-hoax-166810096.html (accessed 12/2/2015).
Simanek, Donald E. "The Moon Hoax." lhup.edu/~dsimanek/hoaxes/moonhoax.htm (accessed 12/2/2015).

17. The *Walam Olum*: 90 Generations of Oral History, or a Hoax?

Sources

Barlow, William, and Powell, David O. "'The Late Dr. Ward of Indiana': Rafinesque's Source of the Walam Olum." *Indiana Magazine of History* 82, 2 (June 1986): 185–193.
Boewe, Charles. "The Manuscripts of C. S. Rafinesque (1783–1840)." *Proceedings of the American Philosophical Society* 102, 6 (Dec. 15, 1958): 590–595.
Brinton, Daniel G., trans. *The Walam Olum* [1885]. Sacred Texts: sacred-texts.com/nam/walam/index.htm (accessed 12/3/2015).
Fitzgerald, Frances. *America Revised: History Schoolbooks in the Twentieth Century.* Boston: Little, Brown, 1979.
Hamilton, Robert. "United States and Native American Relations." itech.fgcu.edu/&/issues/vol3/issue1/united.htm (accessed 12/3/2015).
"Indian Removal Act." Primary Documents in American History, Library of Congress. loc.gov/rr/program/bib/ourdocs/Indian.html (accessed 12/3/2015).
Loewen, James. "Introduction to *Lies My Teachers Told Me.*" sundown.afro.illinois.edu/content.php?file=liesmyteachertoldme-introduction.html (accessed 11/14/2015).
Mann, Charles C. *1491: New Revelations of the Americas Before Columbus,* 2nd ed. New York: Vintage Books, 2011.
Newman, Andrew. "The 'Walam Olum': An Indigenous Apocrypha and Its Readers." *American Literary History* 22, 1 (Spring 2010): 26–56.
Rafinesque, C. S. *A Life of Travels and Researches in North America and South Europe.* Philadelphia: Printed for the author by F. Turner, 1836.
Archaeology Archive. "Walam Olum Hokum." archive.archaeology.org/online/features/hoaxes/walam_olum.html (accessed 12/3/2015).
Wikipedia. "Constantine Samuel Rafinesque." en.wikipedia.org/wiki/Constantine_Samuel_Rafinesque (accessed 10/24/2015).

Additional Resources

U.S. Department of State, Office of the Historian. "Indian Treaties and the Removal Act of 1830." Milestones 1830–1860. history.state.gov/milestones/1830-1860/indian-treaties (accessed 12/3/2015).

"US to 1865: Andrew Jackson and the Indian Removal Act of 1830." *The Daily KOS* (May 27, 2012): dailykos.com/story/2012/05/27/1091008/-US-to-1865-Andrew-Jackson-and-the-Indian-Removal-Act-of-1830-with-a-personal-note# (accessed 12/3/2015).

WGBH. "Indian Removal: 1814–1858." Africans in America, Part 4 (1831–1865). pbs.org/wgbh/aia/part4/4p2959.html (accessed 12/3/2015).

Wikipedia. "Constantine Samuel Rafinesque." en.wikipedia.org/wiki/Constantine_Samuel_Rafinesque (accessed 12/3/2015).

18. Was the Fejee Mermaid a Genuine Fake?

Sources

Barnum, P. T. *Struggles and Triumphs: Or, Forty Years' Recollections.* Buffalo, N.Y.: Warren, Johnson & Co., 1873. archive.org/details/strugglestriumph00barn_1 (accessed 12/3/2015).

"Buxton Mermaid Origins Probed at University of Lincoln." BBC News. (February 15, 2012). bbc.com/news/uk-england-17038668 (accessed 12/3/2015).

"Dead Mermaid Found?" AboutEntertainment. urbanlegends.about.com/od/mythicalcreatures/ss/Pictures-Mermaid-Found-After-Tsunami.htm (accessed 12/3/2015).

Greenberg, Kenneth S. "The Nose, the Lie, and the Duel in the Antebellum South." *The American Historical Review* 95, 1 (February 1990): 57–74.

Harris, Neil. *Humbug: The Art of P.T. Barnum.* Boston: Little, Brown and Company, 1973.

Levi, Steven C. "P.T. Barnum and the Feejee Mermaid." *Western Folklore* 36, 2 (April 1977): 149–154.

"Merman: Part Monkey, Part Fish." British Museum. web.archive.org/web/20151017210533/http://www.britishmuseum.org/explore/highlights/highlight_objects/asia/m/merman_part_monkey,_part_fish.aspx (accessed 12/3/2015).

"Unmasking the Mysterious Merman." Horniman Museum and Gardens. horniman.ac.uk/collections/unmasking-the-mysterious-merman (accessed 12/3/2015).

Viscardi, Paolo. "Mysterious Mermaid Stripped Naked." *The Guardian* (April 16, 2014). theguardian.com/science/animal-magic/2014/apr/16/mermaid-stripped-naked (accessed 12/3/2015).

Wikipedia. "The Little Mermaid." en.wikipedia.org/wiki/The_Little_Mermaid (accessed 12/3/2015).

Wikipedia. "Scudder's American Museum." en.wikipedia.org/wiki/Scudder%27s_American_Museum (accessed 10/24/2015).

Additional Resources

Gods–and–Monsters.com. "Mermaid Mythology." gods-and-monsters.com/mermaid-mythology.html (accessed 12/3/2015).

Hoax Factor. "17 Real Life Mermaid Hoaxes: The Evidence." YouTube. youtube.com/watch?v=Wzd3WFb9V8k (accessed 12/3/2015).

Horniman Museum and Gardens. "Manmade Mermaids." horniman.ac.uk/collections/stories/manmade-mermaids/story-chapter/the-horniman-merman (accessed 12/3/2015).

Peabody Museum of Archaeology and Ethnology. "FeeJee Mermaid." (Uploaded August 12, 2010). youtube.com/watch?v=C1g7QbP4rM4 (accessed 12/3/2015).

Wikipedia. "Ningyo." en.wikipedia.org/wiki/Ningyo (accessed 12/3/2015).

19. The Fox Sisters Invent Spiritual Telegraphy

Sources

Branford, Anna. "Gould and the Fairies." *Australian Journal of Anthropology* 22, 1 (April 2011): 89–103.

Chapin, David. "The Fox Sisters and the Performance of Mystery." *New York History* 81, 2 (2000): 157–188.

Davenport, Reuben Briggs. *The Death-Blow to Spiritualism: Being the True Story of the Fox Sisters, As Revealed by Margaret Fox Kane and Catherine Fox Jencken.* New York: G. W. Dillingham, 1888.

German-American Business Biographies. "German Jews and Peddling in America." Immigrant Entrepreneurship: 1720 to the Present. immigrantentrepreneurship.org/entry.php?rec=191 (accessed 12/5/2015).

Inflation Calculator. davemanuel.com/inflation-calculator.php (accessed 12/5/2015).

McGarry, Molly. *Ghosts of Futures Past: Spiritualism and the Cultural Politics of Nineteenth-Century America.* Berkeley: University of California Press, 2008.

Underhill, A. Leah. *The Missing Link in Modern Spiritualism.* New York: Thomas R. Knox & Co., 1885.

Walker, David. "The Humbug in American Religion: Ritual Theories of Nineteenth-Century Spiritualism." *Religion and American Culture: A Journal of Interpretation* 23, 1 (Winter 2013): 30–74.

Wikipedia. "Electrical Telegraph." http://en.wikipedia.org/wiki/Electrical_telegraph.

Additional Resources

Abbott, Karen. "The Fox Sisters and the Rap on Spiritualism." *Smithsonian.com* (October 30, 2012): smithsonianmag.com/history/the-fox-sisters-and-the-rap-on-spiritualism-99663697/?no-ist (accessed 12/3/2015).

First Spiritual Temple. "Mediumship: The Fox Sisters." fst.org/fxsistrs.htm (accessed 12/3/2015).

"German Jews and Peddling in America." German-American Business Biographies. Immigrant Entrepreneurship: 1720 to the Present. immigrantentrepreneurship.org/entry.php?rec=191 (accessed 12/3/2015).

Nickell, Joe. "A Skeleton's Tale: The Origins of Modern Spiritualism." *Skeptical Inquirer* 32, 4 (July/August 2008): csicop.org/si/show/skeletons_tale_the_origins_of_modern_spiritualism/ (accessed 12/3/2015).

Stuart, Nancy Rubin. "The Raps Heard Around the World." *American History* (August 2005): 42–48, 78, 80

20. Faking a Trip to Gold Rush Territory

Sources

Brooks, J. Tyrwhit, M.D. *Four Months among the Gold-Finders in California: Being the Diary of an Expedition from San Francisco to the Gold Districts.* New York: D. Appleton & Co., 1849. archive.org/details/fourmonthsamongg00vizerich (accessed 12/3/2015).

Gudde, Erwin G. "The Vizetelly Hoax." *Pacific Historical Review* 28, 3 (August 1959): 233–236.

Jordan, Mary A. *They Followed the Sea: Captain Oliver Jordan of Thomaston, Maine, 1789–1879, His Sons and His Daughters and the Ships They Built, Sailed, and Commanded.* Boston, MA: privately printed, 1942.

Library of Congress metadata for *Four Months among the Gold-Finders in Alta California.* lccn.loc.gov/rc01000765 (accessed 12/3/2015).

Ranlett, Charles E. *Master Mariner of Maine: Being the Reminiscences of Charles Everett Ranlett, 1816–1917.* Searsport, ME: Penobscot Marine Museum, 1942.

Shmoop.com. "California Gold Rush Statistics: By the Numbers." shmoop.com/california-gold-rush/statistics.html (accessed 10/25/2015).

Wikipedia. "Treaty of Guadalupe-Hidalgo." en.wikipedia.org/wiki/Treaty_of_Guadalupe_Hidalgo (accessed 12/3/2015).

Wikipedia. "Henry Vizetelly." en.wikipedia.org/wiki/Henry_Vizetelly (accessed 12/3/2015).

Additional Resources

California Gold Rush (1848–1858). Aspiration, Acculturation, and Impact: Immigration to the U.S., 1789–1930. Harvard University Library Open Collections Program. ocp.hul.harvard.edu/immigration/goldrush.html (accessed 12/3/2015).

Gerstäcker, Friedrich. *Narrative of a Journey Round the World.* New York: Harper, 1854. archive.org/details/narrativeajourn02gersgoog (accessed 12/3/2015).

San Francisco Gold Rush Chronology (1846–1849). Virtual Museum of the City of San Francisco. sfmuseum.org/hist/chron1.html (accessed 12/3/2015).

"To California by Sea." Maritime Nation (1800–1850). On the Water. Smithsonian Institution. americanhistory.si.edu/onthewater/exhibition/2_4.html (accessed 12/3/2015).

WGBH. "A Legacy of the War—the Gold Rush and the Foreign Miners' Tax." *The U.S.-Mexican War* (March 14, 2006): pbs.org/kera/usmexicanwar/educators/gold_rush_miners_tax.html (accessed 12/3/2015).

21. When Giants Roamed the Earth

Sources

Fedler, Fred. "A Journalist's Favorite Hoax: Petrifactions." HistoryBuff.com. web.archive.org/web/20150402210830/http://www.historybuff.com/library/refpetrification.html (accessed 12/3/2015).

Franco, Barbara. "The Cardiff Giant: A Hundred Year Old Hoax." *New York History* 50, 4 (October 1969): 420–440.

Marsh, Othniel C. Letter on the Cardiff Giant, November 24, 1869. Printed in Rochester *Daily Union* ("The Cardiff Giant a Humbug"). "December Meeting: The 'Cardiff Giant' Controversy. *Proceedings of the Massachusetts Historical Society* 11 (1869–1870): 159–164.

Pettit, Michael. "'The Joy in Believing': The Cardiff Giant, Commercial Deceptions, and Styles of Observation in Gilded Age America." *Isis* 97, 4 (December 2006): 659–677.

Rose, Mark. "When Giants Roamed the Earth." *Archaeology* 58, 6 (November 2005): 30–35.

Twain, Mark. "Letters from Washington, Number IX, *Territorial Enterprise* (March 7, 1868). Quoted at TwainQuotes.com: twainquotes.com/teindex.html (accessed 12/3/2015).

"Typical Wages in 1860 through 1890." Outrun Change: outrunchange.com/2012/06/14/typical-wages-in-1860-through-1890/ (accessed 12/3/15).

Additional Resources

"The Cardiff Giant." The Farmers' Museum, Cooperstown, NY: farmersmuseum.org/node/2482 (accessed 12/3/2015).

"O.C. Marsh and E.D. Cope: A Rivalry." Dinosaur Wars. American Experience, PBS: pbs.org/wgbh/americanexperience/features/biography/dinosaur-rivalry/ (accessed 12/3/2015).

Rose, Mark. "When Giants Roamed the Earth." *Archaeology* 58, 6 (November 2005): archive.archaeology.org/0511/etc/giants.html

Twain, Mark. "The Petrified Man" [essay]. Read aloud by Cory Doctorow, podcast. archive.org/details/PodcastThePetrifiedManmarkTwain (accessed 12/3/2015).

———. "The Petrified Man" [newspaper hoax]. Virginia City (Nevada), *Territorial Enterprise*, October 26, 1862: twainquotes.com/18621004t.html (accessed 12/3/2015).

22. The Keely Motor Company Promises Efficient World Travel

Sources

Hering, Daniel W. *Foibles and Fallacies of Science: An Account of Celebrated Scientific Vagaries.* New York: Van Nostrand, 1924.

"Inflation Calculator." Dave Manuel.com. davemanuel.com/inflation-calculator.php? (accessed 10/26/2015).

Kuhn, Thomas S. *The Structure of Scientific Revolutions.* 2nd ed., enlarged. Chicago: University of Chicago Press, 1970.

Moore, Clara Jessup. *Keely and His Discoveries: Aerial Navigation.* London: Keegan Paul, 1893.

Ord-Hume, Arthur W. J. G. *Perpetual Motion: The History of an Obsession.* New York: St. Martin's Press, 1977.

Simanek, D. "The Keely Motor Company." lhup.edu/~dsimanek/museum/keely/keely.htm (accessed 12/5/2015).

SVPwiki Home Page. pondscienceinstitute.on-rev.com/svpwiki/tiki-index.php (accessed 12/5/2015).

Wikipedia. "Conservation of Energy." en.wikipedia.org/wiki/Conservation_of_energy (accessed 12/3/2015).

Additional Resources

Allain, Rhett. "An Analysis of a Perpetual Motion Machine." WIRED (November 8, 2012): wired.com/2012/11/an-analysis-of-a-perpetual-motion-machine/ (accessed 12/5/2015).

Historical Documents Relating to Keely: svpvril.com/svpweb5.html#historical (accessed 12/3/2015).

Simanek, D. "The Keely Motor Company." lhup.edu/~dsimanek/museum/keely/keely.htm (accessed 12/3/2015).

23. The Case of the Lying Encyclopedia

Sources

Dobson, John Blythe. "The Spurious Articles in *Appleton's Cyclopaedia of American Biography*—Some New Discoveries and Considerations." *Biography* 16, 4 (Fall 1993): 388–408.

Oates, Titus. "The Wayward Encyclopedias." *The New Yorker* (March 21, 1936): 48–52.

O'Brien, Frank M. "The Wayward Encyclopedias." *The New Yorker* (May 2, 1936): 55–58.

Schindler, Margaret Castle. "Fictitious Biography." *The American Historical Review* 42, 4 (July 1937): 680–690.

Wikipedia. "Reliability of Wikipedia." en.wikipedia.org/wiki/Reliability_of_Wikipedia (accessed 12/5/2015).

Wolchover, Natalie. "How Accurate Is Wikipedia?" *LiveScience.com* (January 24, 2011): livescience.com/32950-how-accurate-is-wikipedia.html (accessed 10/26/2015).

Additional Resources

Blanding, Michael. "Wikipedia or *Encyclopædia Britannica*: Which Has More Bias?" *Forbes* (January 20, 2015): forbes.com/sites/hbsworkingknowledge/2015/01/20/wikipedia-or-encyclopaedia-britannica-which-has-more-bias/ (accessed 12/3/2015).

Cathay. "Is Wikipedia a Reliable Source?" Division of Libraries' Blog, State of Delaware (May 5, 2013): libraries.blogs.delaware.gov/2013/05/05/is-wikipedia-a-reliable-source/ (accessed 12/3/2015).

24. Extracting Gold from Seawater

Sources

"The Electrolytic Marine Salts Company," *Engineering and Mining Journal* 66 (November 12, 1898): 581.

"Gold from the Sea." *Scientific American* 79, 7 (August 13, 1898): 99 (accessed at ia600809.us.archive.org/31/items/scientific-american-1898-08-13/scientific-american-v79-n07-1898-08-13.pdf, 11/15/15).

Multhopp, Jennifer. "Klondike: Lubec's Gold from Sea Water Hoax." *Lubec, Maine: A Border Town Shaped by the Sea.* lubec.mainememory.net/page/960/display.html (accessed 11/15/2015).

Murphy, Jackson. "Prescott Jernegan and the Gold from Seawater Swindle." *The Martha's Vineyard Times* (July 25, 2012): mvtimes.com/2012/07/25/prescott-jernegan-gold-from-seawater-swindle-11663/ (accessed 11/15/2015).

National Ocean Service. "Is There Gold in the Ocean?" oceanservice.noaa.gov/facts/gold.html (accessed 11/15/2015).

"The Salt Water Gold Mine: The Concern May Be Bought for a Sardine Factory." *New York Times* (October 10, 1898).

Spence, Clark C. "I Was a Stranger and Ye Took Me In." *Montana: The Magazine of Western History* 44, 1 (Winter 1994): 42–53.

Stubbs, Brett J. "'Sunbeams from Cucumbers': An Early Twentieth-Century Gold-from-Sea-water Extraction Scheme in Northern New South Wales." *Australasian Historical Archaeology* 26 (2008): 5–12.

Wikipedia. "Lubec, Maine." en.wikipedia.org/wiki/Lubec,_Maine (accessed 11/15/2015).

Additional Resources

"The Gold Accumulator." *Museum of Hoaxes.* hoaxes.org/archive/permalink/the_gold_accumulator (accessed 11/15/2015).

Plazak, Dan. "Gold from Seawater." *Mining Swindles* (10/10/2009): miningswindles.com/html/gold_from_seawater.html (accessed November 15, 2015).

Woods Hole Oceanographic Institute. "Seafloor Mining." whoi.edu/main/topic/seafloor-mining (accessed 12/5/2015).

25. Viking Runes in Minnesota

Sources

Blegen, Theodore C. "Frederick J. Turner and the Kensington Puzzle." *Minnesota History* 39, 4 (Winter 1964): 133–140.

Fridley, Russell W. "Debate Continues over Kensington Rune Stone." *Minnesota History* 45, 4 (Winter 1976): 149–151.

Jackson, Brittany, and Mark Rose. "Saitaphernes' Golden Tiara." *Archaeology* (2009): archive.archaeology.org/online/features/hoaxes/saitaphernes_tiara.html (accessed 8/9/2015).

Larson, Laurence M. "The Kensington Rune Stone." *The Wisconsin Magazine of History* 4, 4 (June 1921): 382–387.

"MHS Collections: The Case of the Gran Tapes: Further Evidence on the Rune Stone Riddle." *Minnesota History* 45, 4 (Winter 1976): 152–156.

Morison, Samuel Eliot. *The European Discovery of America: The Northern Voyages, A.D. 500–1600.* New York: Oxford University Press, 1971.

Powell, Eric A. "The Kensington Code." *Archaeology* 63, 3 (May/June 2010). archive.archaeology.org/1005/abstracts/insider.html (accessed 12/3/2015).

Sotheby's, "291: 'The Rouchomovsky Skeleton,'" sothebys.com/en/auctions/ecatalogue/2013/a-treasured-legacy-steinhardt-n08961/lot.291.html (accessed 11/16/2015).

Wikipedia. "Tiara of Saitaferne." en.wikipedia.org/wiki/Tiara_of_Saitaferne (accessed 11/16/2015).

Additional Resources

Hurstwic. "Other Viking Artifacts in North America." hurstwic.org/history/articles/society/text/other_artifacts.htm (accessed 12/5/2015).

Longfellow, Henry Wadsworth. "The Skeleton in Armor." Poetry Foundation. poetryfoundation.org/poem/173914 (accessed 12/5/2015).

"Maeshowe's Runes—Viking Graffiti." Orkneyjar. orkneyjar.com/history/maeshowe/maeshrunes.htm (accessed 12/3/2015).

26. A Conspiracy to Justify Murder

Sources

Bronner, Stephen Eric. *A Rumor about the Jews: Reflections on Antisemitism and the* Protocols of the Learned Elders of Zion. New York: St. Martin's Press, 2000.

Eaton, Gale. *History of Civilization in 50 Disasters.* Thomaston, ME: Tilbury House, 2015.

Launius, Roger D. "Denying the Apollo Moon Landings: Conspiracy and Questioning in Modern American History." Orlando, FL: 48th AIAA Aerospace Sciences Meeting, January 4–7, 2010.

Plax, Martin J. "On Extremism in Our Time." *Society* 50 (2013): 196–203.

Binjamin W. Segel, *A Lie and a Libel: The History of the* Protocols of the Elders of Zion, translated and edited by
    Richard S. Levy (Lincoln: University of Nebraska Press, 1995), xi.

Wikipedia. "Maurice Joly." en.wikipedia.org/wiki/Maurice_Joly (accessed 12/3/2015).

Wikipedia, "Revolution of 1905," en.wikipedia.org/wiki/Revolution_of_1905 (accessed 10/26/2015).

Additional Resources

"*Protocols of the Elders of Zion* (1927)." The Weimar Republic: The Fragility of Democracy. Facing History and Ourselves. facinghistory.org/weimar-republic-fragility-democracy/society/protocols-elders-zion-1927-society-antisemitism (accessed 12/3/2015).

United States Holocaust Memorial Museum. "Protocols of the Elders of Zion." (June 20, 2014). ushmm.org/wlc/en/article.php?ModuleId=10007058 (accessed 12/3/2015).

Wikipedia. "*The Protocols of the Elders of Zion.*" en.wikipedia.org/wiki/The_Protocols_of_the_Elders_of_Zion (accessed 12/3/2015).

27. A Future Great Novelist Helps Hoax the Royal Navy

Sources

Carter, Miranda. *George, Nicholas and Wilhelm: Three Royal Cousins and the Road to World War I.* New York: Alfred A. Knopf, 2010.

Davis, Wes. "A Fool There Was." *New York Times* (April 1, 2006). nytimes.com/2006/04/01/opinion/01davis.html (accessed 12/3/2015).

"A Dreadnought Hoax: 'Prince Makalin of Abyssinia.'" (London, February 18, 1910; published in the *Hobart Mercury*, Tasmania, 24 March 1910): upload.wikimedia.org/wikipedia/commons/f/f9/DreadnoughtHoaxHobartMercury24March1910.jpg (accessed 12/3/2015).

Jones, Danell. "The Dreadnought Hoax and the Theatres of War." *Literature & History* 22, 1 (Spring 2013): 80–94.

Popova, Maria. "The Dreadnought Hoax: Young Virginia Woolf and Her Bloomsbury Posse Prank the Royal Navy in Drag and a Turban." Brainpickings. brainpickings.org/2014/02/07/dreadnought-hoax-virginia-woolf/ (accessed 12/3/2015).

Wikipedia. "The Dreadnought Hoax." en.wikipedia.org/wiki/Dreadnought_hoax (accessed 12/3/2015).

Additional Resources

Alberge, Dalya. "How a Bearded Virginia Woolf and Her Band of 'Jolly Savages' Hoaxed the Navy." *The Guardian* (February 4, 2012): theguardian.com/books/2012/feb/05/bloomsbury-dreadnought-hoax-recalled-letter (accessed 12/3/2015).

British Library. World War I. bl.uk/world-war-one (accessed 12/3/2015).

Taylor, Alan. "World War I in Photos." *The Atlantic* (2014): theatlantic.com/static/infocus/wwi/ (accessed 12/3/2015).

Wikipedia. "HMS *Dreadnought* (1906)." http://en.wikipedia.org/wiki/HMS_Dreadnought_(1906).

28. Missing Link Found at Piltdown

Sources

Bement, Leland C., Ernest L. Lundelius, Jr. and Richard A. Ketcham. "Hoax or History: A Bison Skull with Embedded Calf Creek Projectile Point." *Plains Anthropologist* 50, 195 (August 2005): 221–226.

Falk, Dean. *The Fossil Chronicles: How Two Controversial Discoveries Changed Our View of Human Evolution.* Berkeley: University of California Press, 2011.

Feder, Kenneth L. *Frauds, Myths, and Mysteries: Science and Pseudoscience in Archaeology.* 4th ed. New York: McGraw-Hill, 2002.

Langdon, John H. "Misinterpreting Piltdown." *Current Anthropology* 32, 5 (December 1991): 627–631.

Museum of Hoaxes. "The Piltdown Chicken." hoaxes.org/archive/permalink/the_piltdown_chicken (accessed 12/6/2015).

Oakley, Kenneth P., and Weiner, J.S. "Piltdown Man." *American Scientist* 43, 4 (October 1955): 573–583; accessible at clarku.edu/~piltdown/map_gen_hist_surveys/piltman_oaklywiener.html (accessed 12/3/2015).

"Piltdown Man Is a Hoax" *Science News Letter* (November 28, 1953): 350.

Reader, John. *Missing Links: In Search of Human Origins.* New York: Oxford University Press, 2011.

Smithsonian National Museum of Natural History. "Ancient DNA and Neanderthals: What Does It Mean to Be Human?" humanorigins.si.edu/evidence/genetics/ancient-dna-and-neanderthals (accessed 12/6/2015).

Washburn, S. L. "The Piltdown Hoax." *American Anthropologist* 55, 5 (December 1953): 759–762.

Wikipedia. "Neanderthal." en.wikipedia.org/wiki/Neanderthal (accessed 12/3/2015).

Additional Resources

"The Boldest Hoax." NOVA Teachers. pbs.org/wgbh/nova/education/activities/3202_hoax.html (accessed 12/3/2015).

Carroll, Robert Todd. "Piltdown Hoax." The Skeptic's Dictionary (2013): skepdic.com/piltdown.html (accessed 12/3/2015).

Harter, Richard. "Piltdown Man: The Bogus Bones Caper." The TalkOrigins Archive (1996–1997). talkorigins.org/faqs/piltdown.html (accessed 12/3/2015).

"Introduction to Human Evolution." *What Does It Mean to Be Human?* Smithsonian Institutions: humanorigins.si.edu/education/intro-human-evolution (accessed 10/27/2015).

"Mystery Skull Interactive." Smithsonian Institutions: humanorigins.si.edu/evidence/human-fossils/mystery-skull-interactive (accessed 10/27/2015).

PBS. *Dawn of Humanity.* NOVA. pbs.org/wgbh/nova/evolution/dawn-of-humanity.html (accessed 10/27/2015).

"Piltdown Man: The Greatest Hoax in the History of Science?" Natural History Museum: nhm.ac.uk/nature-online/science-of-natural-history/the-scientific-process/piltdown-man-hoax/.

29. Naked Man Conquers Maine Woods

Sources

Aliperti, Cliff. "The Half Naked Truth about Harry Reichenbach." Immortal Ephemera (September 17, 2012): immortalephemera.com/23105/press-agent-harry-reichenbach/ (accessed 12/3/2015).

Armagh Planetarium. "Whatever Happened to Biosphere 2?" (March 26, 2013): armaghplanet.com/blog/whatever-happened-to-biosphere-2.html (accessed 12/3/2015).

Boyer, Richard O. "Where Are They Now? The Nature Man." *The New Yorker* (June 18, 1938): 21–25.

Donahue, Bill. "Naked Joe." *Boston Magazine* (April 2013): bostonmagazine.com/news/article/2013/03/26/naked-joe-knowles-nature-man-woods/ (accessed 12/3/2015).

Knowles, Joseph. *Alone in the Wilderness.* Boston: Small, Maynard & Company, 1913.

Motavalli, Jim. *Naked in the Woods: Joseph Knowles and the Legacy of Frontier Fakery.* Cambridge, MA: Da Capo Press, 2007.

Museum of Hoaxes. "The September Morn Hoax." Hoaxes.org. hoaxes.org/archive/permalink/the_september_morn_hoax (accessed 12/3/2015).

Wikipedia. "Biosphere 2." en.wikipedia.org/wiki/Biosphere_2 (accessed 12/3/2015).

Additional Resources

Carson, Gerald. "Yankee Tarzan." *American Heritage Magazine* 32, 3 (April/May 1981): americanheritage.com/content/yankee-tarzan (accessed 12/3/2015).

Mills, Paul. "Joe Knowles and the Legacy of Wilderness Adventures." *Daily Bulldog* (May 12, 2013): dailybulldog.com/db/features/joe-knowles-and-the-legacy-of-wilderness-adventures/ (accessed 12/3/2015).

Motavalli, Jim. "Impressive Wilderness Survival or Elaborate Hoax? The Long, Strange History of Fake Survivalism." *The Daily Green* (March 6, 2008): preview.www.thedailygreen.com/living-green/blogs/cars-transportation/wilderness-survival-hoaxes-460305 (accessed 12/3/2015).

30. The Spectric Poets Unmasked

Sources

Churchill, Suzanne W. "The Lying Game: *Others* and the Great Spectra Hoax of 1917." *American Periodicals* 15, 1 (2005): 23-41.

Poetry Foundation. "Amy Lowell (1874–1925)." poetryfoundation.org/bio/amy-lowell (accessed 12/3/2015).

Russek, Audrey. "So Many Useful Women: The Pseudonymous Poetry of Marjorie Allen Seiffert, 1916–1938." *Tulsa Studies in Women's Literature* 28, 1 (Spring 2009): 75–96.

Smith, William Jay. *The Spectra Hoax.* Middletown, CT: Wesleyan University Press, 1961.

Additional Resources

Daly, Catherine. "Marjorie Allen Seifert and the *Spectra* Hoax." *Jacket Magazine* (2002). jacketmagazine.com/17/daly-spec.html (accessed 12/3/2015).

SCblogger. "The Spectra Hoax." Davenport Library Special Collections (December 8, 2010): blogs.davenportlibrary.com/sc/2010/12/08/the-spectra-hoax/ (accessed 12/3/2015).

Wikipedia. "*Spectra* (book)." en.wikipedia.org/wiki/Spectra_(book) (accessed 12/3/2015).

31. The Original Ponzi Scheme

Sources

Blumenthal, Ralph. "Lost Manuscript Unmasks Details of Original Ponzi." *New York Times* (May 4, 2009): nytimes.com/2009/05/05/nyregion/05ponzi.html?_r=0 (accessed 12/3/2015).

Margolick, David. "His Last Name Is Scheme." *New York Times* (April 10, 2005): nytimes.com/2005/04/10/books/review/his-last-name-is-scheme.html (accessed 12/3/2015).

New York Times. "Times Topics: Ponzi Schemes." topics.nytimes.com/top/reference/timestopics/subjects/f/frauds_and_swindling/ponzi_schemes/index.html?8qa (accessed 12/6/2015).

Scamwatch. "Chain Letters." archive.org/web/20150512002336/http://www.scamwatch.gov.au/content/index.phtml?itemId/694296 (accessed 12/6/2015).

Wikipedia. "Charles Ponzi." en.wikipedia.org/wiki/Charles_Ponzi (accessed 12/3/2015).

Zuckoff, Mitchell. *Ponzi's Scheme: The True Story of a Financial Legend.* New York: Random House, 2005.

Additional Resources

Universal Postal Union. "The UPU." upu.int/en/the-upu/the-upu.html (accessed 12/3/2015).

Wikipedia. "International Reply Coupon." en.wikipedia.org/wiki/International_reply_coupon (accessed 12/3/2015).

Yang, Stephanie. "5 Years Ago Bernie Madoff Was Sentenced to 150 Years in Prison—Here's How His Ponzi Scheme Worked." *Business Insider* (July 1, 2014): businessinsider.com/how-bernie-madoffs-ponzi-scheme-worked-2014-7 (accessed 12/3/2015).

32. Fairies Are Caught on Camera

Sources

Branford, Anna. "Gould and the Fairies." *Australian Journal of Anthropology* 22, 1 (April 2011): 89–103.

Cooper, Joe. "Cottingley: At Last the Truth." *The Unexplained*, No. 117, pp. 2338–2340, 1982. Text reproduced at www.lhup.edu/~dsimanek/cooper.htm (accessed 12/3/2015).

Doyle, Arthur Conan, Sir. *The Coming of the Fairies*. New York: George H. Doran Co., 1922. Accessed at archive.org/details/comingoffairies00doylrich (accessed 12/3/2015).

Fox, Margalit. "Geoffrey Crawley, 83, Dies: Gently Deflated a Fairy Hoax." *New York Times* (November 6, 2010): nytimes.com/2010/11/07/world/europe/07crawley.html (accessed 12/3/2015).

Owen, Alex. "'Borderland Forms': Arthur Conan Doyle, Albion's Daughters, and the Politics of the Cottingley Fairies." *History Workshop* 38 (1994): 48–85.

Wainwright, Martin. "Joe Cooper Obituary: He Got the Cottingley Fairy Fakers to Confess." *The Guardian* (August 24, 2011): theguardian.com/technology/2011/aug/24/joe-cooper-obituary (accessed 12/3/2015).

Wikipedia. "Arthur Conan Doyle." en.wikipedia.org/wiki/Arthur_Conan_Doyle (accessed 12/6/2015).

Additional Resources

Cottingley Connect. cottingleyconnect.org.uk/fairies.shtml (accessed 12/3/2015).

"Cottingley Fairies (Elsie Wright & Frances Griffiths)." Fictive Art. fictive.arts.uci.edu/cottingley_fairies (accessed 12/3/2015).

Fallon, Karl, ed. "The Cottingley Fairies: The Proof That the Photos Captured Fairies." BBC, Antiques Roadshow. youtube.com/watch?v=CN3DpHDKFMg (accessed 12/3/2015).

Junior Skeptic. "Cottingley Fairies." *Skeptic* 15, 3 (2010): 73-81.

"Next Stop, Fairyland!" Where I Live: Bradford & West Yorkshire. BBC (Spring 2004): bbc.co.uk/bradford/sense_of_place/unexplained/cottingley_fairies.shtml (accessed 12/3/2015).

33. Did Grand Duchess Anastasia Survive the Revolution?

Sources

"Appeal in Anastasia Mystery Is Rejected by Hamburg Court: Anna Anderson Loses Plea to Be Acknowledged as Only Survivor in Czar's Family." *New York Times* (March 1, 1967).

Gattrell, Peter. "Europe on the Move: Refugees and World War One." British Library. bl.uk/world-war-one/articles/refugees-europe-on-the-move (accessed 12/3/2015).

Kurth, Peter. *Anastasia: The Riddle of Anna Anderson*. Boston: Little, Brown and Company, 1983.

"Princess Caraboo." The Hoax Museum. hoaxes.org/archive/permalink/princess_caraboo (accessed 12/3/2015).

Welch, Frances. *A Romanov Fantasy: Life at the Court of Anna Anderson*. New York: W. W. Norton, 2007.

Wikipedia. "Aftermath of World War I." en.wikipedia.org/wiki/Aftermath_of_World_War_I (accessed 12/3/2015).

Wikipedia. "Anna Anderson." en.wikipedia.org/?title=Anna_Anderson (accessed 12/3/2015).

Additional Resources

"Anastasia." Biography.com. biography.com/people/anastasia-9184008 (accessed 12/3/2015).

Brewster, Hugh. *Anastasia's Album*. New York: A Hyperion Madison Press Book, 1996.

"The Execution of Tsar Nicholas II, 1918." Eyewitness to History (2005): eyewitnesstohistory. com/nicholas.htm# (accessed 12/3/2015).

Smele, Jonathan. "War and Revolution in Russia 1914–1921." BBC History (March 10, 2011): bbc.co.uk/history/worldwars/wwone/eastern front 01.shtml (accessed 12/3/2015).

34. Houdini Debunks a Medium

Sources

Evans, Henry Ridgely. "Madame Blavatsky." *The Monist* 14, 3 (April 1904): 387–408.

Hix, Lisa. "Ghosts in the Machines: The Devices and Daring Mediums That Spoke for the Dead." *Collectors Weekly* (October 29, 2014): collectorsweekly.com/articles/ghosts-in-the-machines-the-devices-and-defiant-mediums-that-spoke-for-the-spirits/ (accessed 12/13/2015).

Jaher, David. *The Witch of Lime Street: Séance, Seduction, and Houdini in the Spirit World*. New York: Crown, 2015.

Johnson, K. Paul. *The Masters Revealed: Madame Blavatsky and the Myth of the Great White Lodge*. Albany: State University of New York Press, 1994.

Prothero, Stephen. "From Spiritualism to Theosophy: 'Uplifting' a Democratic Tradition." *Religion and American Culture: A Journal of Interpretation* 3, 2 (Summer 1993): 197–216.

Scott, J. Barton. "Miracle Publics: Theosophy, Christianity, and the Coulomb Affair." *History of Religions* 49, 2 (November 2009): 172–196.

Silverman, Kenneth. *Houdini!!! The Career of Ehrich Weiss: American Self-Liberator, Europe's Eclipsing Sensation, World's Handcuff King & Prison Breaker—Nothing on Earth Can Hold HOUDINI a Prisoner!!!* New York: Harper Collins, 1996.

Stashower, Daniel. "Mina Crandon & Harry Houdini: The Medium and the Magician." *American History* (August 1999): historynet.com/mina-crandon-harry-houdini-the-medium-and-the-magician.htm (accessed 12/13/2015)

Wikipedia. "American Society for Psychical Research." en.wikipedia.org/wiki/American_Society_for_Psychical_Research (accessed 12/13/2015).

Wikipedia. "Automatic Writing." en.wikipedia.org/wiki/Automatic_writing (accessed 12/13/2015).

Wikipedia. "Harry Houdini." en.wikipedia.org/wiki/Harry_Houdini (accessed 12/13/2015).

Wikipedia. "Joseph Smith." en.wikipedia.org/wiki/Joseph_Smith (accessed 12/13/2015).

Wikipedia. "Séance." en.wikipedia.org/wiki/S%C3%A9ance (accessed 12/13/2015).

Additional Resources

Carnegie, Dean. "The Spirit Cabinet – A History." *The Magic Detective* (March 13, 2011): themagicdetective.com/2011/03/spirit-cabinet-history.html (accessed 12/13/2015).

Taylor, Troy. "Spirit Cabinets: Communicating with the Spirits." *The Haunted Museum: The Historic & Haunted Guide to the Supernatural* (2003–2008). prairieghosts.com/cabinets.html (accessed 12/13/2015).

Wikipedia. "Mina Crandon." en.wikipedia.org/wiki/Mina_Crandon (accessed 12/13/2015).

35. If You Believe That, I Have a Tower to Sell You

Sources

"'The Count' Escapes Jail on Sheet Rope: International Crook Drops 50 Feet to Street in Sight of Hundreds on West Side." *New York Times* (September 2, 1935). query.nytimes.com/gst/abstract.html?res=9E00E0DB113EE53ABC4A53DFBF66838E629EDE (accessed 12/3/2015).

King, Gilbert. "The Smoothest Con Man That Ever Lived." Smithsonian.com (August 22, 2012): smithsonianmag.com/history/the-smoothest-con-man-that-ever-lived-29861908/?no-ist= (accessed 12/3/2015).

New York Times. "Confidence Man Jailed" (July 8, 1928). query.nytimes.com/gst/abstract.html?res=9902E1D91238E23ABC4053DFB1668383639EDE (accessed 12/6/2015).

Palermo, Elizabeth. "Eiffel Tower: Information and Facts." LiveScience.com (May 7, 2013): livescience.com/29391-eiffel-tower.html (accessed 12/3/2015).

"Victor Lustig." Biography.com. biography.com/people/victor-lustig-20657385 (accessed 12/3/2015).

Wikipedia. "Eiffel Tower." en.wikipedia.org/wiki/Eiffel_Tower (accessed 12/3/2015).

Wikipedia. "George C. Parker." en.wikipedia.org/wiki/George_C._Parker (accessed 12/6/2015).

Wikipedia. "Victor Lustig." en.wikipedia.org/wiki/Victor_Lustig (accessed 12/3/2015).

Additional Resources

"Eiffel Tower." History.com. history.com/topics/eiffel-tower (accessed 12/3/2015).

"Everything about the Tower: The Major Events." toureiffel.paris/en/everything-about-the-tower/the-major-events.html (accessed 12/3/2015).

Pizzoli, Greg. *The Impossibly True Story of Tricky Vic, the Man Who Sold the Eiffel Tower.* New York: Viking, 2015.

Velinger, Jan. "The Man Who (Could Have) Sold the World." Radio Czechoslovakia. radio.cz/en/section/czechs/victor-lustig-the-man-who-could-have-sold-the-world (accessed 12/3/2015).

36. The Loch Ness Monster

Sources

Binns, Ronald. *The Loch Ness Mystery Solved,* Buffalo, NY: Prometheus Books, 1984.

Borch, Karl. "The Monster in Loch Ness." *The Journal of Risk and Insurance* 43, 3 (September 1976): 521–525.

Fields, Liz. "Loch Ness Monster Reportings on the Rise after Sighting on Apple Maps." ABC News (April 20, 2014): abcnews.go.com/International/loch-ness-monster-report-rise-sighting-apple-maps/story?id=23394714 (accessed 12/3/2015).

Fife, Austin E. "Loch Ness Monster." *Western Folklore* 18, 1 (January 1959): 53.

Johnston, T. N. "The Bathymetrical Survey of Loch Ness." *The Geographical Journal* 24, 4 (October 1904): 429–430.

McKelvey, Kevin S., Keith B. Aubry, and Michael K. Schwartz. "Using Anecdotal Occurrence Data for Rare or Elusive Species: The Illusion of Reality and a Call for Evidentiary Standards." *BioScience* 58, 6 (June 2008): 549–555.

Museum of Hoaxes. "The Body of Nessie Found." hoaxes.org/af_database/permalink/the_body_of_nessie_found (accessed 12/3/2015).

Museum of Hoaxes. "The Surgeon's Photo." hoaxes.org/photo_database/image/the_surgeons_photo/ (accessed 12/3/2015).

"'Nessie': What's in an Anagram?" *Science, New Series,* 191, 4222 (January 9, 1976): 54.

The Official Loch Ness Sightings Register. lochnesssightings.com/ (accessed 12/3/2015).

Sheldon, R.W. and Kerr, S.R. "The Population Density of Monsters in Loch Ness." *Limnology and Oceanography* 17, 5 (September 1972): 796–798.

Singleton, Micah. "Google Maps Lets You Search for the Loch Ness Monster from Your Couch." *The Verge* (April 21, 2015): theverge.com/2015/4/21/8463031/google-maps-loch-ness-monster (accessed 12/3/2015).

Oliver Smith, "Has Google Found the Loch Ness Monster?" Telegraph (April 21, 2015): telegraph.co.uk/travel/destinations/europe/uk/scotland/11549549/Has-Google-found-the-Loch-Ness-Monster.html (accessed 12/3/2015).

Wikipedia. "Loch Ness." en.wikipedia.org/wiki/Loch_Ness (accessed 12/3/2015).

Additional Resources

Google Street View. Loch Ness. google.com/maps/@57.186623,-4.617133,3a,75y,146.01h,93.51t/
data=!3m7!1e1!3m5!1s7JaoCK_Mj44h4_9_5brszQ!2e0!3e5!7i13312!8i6656 (accessed
12/3/2015).

Gross, Jennie. "Latest Loch Ness 'Sighting' Causes a Monstrous Fight." *Wall Street Journal* (October 4, 2013): wsj.com/articles/SB10001424052702304795804579099051192907582
(accessed 12/3/2015).

"Loch Ness Sightings through the Years, in Pictures." *Telegraph.* telegraph.co.uk/news/picture-
galleries/howaboutthat/10776095/In-pictures-Loch-Ness-Monster-sightings-through-
the-years.html (accessed 12/3/2015).

Lyons, Stephen. "The Legend of Loch Ness." NOVA (1/12/1999): pbs.org/wgbh/nova/ancient/
legend-loch-ness.html (accessed 12/3/2015).

"Strike-slip Fault, Scotland." geolsoc.org.uk/ks3/gsl/education/resources/rockcycle/page3796.
html (accessed 12/3/2015).

37. Martians Attack

Sources

Bartholomew, Robert E., and Benjamin Radford. *The Martians Have Landed! A History of Media-
Driven Panics and Hoaxes* (Jefferson, NC: McFarland & Company, 2012).

"Broadcasting the Barricades." War of the Worlds Invasion: Historical Perspective. war-ofthe-
worlds.co.uk/broadcasting_the_barricade_ronald_knox.htm (accessed 12/4/2015).

Naremore, James. "The Man Who Caused the Mars Panic." *Humanities* 24,4 (Jul/Aug 2003):
38-39.

"Orson Welles—Mercury Theatre—1938 Recordings." archive.org/details/OrsonWelles-Mer-
curyTheater-1938Recordings (accessed 12/4/2015).

Oxenford, David. "Orson Welles' War of the Worlds 75 Years Later. What Would the FCC
Do Now?" Broadcast Law Blog (October 31, 2013): broadcastlawblog.com/2013/10/
articles/orson-welles-war-of-the-worlds-75-years-later-what-would-the-fcc-do-now/
(accessed 12/4/2015).

"Radio Listeners in Panic, Taking War Drama as Fact." *New York Times* (October 31, 1938).
query.nytimes.com/mem/archive-free/pdf?res=9800E6DA163BEE3ABC4950DFB66783
83629EDE (accessed 12/4/2015).

Rosengren, Karl Erik, Peter Arvidson, and Dahn Sturesson. "The Barsebäck 'Panic': A Radio
Programme as a Negative Summary Event," *Acta Sociologica* 18, 4 (1975): 303–321.

Additional Resources

"The Mercury Theatre on the Air." mercurytheatre.info/ (accessed 12/4/2015).

"Radio's *War of the Worlds* Broadcast: 1938." jeff560.tripod.com/wotw.html (accessed 12/4/2015).

U.S. Holocaust Memorial Museum. "World War II: Timeline." ushmm.org/wlc/en/article.
php?ModuleId=10007306 (accessed 12/4/2015).

Wikipedia. "History of Broadcasting." en.wikipedia.org/wiki/History_of_
broadcasting#United_States (accessed 12/4/2015).

38. Operation Mincemeat Deludes Hitler

Sources

Baker, David. "The Optical Cargo That Wasn't." *Optician* 244, 6382 (December 14, 2012):
18–19.

Cave Brown, Anthony. *Bodyguard of Lies*, Part III, Section 4 ("Mincemeat"), 278–289. New
York: Harper & Row, 1975.

Gladwell, Malcolm. "Pandora's Briefcase." *The New Yorker* (May 10, 2010): newyorker.com/
magazine/2010/05/10/pandoras-briefcase (accessed 7/27/2015).

Gottlieb, Klaus. "The Mincemeat Postmortem: Forensic Aspects of World War II's Boldest Counterintelligence Operation." *Military Medicine* 174, 1 (January 2009): 93–99.

Holt, Thaddeus. *The Deceivers: Allied Military Deception in the Second World War.* New York: Scribner, 2004.

Additional Resources

Ask History. "What Was Operation Mincemeat?" History.com (June 5, 2013): history.com/news/ask-history/what-was-operation-mincemeat (accessed 7/27/2015).

BBC History. "Operation Mincemeat." bbc.co.uk/history/topics/operation_mincemeat (accessed 7/27/2015).

Garner, Dwight. "Floating a Wild Plan and a Dead Man to Defeat the Nazis." *New York Times* (May 11, 2010): nytimes.com/2010/05/12/books/12book.html (accessed 7/27/2015).

"Lady Risdale" [obituary]. *The Telegram* (December 17, 2009): telegraph.co.uk/news/obituaries/military-obituaries/special-forces-obituaries/6835071/Lady-Ridsdale.html (accessed 7/27/2015).

"The Man Who Never Was." The Hitchhiker's Guide to the Galaxy: Earth Edition (December 2, 2010): h2g2.com/edited_entry/A3031949 (accessed 12/4/2015).

NPR. "Dead Man Floating: World War II's Oddest Operation. (June 12, 2010): npr.org/templates/story/story.php?storyId=127742365 (accessed 7/27/2015).

Wikipedia. "Operation Mincemeat." en.wikipedia.org/wiki/Operation_Mincemeat (accessed 7/27/2015).

39. Dutch Artist Arrested for Selling a Vermeer to Hermann Göring

Sources

Cohen, Paula Marantz. "The Meanings of Forgery." *Southwest Review* 97, 3 (2012): 12–25.

Fleming, Stuart. "Art Forgery: Some Scientific Defenses." *Proceedings of the American Philosophical Society* 130, 2 (June 1986): 175–195.

Hoving, Thomas P. F. "The Game of Duplicity." *The Metropolitan Museum of Art Bulletin,* New Series 26, 6 (February 1968): 241–246.

"John Marshall Phillips [obituary]." *Bulletin of the Associates in Fine Arts at Yale* 21, 1 (October, 1953): n.p.

Keats, Jonathon. *Forged: Why Fakes Are the Great Art of Our Age.* New York: Oxford University Press, 2013.

Rousseau, Theodore. "The Stylistic Detection of Forgeries." *The Metropolitan Museum of Art Bulletin,* New Series 26, 6 (February 1968): 247–252.

Werness, Hope B. "Han van Meegeren *fecit,*" in Dennis Dutton, ed., *The Forger's Art: Forgery and the Philosophy of Art,* 1–57. Berkeley: University of California Press, 1983.

Wikipedia. "Netherlands in World War II." en.wikipedia.org/wiki/Netherlands_in_World_War_II.

Additional Resources

Bradsher, Greg. "Documenting Nazi Plunder of European Art." Holocaust-Era Assets. National Archives. archives.gov/research/holocaust/records-and-research/documenting-nazi-plunder-of-european-art.html (accessed 12/4/2015).

Cohen, Patricia. "So Valuable, It Could Almost Be Real." *New York Times* (December 13, 2013): nytimes.com/2014/01/01/arts/design/so-valuable-it-could-almost-be-real.html?_r=0 (accessed 12/4/2015).

Kennedy, Randy. "Elusive Forger, Giving but Never Stealing." *New York Times* (January 11, 2011): artsandartists.org/documents/exhibitions/intenttodeceive/012011_NewYorkTimes.pdf (accessed 12/4/2015).

Nothnagle, Alan. "News: Herman Göring's Art Collection Goes Online." Institute of Museum Ethics (June 24, 2012): museumethics.org/2012/06/news-hermann-gorings-art-collection-goes-online/ (accessed 12/4/2015).

Simpkins, Travis. "Art Crime Illustrated." artcrimeillustrated.com/2015/04/forged-why-fakes-are-great-art-of-our.html (accessed 7/29/2015).

40. The Cursed Tomb of the Last Aztec Emperor

Sources

Fulton, Christopher. "Siqueiros against the Myth: Paeans to Cuautémoc, Last of the Aztec Emperors." *Oxford Art Journal* 32, 1 (2009): 67, 69–93.

Gillingham, Paul. *Cuauhtémoc's Bones: Forging Identity in Modern Mexico*. Albuquerque: University of New Mexico Press, 2011.

———. "The Emperor of Ixcateopan: Fraud, Nationalism and Memory in Modern Mexico." *Journal of Latin American Studies* 37, 3 (Aug., 2005): 561–584.

Henderson, Timothy J. "*Cuauhtémoc's Bones: Forging Identity in Modern Mexico*. By Paul Gillingham (Albuquerque, University of New Mexico Press, 2011)" [review]. *Journal of Interdisciplinary History* 43, 1 (Summer 2012): 148–150.

Jackson, Brittany, and Mark Rose. "Tarragona Two-Step." *Archaeology Archive*: archive.archaeology.org/online/features/hoaxes/ (accessed 12/6/2015).

"Notes and Comments." *The Catholic Historical Review* 36, 3 (October 1950): 338–339.

Wikipedia. "Edward I of England." en.wikipedia.org/wiki/Edward_I_of_England (accessed 10/29/2015).

Additional Resources

"The Aztec Empire." History.Com. aztec-history.com/aztec-empire.html (accessed 12/4/2015).

Cuauhtemoc [pronunciation]: Inogolo—English Pronunciation Guide to the Names of People, Places, and Stuff. inogolo.com/pronunciation/Cuauhtemoc (accessed 12/4/2015).

"Paul Gillingham." Northwestern University. history.northwestern.edu/people/gillingham.html (accessed 12/4/2015).

Tenochtitlán Facts. "Cuauhtémoc." tenochtitlanfacts.com/Cuauhtemoc.html (accessed 12/4/2015).

Wikipedia. "Cuauhtémoc." en.wikipedia.org/wiki/Cuauht%C3%A9moc (accessed 12/4/2015).

Wikipedia. "Indigenismo." en.wikipedia.org/wiki/Indigenismo (accessed 12/4/2015).

41. Donald Crowhurst Vanishes at Sea

Sources

Raban, Jonathan. "Introduction," in Nicholas Tomalin and Ron Hall, *The Strange Last Voyage of Donald Crowhurst* (Camden, ME: International Marine Publications, 1995), xi–xix.

"Science of the 34th America's Cup." National Sailing Hall of Fame. nshof.org/index.php?option=com_content&view=category&id=179:science-of-the-34th-americas-cup&layout=blog&Itemid=281 (accessed 12/4/2015).

"Timeline of Computer History." Computer History Museum. computerhistory.org/timeline/?category=cmptr (accessed 12/4/2015).

Tomalin, Nicholas, and Ron Hall. *The Strange Last Voyage of Donald Crowhurst*. New York: Stein & Day, 1970.

Wikipedia. "Gypsy Moth IV." en.wikipedia.org/wiki/Gipsy_Moth_IV (accessed 12/4/2015).

Additional Resources

Beaumont-Thomas, Ben. "Colin Firth to Set Sail with Biopic of Doomed Yachtsman Donald Crowhurst." *The Guardian* (January 28, 2015): theguardian.com/film/2015/jan/28/colin-firth-biopic-donald-crowhurst-james-marsh (accessed 12/4/2015).

Cummings, Denis. "On This Day: Donald Crowhurst's Boat Found Abandoned." Finding Dulcinea (July 10, 2011): findingdulcinea.com/news/on-this-day/July-August-08/On-this-Day--Donald-Crowhurst-s-Boat-Found-Abandoned.html (accessed 12/4/2015).

"Deep Water." Independent Lens. PBS. pbs.org/independentlens/deepwater/ (accessed 12/4/2015).

42. The Tasaday: a Stone-Age Tribe, or a Hoax?

Sources

Headland, Thomas N., ed. *The Tasaday Controversy: Assessing the Evidence.* Washington, DC: American Anthropological Association, 1992.

Lawler, Andrew. "Do the Amazon's Last Isolated Tribes Have a Future?" *New York Times* (August 8, 2015): nytimes.com/2015/08/09/opinion/sunday/do-the-amazons-last-iso-lated-tribes-have-a-future.html?_r=0 (accessed 12/15/2015).

McDougall, Dan. "Survival Comes First for the Last Stone Age Tribe [in the] World." *The Guardian* (February 11, 2006): theguardian.com/world/2006/feb/12/theobserver.world-news12 (accessed 12/15/2015).

Molony, Carol H. "The Tasaday Language: Evidence for Authenticity?" in Headland, Thomas N., ed. *The Tasaday Controversy: Assessing the Evidence*, 107–16 (Washington, DC: American Anthropological Association, 1992).

Nance, John. *The Gentle Tasaday: A Stone Age People in the Philippine Rain Forest.* New York: Harcourt Brace Jovanovich, 1975.

Scaff, Alvin H. "Cultural Factors in Ecological Change on Mindanao in the Philippines." *Social Forces* 27, 2 (December 1948): 119–128.

Survival International. "The Most Isolated Tribe in the World?" survivalinternational.org/campaigns/mostisolated (accessed 12/15/2015).

Thomas, Benjamin. "*National Geographic*, PANAMIN and the Stone-Age Tribe." *Dialectical Anthropology* 25, 1 (March 2000): 77–88.

Thomas, Robert McG., Jr. "Manuel Elizalde, 60, Dies; Defender of Primitive Tribe." *New York Times* (May 8, 1997): nytimes.com/1997/05/08/world/manuel-elizalde-60-dies-defender-of-primitive-tribe.html (accessed 7/7/2015).

Watson, Traci. "People Without Electricity Don't Get 8 Hours' Sleep Either." *National Geographic* (October 15, 2015): news.nationalgeographic.com/2015/10/20151015-paleo-sleep-time-hadza-san-tsimane-science/ (accessed 12/15/2015).

World Health Organization. "Health of Indigenous Peoples." (October 2007). who.int/mediacentre/factsheets/fs326/en/ (accessed 12/15/2015).

Yen, D. E. "The Tasaday Environment: Seventeen Years On." *Philippine Studies* 50, 1 (2002): 76–92.

Additional Resources

Headland, Thomas. "Tasaday." *Encyclopedia of World Cultures.* 1996. Encyclopedia.com. (July 5, 2015). encyclopedia.com/doc/1G2-3458000904.html (accessed July 7, 2015).

Mydans, Seth. "The Tasaday Revisited: A Hoax or Social Change at Work?" *New York Times* (May 13, 1986): nytimes.com/1986/05/13/science/the-tasaday-revisited-a-hoax-or-social-change-at-work.html (accessed July 7, 2015).

Nance, John. "Tasaday Story." You Tube. youtube.com/watch?v=g8BGW-HwHzA (8:09 min.; accessed July 7, 2015); youtube.com/watch?v=td3G9Yb73Xg (8:45 min.; accessed 7/7/2015).

Smith, Court. "Tasaday History." Oregon State University. (February 19, 2013). oregonstate.edu/instruct/anth210/tasaday.html (accessed 7/7/2015).

43. A Faked Autobiography of Howard Hughes

Sources

Brown, Mick. "You Couldn't Make It Up." *The Telegraph* (July 28, 2007): telegraph.co.uk/culture/3666824/You-couldnt-make-it-up.html (accessed 7/29/2015).

Davies, Martin. "Clifford Irving." Bibliomaniac's Corner, Ibiza History and Culture. liveibiza.com/ibiza_literature/clifford_irving_ibiza.htm (accessed 7/30/2015).

Ford, Dana, and Greg Botelho. "Who Is Rachel Dolezal?" CNN-News (June 17, 2015): cnn.com/2015/06/16/us/rachel-dolezal/ (accessed 8/2/2015).

Hilferty, Robert. "Clifford Irving Faked Hughes Book for Fun, Derides 'Hoax' Movie." *Bloomberg* (April 25, 2007): bloomberg.com/apps/news?pid=newsarchive&sid=afoXTPWZROj0 (accessed 7/30/2015).

Irving, Clifford. *The Hoax.* New York: Hyperion, 2006. (Published in Britain, 1977, as *Project Octavio*.)

Wikipedia. "Howard Hughes." en.wikipedia.org/wiki/Howard_Hughes (accessed 7/30/2015).

Wikipedia. "Misha: A Mémoire of the Holocaust Years." en.wikipedia.org/wiki/Misha:_A_M%C3%A9moire_of_the_Holocaust_Years (accessed 8/2/2015).

Additional Resources

CBS News Staff. "Liar, Liar: Clifford Irving Revisited." CBSNews.net (January 28, 2000): cbsnews.com/news/liar-liar/ (accessed 7/29/2015).

"Howard Hughes, Producer (1905–1976). Biography.com: biography.com/people/howard-hughes-9346282 (accessed 7/30/2015).

Irving, Clifford. "Bio." *The Official Website of Clifford Irving.* cliffordirving.com/clifford-irvings-bio (accessed 7/30/2015).

Wikipedia. "F for Fake." en.wikipedia.org/wiki/F_for_Fake (accessed 7/30/2015).

44. Moon Landing Conspiracy Theories

Sources

Conspiracy Theories: Separating Fact from Fiction. "The Moon Landings Were Faked." *Time* (2009): content.time.com/time/specials/packages/article/0,28804,1860871_1860876_1860992,00.html (accessed 11/8/2015).

Goertzel, Ted. "Belief in Conspiracy Theories." *Political Psychology* 15, 4 (December 1994): 731–742.

Launius, Roger D. "Denying the Apollo Moon Landings: Conspiracy and Questioning in Modern American History." Orlando, FL: 48th AIAA Aerospace Sciences Meeting, January 4–7, 2010.

National Science Foundation. *Science and Engineering Indicators 2014.* "Chapter 7: Science and Technology: Public Attitudes and Understanding." nsf.gov/statistics/seind14/index.cfm/chapter-7/c7h.htm#s2 (accessed 12/16/2015).

Neuman, Scott. "1 in 4 Americans Believes the Sun Goes Around the Earth, Survey Says." npr.org/sections/thetwo-way/2014/02/14/277058739/1-in-4-americans-think-the-sun-goes-around-the-earth-survey-says (accessed 12/4/2015).

Phillips, Tony. "The Great Moon Hoax: Moon Rocks and Common Sense Prove Apollo Astronauts Really Did Visit the Moon." *NASA Science News* (February 23, 2001): science.nasa.gov/science-news/science-at-nasa/2001/ast23feb_2/ (accessed 11/4/2015).

Plait, Philip. "Fox News and the Apollo Moon Hoax." *Bad Astronomy* (February 13, 2001–June 11, 2011): badastronomy.com/bad/tv/foxapollo.html (accessed 11/4/2015).

Schwartz, John. "Vocal Minority Insists It Was All Smoke and Mirrors." *New York Times* (July 13, 2009): nytimes.com/2009/07/14/science/space/14hoax.html (accessed 11/7/2015).

Tyson, Neil deGrasse. "On the First Moon Landing." YouTube (July 28, 2012): youtube.com/watch?v=Q6ClA5f5uu0 (accessed 11/6/2015).

Van Bakel, Rogier. "The Wrong Stuff." *WIRED* (September 1, 1994): wired.com/1994/09/moon-land/?pg=5 (accessed 11/7/2015).

Wikipedia. "Apollo 11 in Popular Culture." en.wikipedia.org/wiki/Apollo_11_in_popular_culture (accessed 11/7/2015).

Wikipedia. "Moon Landing." en.wikipedia.org/wiki/Moon_landing (accessed 11/7/2015).

Windley, Jay. "Moon Base Clavius." clavius.org/index.html (accessed 11/7/2015).

Additional Resources

"A Brief History of Photo Fakery." New York Times (August 23, 2009): nytimes.com/slideshow/2009/08/23/weekinreview/20090823_FAKE_SS_index.html (accessed 11/7/2015).

Cunningham, Darryl. "The Moon Hoax." Darryl Cunningham Investigates (July 20, 2010): darrylcunningham.blogspot.com/2010/07/moon-hoax.html (accessed 11/7/2015).

Kaku, Michio. "On the Moon Landing 'Hoax.'" YouTube (November 28, 2011): youtube.com/watch?v=drSqtwOQywk (accessed 11/6/2015).

Launius, Roger D. "Why Do People Persist in Denying the Moon Landings?" Smithsonian National Air and Space Museum (April 1, 2010): blog.nasm.si.edu/history/why-do-people-persist-in-denying-the-moon-landings/ (accessed 11/9/2015).

Than, Ker. "8 Moon-Landing Hoax Myths—Busted." National Geographic News (July 16, 2009): news.nationalgeographic.com/news/2009/07/photogalleries/apollo-moon-landing-hoax-pictures/ (accessed 11/6/2015).

Wikipedia. "Moon Landing Conspiracy Theories." en.wikipedia.org/wiki/Moon_landing_conspiracy_theories (accessed 11/4/2015).

45. Genuine Fake Hitler Diaries

Sources

Connolly, Kate. "Art Dealer Convicted of Forging Forger's Forgeries." Guardian (September 10, 2010): theguardian.com/artanddesign/2010/sep/10/forgeries-conviction-kujau (accessed 8/12/2015).

"The Currency Converter," Coinmill.com: coinmill.com/DEM_USD.html (accessed 8/13/2015).

Hall, Allan. "Living in Poverty, the Man Who 'Found' Hitler's Diaries." The Independent (April 24, 2008): independent.co.uk/news/world/europe/living-in-poverty-the-man-who-found-hitlers-diaries-814757.html (accessed 8/13/2015).

Markham, James M. "Hitler Diaries Plot, If There Was One, Thickens." New York Times (July 6, 1985): nytimes.com/1985/07/06/world/hitler-diaries-plot-if-there-was-one-thickens.html (accessed 8/9/2015).

Museum of Hoaxes. "The Hitler Diaries." hoaxes.org/archive/permalink/the_hitler_diaries (accessed 8/12/2015).

Pace, Eric. "Konrad Kujau, 62, 'Hitler Diaries' Swindler" [obituary]. New York Times (September 14, 2000): nytimes.com/2000/09/14/world/konrad-kujau-62-hitler-diaries-swindler.html (accessed 8/9/2015).

Rentschler, Eric. "The Fascination of a Fake: The Hitler Diaries." New German Critique 90 (Autumn 2003): 177–192.

Additional Resources

Cottrell, Chris, and Nicholas Kulish. "30 Years Later, Forged Hitler Diaries Enter German Archives." New York Times (April 23, 2013): nytimes.com/2013/04/24/world/europe/forged-hitler-diaries-now-part-of-germanys-archives.html (accessed 8/9/2015).

Duba, Ursula. "How Do Young Germans Deal with the Legacy of the Holocaust and the Third Reich?" PBS Frontline (May 31, 2005): pbs.org/wgbh/pages/frontline/shows/germans/germans/howdo.html (accessed 8/12/2015).

McGrane, Sally. "Diary of the Hitler Diary Hoax." New Yorker (April 25, 2013): newyorker.com/books/page-turner/diary-of-the-hitler-diary-hoax (accessed 8/12/2015).

Markham, James M. "The Hitler Diaries: A Fiasco on Trial." *New York Times* (September 30, 1984): nytimes.com/1984/09/30/world/the-hitler-diaries-a-fiasco-on-trial.html (accessed 8/12/2015).

Mitchell, Robert W. "The Psychology of Human Deception." *Social Research* 63, 3 (Fall 1996): 819–861.

Streisand, Betsy. "100 Percent False." *U.S. News & World Report* 133, 8 (August 26, 2002): 62.

Wikipedia. "Hitler Diaries." en.wikipedia.org/wiki/Hitler_Diaries (accessed 8/12/2015).

46. More Lying Stones: Moroccan Fossils in the Himalayas

Sources

"Fossils Found in Tibet Revise History of Elevation, Climate." *Science Daily* (June 12, 2008): sciencedaily.com/releases/2008/06/080611144021.htm (accessed 7/20/2015).

Holden, Constance. "Indian Geologist Suspended." *Science*, New Series 251 (March 15, 1991): 1310.

Ioannidis, John P. A. "Why Most Published Research Findings Are False." *PLoS* (August 30, 2005): journals.plos.org/plosmedicine/article?id=10.1371/journal.pmed.0020124 (accessed 7/20/2015).

Lewin, Roger. "The Case of the 'Misplaced' Fossils." *Science*, New Series 244, 4902 (April 21, 1989): 277–279.

Stevens, William K. "Scientist Accused of Faking Findings." *New York Times* (April 23, 1989): nytimes.com/1989/04/23/us/scientist-accused-of-faking-findings.html (accessed 7/20/2015).

Talent, John A. "The 'Misplaced' Fossils." *Science*, New Series 246, 4931 (November 10, 1989): 740–741.

Webster, Gary D. "An Evaluation of the V. J. Gupta Echinoderm Papers, 1971–1989." *Journal of Paleontology* 65, 6 (November 1991): 1006–1008.

———, Carl B. Rexroad, and John A. Talent. "An Evaluation of the V. J. Gupta Conodont Papers." *Journal of Paleontology* 67, 3 (May 1993): 486–493.

"What Happens to the Whistleblowers?" *The Science Show*. Radio National (September 3, 2005): griffith.edu.au/__data/assets/pdf_file/0010/159238/radionat3sept05.pdf (accessed 7/20/2015).

Additional Resources

Freedman, David H. "Lies, Damned Lies, and Medical Statistics." *The Atlantic* (November 2010): theatlantic.com/magazine/archive/2010/11/lies-damned-lies-and-medical-science/308269/ (accessed 7/20/2015).

"Himalayan Fossil Hoax." Museum of Hoaxes. hoaxes.org/archive/permalink/the_himalayan_fossils_hoax (accessed 7/20/2015).

Wikipedia. "Geography of the Himalaya." en.wikipedia.org/wiki/Geology_of_the_Himalaya (accessed 7/20/2015).

47. Crop Circle Artists Confess

Sources

Anderson, Alun. "Britain's Crop Circles: Reaping by Whirlwind?" *Science*, New Series 253, 5023 (August 30, 1991): 961–962.

Chorley, Richard David. "Statement of the Chorley Family Concerning Robbert van den Broeke." The Official Website of Colin Andrews (August 19, 2012): colinandrews.net/David_Chorley-Family-Statement-Colin_Andrews-Crop_Circles.html (accessed 7/22/2015).

Dixon, Bernard. "Mind Boggling." *British Medical Journal* 303, 6808 (October 19, 1991): 999.

Geraghty, Paul. "Doug and Dave: The Crop Circle Hoaxers." Spooky Stuff (October 22, 2012): spookystuff.co.uk/douganddavethecropcirclehoaxers.html (accessed 7/22/2015).

Hernando, Harriet. "First Crop Circle." *Daily Mail* (July 14, 2014): dailymail.co.uk/news/article-2691479/First-crop-circle-year-appears-overnight-Dorset-wheat-field-sparking-new-it.html (accessed 7/22/2015).

Nolan, Steve. "Worst. Crop Circles. Ever. What Happened to the Patterns That Delighted and Baffled the World?" *Daily Mail* (July 31, 2013): dailymail.co.uk/news/article-2381877/Worst-crop-circles-What-happened-patterns-delighted-baffled-world.html (accessed 7/22/2015).

Parry, Wynne. "Crop-Circle Artists Becoming High Tech." LiveScience (August 2, 2011): livescience.com/15353-crop-circle-artists-technology-physics-hoax.html (accessed 7/22/2015).

Radford, Benjamin. "Crop Circles Explained." LiveScience (January 23, 2013): livescience.com/26540-crop-circles.html (accessed 7/22/2015).

———. "Crop Circle Was a Publicity Stunt: Why 'Experts' Were Fooled." LiveScience (January 7, 2014): livescience.com/42368-crop-circle-hoaxes.html (accessed 7/22/2015).

Roberts, John. "Trickster." *Oxford Art Journal* 22, 1 (1999): 83–101.

Schnabel, Jim. "Puck in the Laboratory: The Construction and Deconstruction of Hoaxlike Deception in Science." *Science, Technology, & Human Values* 19, 4 (Autumn 1994): 459–492.

"Stoned Wallabies Make Crop Circles." BBC News (June 25, 2009): news.bbc.co.uk/2/hi/asia-pacific/8118257.stm (accessed 7/22/2015).

Watson, Stephanie. "How Crop Circles Work." How Stuff Works: science.howstuffworks.com/science-vs-myth/unexplained-phenomena/crop-circle4.htm (accessed 7/22/2015).

"Why Is the Crop Circle Access Donation Initiative Needed?" Crop Circle Access Centre: cropcircleaccess.com/crop-circle-access-donation-initiative/why-is-an-access-pass-needed/ (accessed 7/22/2015).

Additional Resources

"The Beautiful Geometry of Crop Circles." Mathematics Awareness Month 2014: Mathematics, Magic, and Mystery. mathaware.org/mam/2014/calendar/cropcircles.html (accessed 7/22/2015).

"Crop Circles: The Human Angle." mysteriousuniverse.org/2012/08/crop-circles-the-human-angle/ (accessed 7/22/2015).

"Doug and Dave—South Today 1991." youtube.com/watch?v=Qzvuqs9Bf7Q (accessed 7/22/2015).

Lundberg, John. "Circlemakers: Case History." circlemakers.org/case_history.html (accessed 7/22/2015).

Wikipedia. "Crop Circle." en.wikipedia.org/wiki/Crop_circle (accessed 7/22/2015).

48. Physicist Alan Sokal Spoofs Postmodern Scholarship

Sources

McCook, Alison. "Cancer Researcher Cleared of Misconduct." Retraction Watch (December 15, 2015): retractionwatch.com/2015/12/15/cancer-researcher-cleared-of-misconduct-inquiry-finds-genuine-error-or-honest-oversight/#more-35279 (accessed 12/15/2015).

"Mystery Science Theatre." *Lingua Franca.* linguafranca.mirror.theinfo.org/9607/mst.html (accessed 8/4/2015).

Reynolds, Jonathan. "The Sokal Hoax Fifteen Years Later: A Philosophical Reading of the Controversy." *Spike Magazine:* spikemagazine.com/the-sokal-hoax.php (accessed 8/7/2015).

Ross, Andrew. "Reflections on the Sokal Affair." *Social Text,* 50 (Spring 1997): 149–152.

Sokal, Alan. "A Physicist Experiments with Cultural Studies." physics.nyu.edu/faculty/sokal/lingua_franca_v4/lingua_franca_v4.html (accessed 8/6/2015).

———, and Jean Bricmont. *Fashionable Nonsense: Postmodern Intellectuals' Abuse of Science.* New York: Picador, 1998.

"The Sokal Hoax: A Forum." *Lingua Franca* (July/August 1996): linguafranca.mirror.theinfo. org/9607/tsh.html (accessed 8/4/2015).

Wikipedia. "C. P. Snow." en.wikipedia.org/wiki/C._P._Snow (accessed 8/7/2015).

Wikipedia. "Scholarly Peer Review." en.wikipedia.org/wiki/Scholarly_peer_review (accessed 8/7/2015).

Wikipedia. "Science Wars." en.wikipedia.org/wiki/Science_wars (accessed 8/4/2015).

Additional Resources

Borsten, Leron. "What Is Quantum Gravity?" Physicsworld.com (May 9, 2013): physicsworld. com/cws/article/multimedia/2013/may/09/what-is-quantum-gravity (accessed 8/6/2015).

Fish, Stanley. "Professor Sokal's Bad Joke." *New York Times* (May 21, 1996): nytimes. com/1996/05/21/opinion/professor-sokal-s-bad-joke.html (accessed 8/7/2015).

"Sokal Hoax." Skeptic's Dictionary. skepdic.com/sokal.html (accessed 8/7/2015).

"The Sokal Hoax." Museum of Hoaxes. hoaxes.org/archive/permalink/the_sokal_hoax (accessed 8/7/2015).

49. Joining the Campaign to Ban DHMO

Sources

"Ban Dihydrogen Monoxide." bandhmo.org/ (accessed 8/8/2015).

Bracey, Gerald W. "Research." *The Phi Delta Kappan* 79, 5 (January 1998): 406, 408.

"DHMO: Your All-Natural Friend." armory.com/~crisper/DHMO/ (accessed 8/9/2015).

Kluger, Jeffrey "Why Science Is Winning the Vaccine Wars." *Time* (July 27, 2015): 25.

"Timeline: The Modern Environmental Movement," American Experience, PBS, pbs.org/ wgbh/americanexperience/features/timeline/earthdays/ (accessed 8/8/2015).

United States Centers for Disease Control and Prevention. "Unintentional Drowning: Get the Facts." cdc.gov/HomeandRecreationalSafety/Water-Safety/waterinjuries-factsheet.html (accessed 8/9/2015).

United States Environmental Assessment Center, Dihydrogen Monoxide Research Division. "Dihydrogen Monoxide FAQ." DHMO.org/facts.html (accessed 8/9/2015).

"Water Works." Snopes.com (March 8, 2015): snopes.com/science/dhmo.asp (accessed 8/9/2015).

Wikipedia. "DDT." en.wikipedia.org/wiki/DDT (accessed 8/8/2015).

Wikipedia. "Dihydrogen Monoxide Hoax." en.wikipedia.org/wiki/Dihydrogen_monoxide_ hoax (accessed 8/9/2015).

Wikipedia. "Nevada Test Site." en.wikipedia.org/wiki/Nevada_Test_Site (accessed 8/8/2015).

Additional Resources

Burns, Anna. "Is Dihydrogen Monoxide (DHMO) Contaminating Our Water?" YouTube (September 28, 2007): youtube.com/watch?v=jAI1JAYj53k (accessed 8/9/2015).

"Penn and Teller Get Hippies to Sign Water Banning Petition." YouTube (December 6, 2006): youtube.com/watch?v=yi3erdgVVTw (accessed 8/9/2015).

Schrock, Kathy. "Critical Evaluation Page." (2002). schrockguide.net/critical-evaluation-les-son-plan.html (accessed 8/9/2015).

50. Microsoft Technical Support

Sources

Anderson, Nate. "Inside the U.S. Government's War on Tech Support Scammers." *Ars Technica* (May 18, 2014): arstechnica.com/tech-policy/2014/05/stains-of-deceitfulness-inside-the-us-governments-war-on-tech-support-scammers/ (accessed 7/25/2015).

Brodkin, Jon. "Hello, I'm Definitely Not Calling from India. Can I Take Control of Your PC?" *Ars Technica* (October 3, 2012): arstechnica.com/tech-policy/2012/10/

hello-im-definitely-not-calling-from-india-can-i-take-control-of-your-pc/ (accessed 7/24/2015).

George-Parkin, Hilary. "When Is Fortune-Telling a Crime?" *The Atlantic* (November 14, 2014): theatlantic.com/features/archive/2014/11/when-is-fortunetelling-a-crime/382738/ (accessed 7/25/2015).

"Microsoft Scam Man Is Sentenced in 'Landmark' Case." BBC News (March 31, 2014): bbc.com/news/technology-26818745 (accessed 7/24/2015).

Museum of Hoaxes. "Microsoft Buys the Catholic Church." hoaxes.org/archive/permalink/microsoft_buys_the_catholic_church (accessed 7/25/2015).

Pogrebin, Robin. "It Seems the Cards Do Lie; A Police Sting Cracks Down on Fortunetelling Fraud." *New York Times* (June 30, 1999): nytimes.com/1999/06/30/nyregion/it-seems-the-cards-do-lie-a-police-sting-cracks-down-on-fortunetelling-fraud.html (accessed 7/25/2015).

Segura, Jerome. "Tech Support Scams – Help & Resource Page." Malwarebytes Labs (October 4, 2013): blog.malwarebytes.org/tech-support-scams/ (accessed 7/24/2015).

Solon, Olivia. "What Happens If You Play Along with a Microsoft 'Tech Support' Scam?" *WIRED.Co.UK* (April 11, 2013): wired.co.uk/news/archive/2013-04/11/malwarebytes (accessed 7/24/2015).

Whitney, Lance. "Microsoft Combats Tech Support Scammers with Lawsuit." CNET (December 19, 2014): cnet.com/news/microsoft-combats-tech-support-scammers-with-lawsuit/ (accessed 7/24/2015).

Wikipedia. "Fortune-Telling Fraud." en.wikipedia.org/wiki/Fortune_telling_fraud (accessed 7/25/2015).

Wikipedia. "Microsoft Joke." en.wikipedia.org/wiki/Microsoft_joke (accessed 7/24/2015).

Additional Resources

Arthur, Charles. "Virus Phone Scam Being Run from Call Centres in India." *The Guardian*, U.S. Edition (July 18, 2010): theguardian.com/world/2010/jul/18/phone-scam-india-call-centres (accessed 7/24/2015).

Marvin, Ginny. "Despite Crackdowns, Tech Support Ads in Search Are Still Cause for Consumer Confusion." *Search Engine Land* (August 5, 2014): searchengineland.com/tech-support-ads-search-still-consumer-quagmire-197905 (accessed 7/24/2015).

Schifferle, Lisa Weintraub. "FTC Cracks Down on Tech Support Scams." Federal Trade Commission, Consumer Information blog (November 19, 2014): consumer.ftc.gov/blog/ftc-cracks-down-tech-support-scams (accessed 7/25/2015).

Wikipedia. "Technical Support Scams." en.wikipedia.org/wiki/Technical_support_scam (accessed 7/24/2015).

Endnotes

Introduction

1. P.T. Barnum, *The Humbugs of the World* (London: John Camden Hotten, 1866), 1.

Chapter 1

1. Virgil, *The Aeneid of Virgil: A Verse Translation by Allen Mandelbaum* (Berkeley: University of California Press, 1981).
2. Eric H. Cline, *1177 B.C.: The Year Civilization Collapsed* (Princeton, NJ: Princeton University Press, 2014).
3. B. A. Sparkes, "The Trojan Horse in Classical Art," *Greece & Rome* 18, 1 (1971): 54–70.
4. "Trojan Horse," Wikipedia, http://en.wikipedia.org/wiki/Trojan_Horse.

Chapter 2

1. Joseph Rosenblum, *Practice to Deceive: The Amazing Stories of Literary Forgery's Most Notorious Practitioners* (New Castle, Delaware: Oak Knoll Press, 2000), xvi.
2. Rosenbloom, *Practice to Deceive*, xvi.
3. Charles L. Wells, *The Age of Charlemagne*, Volume 4 of *Ten Epochs of Church History*, ed. by John Fulton (New York: The Christian Literature Company, 1898), .
4. Paul Johnson, *A History of Christianity* (New York: Atheneum, 1976), 169–170.
5. Paolo Liverani, "Saint Peter's, Leo the Great and the Leprosy of Constantine," *Papers of the British School at Rome* 76 (2008): 155–172.
6. Eamon Duff, *Saints & Sinners: A History of the Popes* (New Haven: Yale University Press, 2001), 86–87.
7. John W. O'Malley, *A History of the Popes* (New York: Rowman & Littlefield, 2010), 59.
8. Peter E. Prosser, "Church History's Biggest Hoax," *Christian History* 20, 4 (2001).
9. David M. Whitford, "The Papal Antichrist: Martin Luther and the Underappreciated Influence of Lorenzo Valla," *Renaissance Quarterly* 61 (2008): 26–52
10. G. W. Bowersock, "Introduction," in Lorenzo Valla, *On the Donation of Constantine* (Cambridge, Massachusetts: Harvard University Press, 2007).
11. Whitford.
12. "Languages of the Roman Empire." Wikipedia. http://en.wikipedia.org/wiki/Languages_of_the_Roman_Empire.
13. "Constantine the Great and Christianity." Wikipedia. http://en.wikipedia.org/wiki/Constantine_the_Great_and_Christianity.
14. Eusebius, *Church History. Life of Constantine the Great, Oration in Praise of Constantine.* Ed. Philip Schaff and Henry Wace. Select Library of the Nicene and Post-Nicene Fathers of the Christian Church, Second Series. New York: Christian Literature Company, 1890–1900. Sage Digital Library (found at archive.org).

Chapter 3

1. Matteo Salvadore, "The Ethiopian Age of Exploration: Prester John's Discovery of Europe, 1306–1458," *Journal of World History* 21, 4 (December 2010): 593–627.
2. Karl F. Helleiner, "Prester John's Letter: A Mediaeval Utopia," *Phoenix* 13, 2 (Summer 1959): 47–57.
3. Helleiner.
4. Charles E. Nowell, "The Historical Prester John," *Speculum* 28, 3 (1953): 435–445.

5. Helleiner.

6. Nowell.

7. Helleiner.

8. "Tales of Land and Sea: More on Medieval Mappae Mundi." *In Romaunce as We Rede* (April 27, 2012): inromaunce.blogspot.com/2012/04/tales-of-land-and-sea-more-on-medieval.html (accessed 10/21/2015).

9. Elizabeth L. Eisenstein, *The Printing Revolution in Early Modern Europe* (New York: Cambridge University Press, 1983), 195–200.

Chapter 4

1. Frances Woods, *Did Marco Polo Go to China?* (Boulder, CO: Westview Press, 1996), 5.

2. Woods, 7.

3. Kublai Khan, *Wikipedia*, http://en.wikipedia.org/wiki/Kublai_Khan#Emperor_of_the_Yuan_Dynasty.

4. Woods, 43, 140.

5. Woods.

6. Peter Jackson, "Marco Polo and His 'Travels,'" *Bulletin of the School of Oriental and African Studies, University of London*, 61, 1 (1998): 82–101.

7. Jackson.

8. Tamarah Kohanski and C. David Benson, "The Book of John Mandeville: Introduction," TEAMS Middle English Text Series, Robbins Library Digital Projects, University of Rochester, 2007. http://d.lib.rochester.edu/teams/text/kohanski-and-benson-the-book-of-john-mandeville-introduction.

9. C. W. R. D. Mosely, "'New Things to Speak of': Money, Memory, and *Mandeville's Travels* in Early Modern England," *The Yearbook of English Studies*, 41, 1 (2011): 5–20.

10. Andrew Fleck, "Here, There, and In Between: Representing Difference in the 'Travels' of Sir John Mandeville," *Studies in Philology*, 97, 4 (Autumn 2000): 379–400.

Chapter 5

1. Lawrence and Nancy Goldstone, *The Friar and the Cipher: Roger Bacon and the Unsolved Mystery of the Most Unusual Manuscript in the World* (New York: Doubleday, 2005), 199.

2. Goldstone, 200.

3. John Matthews Manly, "Roger Bacon and the Voynich MS," *Speculum* 6, 3 (July 1931): 345–391.

4. René Zandbergen, "The Voynich Manuscript" (2004–2015): http://www.voynich.nu/.

5. James Child, "The Voynich Manuscript Revisited," https://www.nsa.gov/public_info/_files/tech_journals/Voynich_Manuscript_Revisited.pdf.

6. Lisa Grossman, "Mexican Plants Could Break Code on Gibberish Manuscript," *New Scientist* (February 7, 2014): http://www.newscientist.com/article/dn24987-mexican-plants-could-break-code-on-gibberish-manuscript.html#.VUDMQ5V0zwp.

7. Diego R. Amancio *et al.*, "Probing the statistical properties of unknown texts: application to the Voynich Manuscript," 2013. https://ia601901.us.archive.org/28/items/arxiv-1303.0347/1303.0347.pdf; Andreas Schinner, "The Voynich Manuscript: Evidence of the Hoax Hypothesis," *Cryptologia* 31, 2 (April 2007): http://www.tandfonline.com/doi/abs/10.1080/01611190601133539.

8. Rich McCormick, "Decrypting the Most Mysterious Book in the World," *The Verge* (February 28, 2014): http://www.theverge.com/2014/2/28/5453596/voynich-manuscript-decrypting-the-most-mysterious-book-in-the-world.

9. Joseph D'Agnese, "Scientific Method Man," *Wired* 12, 9 (September, 2004): http://archive.wired.com/wired/archive/12.09/rugg.html.

10. Nick Rigby, "Breakthrough over 600-Year-Old Mystery Manuscript," BBC News (February 18, 2014): http://www.bbc.com/news/uk-england-beds-bucks-herts-26198471.
11. Sukhwant Singh, "Voynich Manuscript Is Written in Landa Khojki Scripts and Belongs to Sindh Regions Mahajan": http://www.voynich-manuscript-landa-khojki-scripts-sindhi-mahajans-book.net/home.html.
12. "Romani People," Wikipedia, http://en.wikipedia.org/wiki/Romani_people.
13. "Esperanto," Wikipedia, http://en.wikipedia.org/wiki/Esperanto.
14. "Tengwar," Omniglot, http://www.omniglot.com/writing/tengwar.htm.

Chapter 6

1. Peter Holmes, "The Great Council in the Reign of Henry VII," *The English Historical Review* 101, 401 (October 1986): 840–862.
2. Michael Bennett, *Lambert Simnel and the Battle of Stoke* (New York: St. Martin's Press, 1987).
3. F. X. Martin, "The Crowning of a King at Dublin, 24 May 1487," *Hermathena* 144 (Summer 1988): 7–34.
4. Bennett, *Lambert Simnel*.
5. "Succession to the British Throne." Wikipedia, http://en.wikipedia.org/wiki/Succession_to_the_British_throne.
6. Michael Hicks, "The Second Anonymous Continuation of the Crowland Abbey Chronicle 1459–86 Revisited," *The English Historical Review* 122, 496 (April 2007): 349–370.
7. "The History of Crowland." The Museum of Hoaxes. http://hoaxes.org/archive/permalink/the_history_of_crowland.
8. Roffe, David, "The Historia Croylandensis: A Plea for Reassessment," *The English Historical Review* 110, 435 (February 1995): 93–108.

Chapter 7

1. Ruth Rubinstein, "Michelangelo's Lost *Sleeping Cupid* and Fetti's *Vertumnus and Pomona*," *Journal of the Warburg and Courtauld Institutes* 49 (1986): 257–259.
2. Brown, Mark. "Michelangelo's Bronze Panther Riders Revealed after 'Renaissance whodunnit.'" *The Guardian* (February 1, 2015). http://www.theguardian.com/artanddesign/2015/feb/02/michelangelo-bronzes-sculptures-fitzwilliam-museum-cambridge.
3. Russell, John. "A Michelangelo on 5th Avenue? It Seems So." *New York Times* (January 23, 1996): http://www.nytimes.com/1996/01/23/arts/a-michelangelo-on-5th-ave-it-seems-so.html.
4. Brown.
5. "The Rise, Fall, and Resurrection of Ancient Rome," Italian Renaissance Resources, http://italianrenaissanceresources.com/units/unit-7/essays/rise-fall-and-resurrection-of-ancient-rome/.
6. Michael Koortbojian, "Pliny's Laocoön?" In *Antiquity and Its Interpreters*, ed. Alina Payne, Ann Kuttner, & Rebekah Smick (New York: Cambridge University Press, 2010), 208.
7. Paul F. Norton, "The Lost Sleeping Cupid of Michelangelo," *The Art Bulletin* 39, 4 (December 1957): 251.
8. Deborah Parker, *Michelangelo and the Art of Letter Writing* (New York: Cambridge University Press, 2010), 11.
9. Miles J. Unger, *Michelangelo: A Life in Six Masterpieces* (New York: Simon & Schuster, 2014), 40–41.
10. Norton, 252.
11. Norton.

12. "Annio da Viterbo," Wikipedia, http://en.wikipedia.org/wiki/Annio_da_Viterbo.
13. John Glassie, *A Man of Misconceptions: The Life of an Eccentric in an Age of Change* (New York: Riverhead Books, 2012), 173–174.

Chapter 8
1. Fred W. Lucas, *The Annals of the Voyages of the Brothers Nicolò and Antonio Zeno* (London: H. Stevens Son & Stiles, 1898).
2. Lucas, 8.
3. Donald S. Johnson, *Phantom Islands of the Atlantic: The Legends of Seven Lands That Never Were* (New York: Walker and Company, 1994), 46–47.
4. Helen Wallis, "England's Search for the Northern Passages in the Sixteenth and Early Seventeenth Centuries," *Arctic* 37, 4 (December 1984): 453–472.
5. Johnson, 46.
6. Elizabeth L. Eisenstein, *The Printing Revolution in Early Modern Europe* (New York: Cambridge University Press, 1983), 195–200.
7. Lucas, 6.
8. Admiral Irminger, "Zeno's Frisland Is Iceland and Not the Faeroes," *Journal of the Royal Geographical Society of London* 49 (1879): 398–412.
9. E. C. S. Rye, "New Books," *Proceedings of the Royal Geographical Society and Monthly Record of Geography* 5, 11 (November 1883): 676–682.
10. R. H. Major, "The Site of the Lost Colony of Greenland Determined, and Pre-Columbian Discoveries of America Confirmed," *Proceedings of the Royal Geographical Society of London* 17, 5 (1872–1873): 312–321.
11. Brian Smith, "Earl Henry Sinclair's fictitious trip to America," orig. *New Orkney Antiquarian Journal*, 2 (2002).
12. Nate Probasco, "Cartography as a Tool of Colonization: Sir Humphrey Gilbert's 1583 Voyage to North America," *Renaissance Quarterly* 67, 2 (Summer 2014): 425–472.
13. Johnson, 183.
14. "Thule," Wikipedia, http://en.wikipedia.org/wiki/Thule.
15. Johnson, 63–90.

Chapter 9
1. Lawrence M. Principe, *The Secrets of Alchemy* (Chicago: University of Chicago Press, 2013), 49.
2. Principe, *Secrets of Alchemy*, 61.
3. Principe, *Secrets of Alchemy*.
4. Principe, *Secrets of Alchemy*, 62–63.
5. John Maxson Stillman, "Basil Valentine: A Seventeenth-Century Hoax," *Popular Science Monthly* 81 (December 1912).
6. C. S. Pierce, "Note on the Age of Basil Valentine," *Science, New Series*, 8, 189 (August 12, 1898): 169–176.
7. "Basil Valentine," Wikipedia, en.wikipedia.org/wiki/Basil_Valentine.
8. Pierce, "Note."
9. Stillman, "Basil Valentine."
10. Stillman, "Basil Valentine."
11. Stillman, "Basil Valentine."
12. Stillman, "Basil Valentine"; "Paracelsus," Wikipedia, en.wikipedia.org/wiki/Paracelsus.

Chapter 10

1. John Glassie, *A Man of Misconceptions: The Life of an Eccentric in an Age of Change* (New York: Riverhead Books, 2012).
2. Elizabeth L. Eisenstein, *The Printing Revolution in Early Modern Europe* (New York: Cambridge University Press, 1983).
3. Glassie, 71–72.
4. Glassie, 70–71.
5. Glassie, 96.
6. Glassie, 166.
7. Joscelyn Godwin, *Athanasius Kircher's Theatre of the World: The Life and Work of the Last Man to Search for Universal Knowledge* (Rochester, VT: Inner Traditions, 2009), 110.
8. "Athanasius Kircher, Victim of Pranks," Museum of Hoaxes, http://hoaxes.org/archive/permalink/athanasius_kircher (accessed 10/23/2015).
9. Glassie, 208.
10. Glassie, 241.
11. "Cabinet of Curiosities: 1710," *Learning Timelines*, British Library: http://www.bl.uk/learning/timeline/itcm107648.html (accessed 10/22/2015).
12. Glassie, 146.
13. Wikipedia, "Scientific Revolution," https://en.wikipedia.org/wiki/Scientific_revolution (accessed 10/23/15).

Chapter 11

1. Melvin E. Jahn and Daniel J. Woolf, *The Lying Stones of Dr. Johann Bartholomew Adam Beringer* (Los Angeles: University of California Press, 1963): 137.
2. Jahn and Woolf, 137.
3. Jahn and Woolf, 139.
4. Jahn and Woolf, 18.
5. Jahn and Woolf, 20–21.
6. Stephen Jay Gould, *The Lying Stones of Marrakech* (New York: Harmony Books, 2000), 22.
7. Jahn and Woolf, 93.
8. Jahn and Woolf, 106.
9. Gould, 13.
10. "Fossils: History of the Study of Fossils," Wikipedia, http://en.wikipedia.org/wiki/Fossil#History_of_the_study_of_fossils.
11. Stephen Jay Gould, *The Lying Stones of Marrakech* (New York: Harmony Books, 2000), 20.
12. Jahn and Woolf, 45.

Chapter 12

1. Peter T. Murphy, "Fool's Gold: The Highland Treasures of MacPherson's Ossian," *ELH* 53, 3 (Autumn 1986): 567–591
2. Joseph Rosenblum, "'Ossian' James Macpherson," in *Practice to Deceive: The Amazing Stories of Literary Forgery's Most Notorious Practitioners* (New Castle, Delaware: Oak Knoll Press, 1999), 19–54.
3. Rosenblum, 32.
4. Rosenblum, 28–29.
5. Quoted in James Porter, "'Bring Me the Head of James Macpherson': The Execution of Ossian and the Wellsprings of Folkloristic Discourse," *The Journal of American Folklore* 114, 454 (Autumn 2001): 407.
6. Porter, 396.
7. Quoted in Rosenblum, 47.

8. Rosenblum, 19.
9. Porter, 408.

Chapter 13

1. Max Hall, "An Amateur Detective on the Trail of B. Franklin, Hoaxer," *Proceedings of the Massachusetts Historical Society*, Third Series, 84 (1972): 28.
2. Prudence L. Steiner, "Benjamin Franklin's Biblical Hoaxes," *Proceedings of the American Philosophical Society* 131, 2 (June 1987): 183.
3. Hall, "Amateur Detective."
4. Benjamin Franklin, "An Edict by the King of Prussia," *The Public Advertiser* (September 22, 1773): founders.archives.gov/documents/Franklin/01-20-02-0223.
5. Quoted by Steiner, 187.
6. Carla Mulford, "Benjamin Franklin's Savage Eloquence: Hoaxes from the Press at Passy, 1782," *Proceedings of the American Philosophical Society* 152, 4 (December 2008): 490–530.
7. [Benjamin Franklin], "A Witch Trial at Mount Holly," *Pennsylvania Gazette* (October 22, 1730): founders.archives.gov/documents/Franklin/01-01-02-0056#BNFN-01-01-02-0056-fn-0001-ptr.
8. Owen Davies, *America Bewitched: The Story of Witchcraft after Salem* (Oxford: Oxford University Press, 2013).

Chapter 14

1. Wikipedia, "Potemkin Village," en.wikipedia.org/wiki/Potemkin_village.
2. David M. Griffiths, "Catherine II Discovers the Crimea," *Jahrbücher für Geschichte Osteuropas, Neue Folge* 56, 3 (2008): 339–48.
3. George Soloveytchik, *Potemkin: Soldier, Statesman, Lover and Consort of Catherine of Russia* (New York: W. W. Norton, 1947), xi.
4. Sebag Montefiore, *Prince of Princes: The Life of Potemkin* (New York: Thomas Dunne Books, 2000), 380.
5. Griffiths, "Catherine II Discovers the Crimea."
6. Montefiore, *Prince of Princes*, 293.
7. Montefiore, *Prince of Princes*, 294.
8. Montefiore, *Prince of Princes*, 267–268.
9. Montefiore, *Prince of Princes*, 294.
10. James A. Duran, "Catherine II, Potemkin, and Colonization Policy in Southern Russia," *The Russian Review* 28, 1 (January 1969): 30.

Chapter 15

1. Joseph Rosenblum, "'Shakespearean Forgery 101," in *Practice to Deceive: The Amazing Stories of Literary Forgery's Most Notorious Practitioners* (New Castle, Delaware: Oak Knoll Press, 1999), 107–155.
2. William-Henry Ireland, *Confessions of William-Henry Ireland, Containing the Particulars of His Fabrication of the Shakespeare Manuscripts* (New York: Burt Franklin, 1969 [reprint of the 1874 edition]).
3. Rosenblum, 113.
4. Ireland, 62.
5. Robert Miles, "Trouble in the Republic of Letters: The Reception of the Shakespeare Forgeries," *Studies in Romanticism* 44, 3 (Fall 2005): 317–340.

6. Michael Wiley, "Coleridge's 'The Raven' and the Forging of Radicalism," *Studies in English Literature, 1500-1900* 43, 4 (Autumn 2003): 799–813.
7. Joseph Rosenblum, "The Marvelous Thomas Chatterton," in *Practice to Deceive: The Amazing Stories of Literary Forgery's Most Notorious Practitioners* (New Castle, Delaware: Oak Knoll Press, 1999), 57–105.
8. Rosenblum, 74.
9. Rosenblum, 98.

Chapter 16

1. "John Herschel." *Wikipedia*. http://en.wikipedia.org/wiki/John_Herschel.
2. "Telegraphy." *Wikipedia*. http://en.wikipedia.org/wiki/Telegraph.
3. J. Donald Fernie, "Marginalia: The Great Moon Hoax," *American Scientist* 81, 2 (March 1993): 120–122.
4. "John Herschel," Wikipedia.
5. Locke, Richard Adams. *Moon Hoax: Or, A Discovery That the Moon Has a Vast Population of Human Beings* [reprint of the 1835 series]. New York: William Gowans, 1859.
6. Maliszewski, Paul. "Paper Moon." *The Wilson Quarterly* 29, 1 (Winter 2005): 26–34.
7. Maliszewski, "Paper Moon."
8. Castagnaro, Mario. "Lunar Fancies and Earthly Truths: The Moon Hoax of 1835 and the Penny Press." *Nineteenth-Century Contexts* 34, 3 (July 2012): 253–268.
9. Maliszewski, "Paper Moon."
10. Fernie, "Marginalia."
11. Maliszewski, "Paper Moon."
12. Fernie, "Marginalia."
13. Maliszewski, "Paper Moon."
14. Heber D. Curtis, "Voyages to the Moon," *Publications of the Astronomical Society of the Pacific* 32, 186 (April 1920): 145–150.
15. "*Comical History of the States and Empires of the Moon,*" Wikipedia, http://en.wikipedia.org/wiki/Comical_History_of_the_States_and_Empires_of_the_Moon.
16. "The Unparalleled Adventure of One Hans Pfaall," Wikipedia, http://en.wikipedia.org/wiki/The_Unparalleled_Adventure_of_One_Hans_Pfaall.
17. Castagnaro, "Lunar Fancies and Earthly Truths."
18. Castagnaro, "Lunar Fancies and Earthly Truths."
19. Smith, Moira. "Arbiters of Truth at Play: Media April Fools' Day Hoaxes." *Folklore* 120, 3 (December 2009): 274–290.

Chapter 17

1. Andrew Newman, "The 'Walam Olum': An Indigenous Apocrypha and Its Readers," *American Literary History* 22, 1 (Spring 2010): 27.
2. "Indian Removal Act," Primary Documents in American History, Library of Congress, https://www.loc.gov/rr/program/bib/ourdocs/Indian.html.
3. Rafinesque, *American Nations*, quoted by Newman, 39.
4. C.S. Rafinesque, *A Life of Travels and Researches in North America and South Europe* (Philadelphia: Printed for the author by F. Turner, 1836).
5. Charles Boewe, "The Manuscripts of C. S. Rafinesque (1783–1840)," *Proceedings of the American Philosophical Society* 102, 6 (December 15, 1958): 590–595.
6. "Constantine Samuel Rafinesque," Wikipedia. http://en.wikipedia.org/wiki/Constantine_Samuel_Rafinesque (accessed 10/24/2015).
7. Newman, 31.

8. For example, William Barlow and David O. Powell, "'The Late Dr. Ward of Indiana': Rafinesque's Source of the Walam Olum," *Indiana Magazine of History* 82, 2 (June 1986): 185–193.
9. Newman, 31.
10. Newman, 36.
11. Newman, 37.
12. James Loewen, "Introduction to *Lies My Teachers Told Me*," sundown.afro.illinois.edu/content.php?file=liesmyteachertoldme-introduction.html (accessed 11/14/2015).
13. Frances Fitzgerald, *America Revised: History Schoolbooks in the Twentieth Century* (Boston: Little, Brown, 1979).
14. Charles C. Mann, *1491: New Revelations of the Americas Before Columbus*, 2nd ed. (New York: Vintage Books, 2011).
15. James Loewen, "Introduction to *Lies My Teachers Told Me*."

Chapter 18

1. Kenneth S. Greenberg, "The Nose, the Lie, and the Duel in the Antebellum South." *The American Historical Review* 95, 1 (February 1990): 57–74.
2. Neil Harris, *Humbug: The Art of P.T. Barnum* (Boston: Little, Brown and Company, 1973), 63.
3. Greenberg.
4. Wikipedia, "Scudder's American Museum," https://en.wikipedia.org/wiki/Scudder%27s_American_Museum (accessed 10/24/2015).
5. "Merman: Part Monkey, Part Fish," British Museum, archive.org/web/20151017210533/http://www.britishmuseum.org/explore/highlights/highlight_objects/asia/m/merman_part_monkey,_part_fish.aspx.
6. Steven C. Levi, "P.T. Barnum and the Feejee Mermaid," *Western Folklore* 36, 2 (April 1977): 149–154.
7. Harris, 65.
8. Barnum, P. T. *Struggles and Triumphs: Or, Forty Years' Recollections* (Buffalo, NY: Warren, Johnson & Co., 1873),
9. "Dead Mermaid Found?" AboutEntertainment. http://urbanlegends.about.com/od/mythicalcreatures/ss/Pictures-Mermaid-Found-After-Tsunami.htm.
10. "Unmasking the Mysterious Merman." Horniman Museum and Gardens. http://www.horniman.ac.uk/collections/unmasking-the-mysterious-merman.
11. "Buxton Mermaid Origins Probed at University of Lincoln," BBC News (February 15, 2012): http://www.bbc.com/news/uk-england-17038668.
12. Paolo Viscardi, "Mysterious Mermaid Stripped Naked," *The Guardian* (April 16, 2014): http://www.theguardian.com/science/animal-magic/2014/apr/16/mermaid-stripped-naked.

Chapter 19

1. A. Leah Underhill, *The Missing Link in Modern Spiritualism* (New York: Thomas R. Knox & Co., 1885), 6.
2. Reuben Briggs Davenport, *The Death-Blow to Spiritualism: Being the True Story of the Fox Sisters, As Revealed by Margaret Fox Kane and Catherine Fox Jencken* (New York: G. W. Dillingham, 1888), 36.
3. Davenport, 116.
4. Underhill, *The Missing Link*, 55.
5. David Chapin, "The Fox Sisters and the Performance of Mystery," *New York History* 81, 2 (2000): 168.

6. Anna Branford, "Gould and the Fairies," *Australian Journal of Anthropology* 22, 1 (April 2011): 89–103.
7. Davenport, 16.
8. Walker, "Humbug," 56.

9. Walker, "Humbug," 55.
10. Inflation Calculator, http://www.davemanuel.com/inflation-calculator.php.
11. "German Jews and Peddling in America." German-American Business Biographies. Immigrant Entrepreneurship: 1720 to the Present. http://immigrantentrepreneurship.org/entry.php?rec=191.
12. "Electrical Telegraph," Wikipedia, http://en.wikipedia.org/wiki/Electrical_telegraph.
13. Molly McGarry, *Ghosts of Futures Past: Spiritualism and the Cultural Politics of Nineteenth-Century America* (Berkeley: University of California Press, 2008), 20.
14. Underhill, *The Missing Link*, 55–56.

Chapter 20
1. Erwin G. Gudde, "The Vizetelly Hoax," *Pacific Historical Review* 28, 3 (August, 1959): 233–236.
2. Brooks, J. Tyrwhit, M.D. *Four Months among the Gold-Finders in California: Being the Diary of an Expedition from San Francisco to the Gold Districts.* New York: D. Appleton & Co., 1849. https://archive.org/details/fourmonthsamongg00vizerich.
3. Gudde, "The Vizetelly Hoax."
4. Library of Congress metadata for *Four Months among the Gold-Finders in Alta California.* http://lccn.loc.gov/rc01000765.
5. Gudde, "Vizetelly Hoax."
6. "Treaty of Guadalupe Hidalgo," Wikipedia, http://en.wikipedia.org/wiki/Treaty_of_Guadalupe_Hidalgo.
7. "California Gold Rush Statistics: By the Numbers," Shmoop.com, http://www.shmoop.com/california-gold-rush/statistics.html (accessed 10/25/2015).
8. Mary A. Jordan, *They Followed the Sea. Captain Oliver Jordan of Thomaston, Maine, 1789–1879, His Sons and His Daughters and the Ships They Built, Sailed, and Commanded* (Boston, MA: privately printed, 1942), 11; Charles E. Ranlett, *Master Mariner of Maine: Being the Reminiscences of Charles Everett Ranlett, 1816–1917* (Searsport, ME: Penobscot Marine Museum, 1942).

Chapter 21
1. Mark Rose, "When Giants Roamed the Earth," *Archaeology* 58, 6 (November 2005): 30–35.
2. Barbara Franco, "The Cardiff Giant: A Hundred Year Old Hoax," *New York History* 50, 4 (October 1969): 420–440.
3. Franco.
4. Othniel C. Marsh, Letter on the Cardiff Giant, November 24, 1869. Printed in Rochester *Daily Union* ("The Cardiff Giant a Humbug"). "December Meeting: The 'Cardiff Giant' Controversy." *Proceedings of the Massachusetts Historical Society* 11 (1869–1870): 161–162.
5. Franco.
6. Michael Pettit, "'The Joy in Believing': The Cardiff Giant, Commercial Deceptions, and Styles of Observation in Gilded Age America," *Isis* 97, 4 (December 2006): 659–677.
7. Franco.

8. "Typical Wages in 1860 through 1890." Outrun Change: http://outrunchange.com/2012/06/14/typical-wages-in-1860-through-1890/.

9. Franco.

10. Rose.

11. Pettit.

12. Franco.

13. Pettit.

14. Mark Twain, "Letters from Washington, Number IX, *Territorial Enterprise*" (March 7, 1868). Quoted at TwainQuotes.com: twainquotes.com/teindex.html.

15. Fred Fedler, "A Journalist's Favorite Hoax: Petrifactions." HistoryBuff.com: web.archive.org/web/20150402210830/http://www.historybuff.com/library/refpetrification.html.

Chapter 22

1. Arthur W. J. G. Ord-Hume, *Perpetual Motion: The History of an Obsession* (New York: St. Martin's Press, 1977), 139.

2. Daniel W. Hering, *Foibles and Fallacies of Science: An Account of Celebrated Scientific Vagaries* (New York: Van Nostrand, 1924), 94.

3. "Inflation Calculator," Dave Manuel.com, davemanuel.com/inflation-calculator.php? (accessed 10/26/2015).

4. Hering, 93.

5. Ord-Hume, 141.

6. Hering, 94.

7. D. Simanek, "The Keely Motor Company," https://www.lhup.edu/~dsimanek/museum/keely/keely.htm.

8. Ord-Hume, 142.

9. Ord-Hume, 147–149.

10. SVPwiki Home Page, http://pondscienceinstitute.on-rev.com/svpwiki/tiki-index.php.

11. Thomas S. Kuhn, *The Structure of Scientific Revolutions*, 2nd ed., enlarged (Chicago: University of Chicago Press, 1970), 18.

12. Daniel W. Hering, *Foibles and Fallacies of Science: An Account of Celebrated Scientific Vagaries* (New York: Van Nostrand, 1924), 72, 76.

13. Wikipedia, "Conservation of Energy," http://en.wikipedia.org/wiki/Conservation_of_energy; "First Law of Thermodynamics," http://en.wikipedia.org/wiki/First_law_of_thermodynamics.

14. Clara Jessup Moore, *Keely and His Discoveries: Aerial Navigation* (London: Keegan Paul, 1893), 353.

Chapter 23

1. Titus Oates, "The Wayward Encyclopedias," *The New Yorker* (March 31): 48–52.

2. Frank M. O'Brien, "The Wayward Encyclopedias," *New Yorker* (May 2, 1936): 55–58.

3. Margaret Castle Schindler, "Fictitious Biography," *The American Historical Review* 42, 4 (July 1937): 682.

4. Schindler, 683–684.

5. John Blythe Dobson, "The Spurious Articles in *Appleton's Cyclopaedia of American Biography*—Some New Discoveries and Considerations," *Biography* 16, 4 (Fall 1993): 400.

6. Schindler, 688.

7. Dobson, 399.

8. Schindler, 689.

9. Dobson, 400.

10. Wikipedia, "Reliability of Wikipedia," http://en.wikipedia.org/wiki/Reliability_of_Wikipedia.
11. Natalie Wolchover, "How Accurate Is Wikipedia?" *LiveScience.com* (January 24, 2011): livescience.com/32950-how-accurate-is-wikipedia.html.

Chapter 24

1. Wikipedia. "Lubec, Maine." en.wikipedia.org/wiki/Lubec,_Maine.
2. Jackson Murphy, "Prescott Jernegan and the Gold from Seawater Swindle," *The Martha's Vineyard Times* (July 25, 2012): mvtimes.com/2012/07/25/prescott-jernegan-gold-from-seawater-swindle-11663/.
3. Brett J. Stubbs, "'Sunbeams from Cucumbers': An Early Twentieth-Century Gold-from-Seawater Extraction Scheme in Northern New South Wales," *Australasian Historical Archaeology* 26 (2008): 5–12.
4. Clark C. Spence, "I Was a Stranger and Ye Took Me In," *Montana: The Magazine of Western History* 44, 1 (Winter 1994): 42–53.
5. Murphy, "Prescott Jernegan."
6. Murphy, "Prescott Jernegan."
7. "Gold from the Sea." *Scientific American* 79, 7 (August 13, 1898): 99.
8. Murphy, "Prescott Jernegan."
9. Jennifer Multhopp, "Klondike: Lubec's Gold from Sea Water Hoax," *Lubec, Maine: A Border Town Shaped by the Sea*: lubec.mainememory.net/page/960/display.html.
10. "The Salt Water Gold Mine: The Concern May Be Bought for a Sardine Factory," *New York Times* (October 10, 1898).
11. Murphy, "Prescott Jernegan."
12. "Gold from the Sea." *Scientific American* 79, 7 (August 13, 1898): 99.
13. National Ocean Service, "Is There Gold in the Ocean?" oceanservice.noaa.gov/facts/gold.html.

Chapter 25

1. Samuel Eliot Morison, *The European Discovery of America: The Northern Voyages, A.D. 500–1600* (New York: Oxford University Press, 1971), 76.
2. Laurence M. Larson, "The Kensington Rune Stone," *The Wisconsin Magazine of History* 4, 4 (June 1921): 382–387.
3. Theodore C. Blegen, "Frederick J. Turner and the Kensington Puzzle," *Minnesota History* 39, 4 (Winter 1964): 133–140.
4. MHS Collections, "The Case of the Gran Tapes: Further Evidence on the Rune Stone Riddle," *Minnesota History* 45, 4 (Winter 1976): 152–156.
5. MHS, "The Case of the Gran Tapes."
6. MHS, "The Case of the Gran Tapes."
7. Russell W. Fridley, "Debate Continues over Kensington Rune Stone," *Minnesota History* 45, 4 (Winter 1976): 149–151.
8. Morison, 76.
9. Russell W. Fridley, "Debate Continues over Kensington Rune Stone," *Minnesota History* 45, 4 (Winter 1976): 149–151.
10. MHS, "The Case of the Gran Tapes."
11. Eric A. Powell, "The Kensington Code," *Archaeology* 63, 3 (May/June 2010). http://archive.archaeology.org/1005/abstracts/insider.html.
12. MHS, "The Case of the Gran Tapes."

13. Brittany Jackson and Mark Rose, "Saitaphernes' Golden Tiara," *Archaeology* (2009): archive.archaeology.org/online/features/hoaxes/saitaphernes_tiara.html (accessed 11/16/2015).
14. Wikipedia, "Tiara of Saitaferne," en.wikipedia.org/wiki/Tiara_of_Saitaferne (accessed 11/16/2015).
15. Sotheby's, "291: 'The Rouchomovsky Skeleton,'" sothebys.com/en/auctions/ecatalogue/2013/a-treasured-legacy-steinhardt-n08961/lot.291.html (accessed 11/16/2015).

Chapter 26

1. Binjamin W. Segel, *A Lie and a Libel: The History of the* Protocols of the Elders of Zion, translated and edited by Richard S. Levy (Lincoln: University of Nebraska Press, 1995), xi.
2. Wikipedia, "Maurice Joly," http://en.wikipedia.org/wiki/Maurice_Joly.
3. Stephen Eric Bronner, *A Rumor about the Jews: Reflections on Antisemitism and the* Protocols of the Learned Elders of Zion (New York: St. Martin's Press, 2000), 88–89.
4. Bronner, 89.
5. Wikipedia, "Revolution of 1905," en.wikipedia.org/wiki/Revolution_of_1905 (accessed 10/26/2015).
6. Bronner, 89.
7. Binjamin W. Segel, *A Lie and a Libel* (Lincoln: University of Nebraska Press, 1995), 60.
8. Bronner, 80.
9. Segel, xii–xiii.
10. Segel, 29.
11. Bronner, 118–123.
12. Segel, xiii.
13. Martin J. Plax, "On Extremism in Our Time," *Society 50* (2013): 196–203. (199)
14. Gale Eaton, *History of Civilization in 50 Disasters* (Thomaston, ME: Tilbury House, 2015).
15. Roger D. Launius, "Denying the Apollo Moon Landings: Conspiracy and Questioning in Modern American History" (Orlando, FL: 48th AIAA Aerospace Sciences Meeting, January 4–7, 2010).

Chapter 27

1. Davis, Wes. "A Fool There Was." *New York Times* (April 1, 2006): http://www.nytimes.com/2006/04/01/opinion/01davis.html.
2. "The Dreadnought Hoax." Wikipedia. http://en.wikipedia.org/wiki/Dreadnought_hoax.
3. "A Dreadnought Hoax: 'Prince Makalin of Abyssinia.'" (London, February 18, 1910; published in the *Hobart Mercury*, Tasmania, 24 March 1910): http://upload.wikimedia.org/wikipedia/commons/f/f9/DreadnoughtHoaxHobartMercury24March1910.jpg.
4. Popova, Maria. "The Dreadnought Hoax: Young Virginia Woolf and Her Bloomsbury Posse Prank the Royal Navy in Drag and a Turban." Brainpickings. http://www.brainpickings.org/2014/02/07/dreadnought-hoax-virginia-woolf/ (accessed 10/26/2015).
5. "A Dreadnought Hoax."
6. Popova, "The Dreadnought Hoax."
7. Jones, Danell. "The Dreadnought Hoax and the Theatres of War." *Literature & History* 22, 1 (Spring 2013): 80–94.
8. Jones.
9. Jones.

10. Miranda Carter, *George, Nicholas and Wilhelm: Three Royal Cousins and the Road to World War I* (New York: Alfred A. Knopf, 2010), 298.
11. "HMS *Dreadnought* (1906)." Wikipedia. http://en.wikipedia.org/wiki/HMS_Dreadnought_(1906).
12. Wikipedia, "Dreadnought Hoax," en.wikipedia.org/wiki/Dreadnought_hoax (accessed 10/26/2015).

Chapter 28

1. Martin Hinton, letter to Joseph Weiner, May 11, 1955; quoted in Dean Falk, *The Fossil Chronicles* (Berkeley: University of California Press, 2011), 18.
2. Kenneth P. Oakley, and J.S. Weiner, "Piltdown Man," *American Scientist* 43, 4 (October 1955): 573–583.
3. Oakley and Weiner, "Piltdown Man."
4. John H. Langdon, "Misinterpreting Piltdown," *Current Anthropology* 32, 5 (December 1991): 627–631.
5. Dean Falk, *Fossil Chronicles*.
6. Kenneth L. Feder, *Frauds, Myths, and Mysteries: Science and Pseudoscience in Archaeology*. 4th ed. (New York: McGraw-Hill, 2002), 72.
7. Oakley and Weiner, "Piltdown Man."
8. Langdon, "Misinterpreting Piltdown."
9. Langdon, "Misinterpreting Piltdown."
10. Falk, *Fossil Chronicles*, 19.
11. S. L. Washburn, "The Piltdown Hoax," *American Anthropologist* 55, 5 (December 1953): 759–762.
12. "Piltdown Man Is a Hoax" *Science News Letter* (November 28, 1953): 350.
13. "Neanderthal," Wikipedia, http://en.wikipedia.org/wiki/Neanderthal.
14. "Ancient DNA and Neanderthals: What Does It Mean to Be Human?" Smithsonian National Museum of Natural History. http://humanorigins.si.edu/evidence/genetics/ancient-dna-and-neanderthals.
15. Leland C. Bement, Ernest L. Lundelius Jr., and Richard A. Ketcham, "Hoax or History: A Bison Skull with Embedded Calf Creek Projectile Point," *Plains Anthropologist* 50, 195 (August 2005): 221–226.
16. "The Piltdown Chicken," Hoaxes.org: hoaxes.org/archive/permalink/the_piltdown_chicken.

Chapter 29

1. Joseph Knowles, *Alone in the Wilderness* (Boston: Small, Maynard & Company, 1913), 70.
2. Knowles, *Alone*, 4.
3. Jim Motavalli, *Naked in the Woods: Joseph Knowles and the Legacy of Frontier Fakery* (Cambridge, MA: Da Capo Press, 2007), 2.
4. Motavalli, *Naked*, 63.
5. Motavalli, *Naked*, 68.
6. Motavalli, *Naked*, 200.
7. Boyer, Richard O. "Where Are They Now? The Nature Man." *The New Yorker* (June 18, 1938): 21–25.
8. Cliff Aliperti, "The Half Naked Truth about Harry Reichenbach," Immortal Ephemera (September 17, 2012): http://immortalephemera.com/23105/press-agent-harry-reichenbach/.
9. "The September Morn Hoax," Hoaxes.org, http://hoaxes.org/archive/permalink/the_september_morn_hoax.

10. "Biosphere 2." Wikipedia. https://en.wikipedia.org/wiki/Biosphere_2.
11. Armagh Planetarium. "Whatever Happened to Biosphere 2?" (March 26, 2013): http://www.armaghplanet.com/blog/whatever-happened-to-biosphere-2.html.
12. Knowles, *Alone*, 79–80.

Chapter 30

1. William Jay Smith, *The Spectra Hoax* (Middletown, CT: Wesleyan University Press, 1961), 15.
2. "Amy Lowell (1874–1925)," Poetry Foundation, http://www.poetryfoundation.org/bio/amy-lowell.
3. William Jay Smith, *The Spectra Hoax* (Middletown, CT: Wesleyan University Press, 1961), 3–4.
4. Smith, *Spectra Hoax*, 27.
5. Smith, *Spectra Hoax*, 28.
6. Smith, *Spectra Hoax*, 28.
7. Smith, *Spectra Hoax*, 28–29.
8. Audrey Russek, "'So Many Useful Women': The Pseudonymous Poetry of Marjorie Allen Seiffert, 1916–1938," *Tulsa Studies in Women's Literature* 28, 1 (Spring 2009): 75–96.
9. Suzanne W. Churchill, "The Lying Game: *Others* and the Great Spectra Hoax of 1917," *American Periodicals* 15, 1 (2005): 24.
10. Smith, *Spectra Hoax*, 112.
11. Smith, *Spectra Hoax*, 141.

Chapter 31

1. Mitchell Zuckoff, "Ponzi's Scheme: The True Story of a Financial Legend" (New York: Random House, 2005), 19–25.
2. "Charles Ponzi," Wikipedia, https://en.wikipedia.org/wiki/Charles_Ponzi.
3. Zuckoff, 84–85.
4. Zuckoff, 93–95.
5. Zuckoff, 116.
6. Zuckoff, 187.
7. Ralph Blumenthal, "Lost Manuscript Unmasks Details of Original Ponzi," *New York Times* (May 4, 2009): http://www.nytimes.com/2009/05/05/nyregion/05ponzi.html?_r=0.
8. Zuckoff, 297.
9. "Chain Letters," Scamwatch, http://www.scamwatch.gov.au/content/index.phtml/itemId/694296.
10. New York Times, "Times Topics: Ponzi Schemes," topics.nytimes.com/top/reference/timestopics/subjects/f/frauds_and_swindling/ponzi_schemes/index.html?8qa.

Chapter 32

1. Alex Owen, "'Borderland Forms': Arthur Conan Doyle, Albion's Daughters, and the Politics of the Cottingley Fairies," *History Workshop* 38 (1994): 48–85.
2. Joe Cooper, "Cottingley: At Last the Truth," *The Unexplained*, 117 (1982): 2338–40. Text reproduced at https://www.lhup.edu/~dsimanek/cooper.htm.
3. Sir Arthur Conan Doyle, *The Coming of the Fairies* (New York: George H. Doran Co., 1922), 13. Accessed at https://archive.org/details/comingoffairies00doylrich.
4. Doyle, 25.
5. Cooper.
6. "Arthur Conan Doyle," Wikipedia, http://en.wikipedia.org/wiki/Arthur_Conan_Doyle.

7. Owen.
8. Anna Branford, "Gould and the Fairies," *Australian Journal of Anthropology* 22, 1 (April 2011): 97.
9. Doyle, *Coming of the Fairies*, 41.
10. Doyle, 124.
11. Doyle, v.

Chapter 33
1. Peter Kurth, *Anastasia: The Riddle of Anna Anderson* (Boston: Little, Brown and Company, 1983).
2. "Appeal in Anastasia Mystery Is Rejected by Hamburg Court: Anna Anderson Loses Plea to Be Acknowledged as Only Survivor in Czar's Family," *New York Times* (March 1, 1967).
3. Hugh Brewster, *Anastasia's Album* (New York: A Hyperion Madison Press Book, 1996).
4. Brewster, *Anastasia's Album*, 46.
5. Frances Welch, *A Romanov Fantasy: Life at the Court of Anna Anderson* (New York: W. W. Norton, 2007), 98–101.
6. Kurth, *Anastasia*, 34.
7. Kurth, *Anastasia*, 144.
8. "Anna Anderson." Wikipedia. https://en.wikipedia.org/?title=Anna_Anderson.
9. "Princess Caraboo," The Hoax Museum, http://hoaxes.org/archive/permalink/princess_caraboo.

Chapter 34
1. David Jaher, *The Witch of Lime Street* (New York: Crown, 2015), 82.
2. Wikipedia, "Séance," en.wikipedia.org/wiki/S%C3%A9ance#S.C3.A9ance_tools_and_techniques.
3. Wikipedia, "Automatic Writing," en.wikipedia.org/wiki/Automatic_writing.
4. Kenneth Silverman, *Houdini!!! The Career of Ehrich Weiss* (New York: Harper Collins, 1996), 281–84.
5. Jaher, *Witch*, 84–85, 122–126.
6. Lisa Hix, "Ghosts in the Machines: The Devices and Daring Mediums That Spoke for the Dead," *Collectors Weekly* (October 29, 2014): collectorsweekly.com/articles/ghosts-in-the-machines-the-devices-and-defiant-mediums-that-spoke-for-the-spirits/.
7. Daniel Stashower, "Mina Crandon & Harry Houdini: The Medium and the Magician," *American History* (August 1999): historynet.com/mina-crandon-harry-houdini-the-medium-and-the-magician.htm.
8. Wikipedia, "Harry Houdini," https://en.wikipedia.org/wiki/Harry_Houdini.
9. Henry Ridgely Evans, "Madame Blavatsky," *The Monist* 14, 3 (April 1904): 387.
10. Wikipedia, "Joseph Smith," https://en.wikipedia.org/wiki/Joseph_Smith.
11. K. Paul Johnson, *The Masters Revealed: Madame Blavatsky and the Myth of the Great White Lodge* (Albany: State University of New York Press, 1994).
12. Evans, "Madame Blavatsky."
13. J. Barton Scott, "Miracle Publics: Theosophy, Christianity, and the Coulomb Affair," *History of Religions* 49, 2 (November 2009): 172–196.
14. Stephen Prothero, "From Spiritualism to Theosophy: 'Uplifting' a Democratic Tradition," *Religion and American Culture: A Journal of Interpretation* 3, 2 (Summer 1993): 197–216.

Chapter 35

1. "'The Count' Escapes Jail on Sheet Rope: International Crook Drops 50 Feet to Street in Sight of Hundreds on West Side," *New York Times* (September 2, 1935): http://query.nytimes.com/gst/abstract.html?res=9E00E0DB113EE53ABC4A53DFBF66838E629 EDE.
2. Pizzoli, Greg. *The Impossibly True Story of Tricky Vic, the Man Who Sold the Eiffel Tower*. New York: Viking, 2015.
3. "Victor Lustig," Wikipedia, https://en.wikipedia.org/wiki/Victor_Lustig.
4. "'The Count' Escapes."
5. Gilbert King, "The Smoothest Con Man That Ever Lived," Smithsonian.com (August 22, 2012): http://www.smithsonianmag.com/history/the-smoothest-con-man-that-ever-lived-29861908/?no-ist=.
6. "Confidence Man Jailed," *New York Times* (July 8, 1928): http://query.nytimes.com/gst/abstract.html?res=9902E1D91238E23ABC4053DFB1668383639EDE.
7. "George C. Parker," Wikipedia, https://en.wikipedia.org/wiki/George_C._Parker.
8. Elizabeth Palermo, "Eiffel Tower: Information and Facts," LiveScience.com (May 7, 2013): http://www.livescience.com/29391-eiffel-tower.html.
9. "Eiffel Tower." Wikipedia. https://en.wikipedia.org/wiki/Eiffel_Tower.

Chapter 36

1. "Loch Ness." Wikipedia. https://en.wikipedia.org/wiki/Loch_Ness.
2. T. N. Johnston, "The Bathymetrical Survey of Loch Ness," *The Geographical Journal* 24, 4 (October 1904): 429–430.
3. "Strange Spectacle on Loch Ness," *Inverness Courier* (May 2, 1933), quoted in Ronald Binns, *The Loch Ness Mystery Solved* (Buffalo, NY: Prometheus Books, 1984), 9–10.
4. Binns, *Loch Ness Mystery Solved*, 11.
5. Binns, *Loch Ness Mystery Solved*, 28.
6. "The Surgeon's Photo," Museum of Hoaxes, http://hoaxes.org/photo_database/image/the_surgeons_photo/.
7. Austin E. Fife, contributor, "Loch Ness Monster," *Western Folklore*, 18, 1 (January 1959): 53.
8. Karl Borch, "The Monster in Loch Ness," *The Journal of Risk and Insurance* 43, 3 (September 1976): 521–525.
9. Binns, 154.
10. "The Body of Nessie Found," Museum of Hoaxes: hoaxes.org/af_database/permalink/the_body_of_nessie_found.
11. R.W. Sheldon and S.R. Kerr, "The Population Density of Monsters in Loch Ness," *Limnology and Oceanography* 17, 5 (Sep., 1972): 796–798.
12. The Official Loch Ness Sightings Register, http://www.lochnesssightings.com/.
13. Liz Fields, "Loch Ness Monster Reportings on the Rise after Sighting on Apple Maps." ABC News (April 20, 2014): http://abcnews.go.com/International/loch-ness-monster-report-rise-sighting-apple-maps/story?id=23394714.
14. Oliver Smith, "Has Google Found the Loch Ness Monster?" Telegraph (April 21, 2015): http://www.telegraph.co.uk/travel/destinations/europe/uk/scotland/11549549/Has-Google-found-the-Loch-Ness-Monster.html.
15. Micah Singleton, "Google Maps Lets You Search for the Loch Ness Monster from Your Couch," *The Verge* (April 21, 2015): http://www.theverge.com/2015/4/21/8463031/google-maps-loch-ness-monster.

16. Kevin S. McKelvey, Keith B. Aubry, and Michael K. Schwartz, "Using Anecdotal Occurrence Data for Rare or Elusive Species: The Illusion of Reality and a Call for Evidentiary Standards," *BioScience* 58, 6 (June 2008): 549–555.
17. "'Nessie': What's in an Anagram?" *Science, New Series*, 191, 4222 (January 9, 1976): 54.

Chapter 37

1. Robert E. Bartholomew and Benjamin Radford, *The Martians Have Landed! A History of Media-Driven Panics and Hoaxes* (Jefferson, NC: McFarland & Company, 2012), 16.
2. Bartholomew and Radford, 16–17.
3. "Orson Welles—Mercury Theatre—1938 Recordings." https://archive.org/details/OrsonWelles-MercuryTheater-1938Recordings.
4. Karl Erik Rosengren, Peter Arvidson, and Dahn Sturesson, "The Barsebäck 'Panic': A Radio Programme as a Negative Summary Event," *Acta Sociologica* 18, 4 (1975): 303–321.
5. "Radio Listeners in Panic, Taking War Drama as Fact." *New York Times* (October 31, 1938): http://query.nytimes.com/mem/archive-free/pdf?res=9800E6DA163BEE3ABC4950DFB6678383629EDE.
6. "Radio Listeners in Panic."
7. "Orson Welles—Mercury Theatre—1938 Recordings."
8. Bartholomew and Radford, 18.
9. "Radio Listeners in Panic."
10. "Radio's *War of the Worlds* Broadcast: 1938." http://jeff560.tripod.com/wotw.html.
11. "Radio Listeners in Panic."
12. Oxenford, David. "Orson Welles' War of the Worlds 75 Years Later: What Would the FCC Do Now?" Broadcast Law Blog (October 31, 2013): http://www.broadcastlawblog.com/2013/10/articles/orson-welles-war-of-the-worlds-75-years-later-what-would-the-fcc-do-now/.
13. "Broadcasting the Barricades," War of the Worlds Invasion: Historical Perspective, http://www.war-of-the-worlds.co.uk/broadcasting_the_barricade_ronald_knox.htm.

Chapter 38

1. Anthony Cave Brown, *Bodyguard of Lies* (New York: Harper & Row, 1975): 278–289.
2. Cave Brown, *Bodyguard*, 285.
3. Klaus Gottlieb, "The Mincemeat Postmortem: Forensic Aspects of World War II's Boldest Counterintelligence Operation," *Military Medicine* 174, 1 (January 2009): 93–99.
4. Cave Brown, *Bodyguard*.
5. Thaddeus Holt, *The Deceivers: Allied Military Deception in the Second World War* (New York: Scribner, 2004), 371.
6. Gottlieb, "Mincemeat Postmortem."
7. Gottlieb, "Mincemeat Postmortem," 95.
8. Malcolm Gladwell, "Pandora's Briefcase," *The New Yorker* (May 10, 2010): newyorker.com/magazine/2010/05/10/pandoras-briefcase.
9. Holt, *Deceivers*, 375.
10. Gladwell, "Pandora's Briefcase."
11. Holt, *Deceivers*, 372.
12. David Baker, "The Optical Cargo That Wasn't," *Optician* 244, 6382 (December 14, 2012): 18–19.
13. Holt, *Deceivers*, 377.
14. Holt, *Deceivers*, 378.
15. Holt, *Deceivers*, 379.
16. Cave Brown, *Bodyguard*, 279–281.

Chapter 39

1. Wikipedia, "Netherlands in World War II," en.wikipedia.org/wiki/Netherlands_in_World_War_II.
2. Jonathon Keats, *Forged: Why Fakes Are the Great Art of Our Age* (New York: Oxford University Press, 2013), 86.
3. Hope B. Werness, "Han van Meegeren *fecit*," in Dennis Dutton, ed., *The Forger's Art: Forgery and the Philosophy of Art* (Berkeley: University of California Press, 1983), 4–5.
4. Werness, "Han van Meegeren *fecit*," 18.
5. Werness, "Han van Meegeren *fecit*," 31.
6. Paula Marantz Cohen, "The Meanings of Forgery," *Southwest Review* 97, 3 (2012): 15.
7. Thomas P. F. Hoving, "The Game of Duplicity," *The Metropolitan Museum of Art Bulletin*, New Series 26, 6 (February 1968): 241–246.
8. Theodore Rousseau, "The Stylistic Detection of Forgeries," *The Metropolitan Museum of Art Bulletin*, New Series 26, 6 (February 1968): 247–252.
9. Werness, "Han van Meegeren *fecit*," 30.
10. Stuart Fleming, "Art Forgery: Some Scientific Defenses," *Proceedings of the American Philosophical Society* 130, 2 (June 1986): 175–195.
11. Rousseau, "Stylistic Detection."
12. Werness, "Han van Meegeren *fecit*," 45.
13. "John Marshall Phillips [obituary]," *Bulletin of the Associates in Fine Arts at Yale* 21, 1 (October 1953): n.p.

Chapter 40

1. Paul Gillingham, *Cuauhtémoc's Bones: Forging Identity in Modern Mexico* (Albuquerque: University of New Mexico Press, 2011), 62.
2. Gillingham, 66–67.
3. Gillingham, Paul. "The Emperor of Ixcateopan: Fraud, Nationalism and Memory in Modern Mexico," *Journal of Latin American Studies* 37, 3 (August 2005): 561–584.
4. Christopher Fulton, "Siqueiros against the Myth: Paeans to Cuautémoc, Last of the Aztec Emperors," *Oxford Art Journal* 32, 1 (2009): 67, 69–93
5. "Notes and Comments," *The Catholic Historical Review* 36, 3 (October 1950): 338–339.
6. Wikipedia, "Edward I of England," en.wikipedia.org/wiki/Edward_I_of_England (accessed 10/29/2015).
7. Brittany Jackson and Mark Rose, "Tarragona Two-Step," *Archaeology Archive*: http://archive.archaeology.org/online/features/hoaxes/.

Chapter 41

1. "Gypsy Moth IV," Wikipedia, https://en.wikipedia.org/wiki/Gipsy_Moth_IV.
2. Nicholas Tomalin and Ron Hall, *The Strange Last Voyage of Donald Crowhurst* (New York: Stein & Day, 1970), 53–54.
3. Tomalin and Hall, 116.
4. Jonathan Raban, introduction, Nicholas Tomalin and Ron Hall, *The Strange Last Voyage of Donald Crowhurst* (Camden, ME: International Marine Publications, 1995), xv.
5. "Timeline of Computer History," Computer History Museum, http://www.computerhistory.org/timeline/?category=cmptr.
6. Science of the 34th America's Cup, National Sailing Hall of Fame, http://www.nshof.org/index.php?option=com_content&view=category&id=179:science-of-the-34th-americas-cup&layout=blog&Itemid=281.

Chapter 42

1. John Nance, *The Gentle Tasaday: A Stone Age People in the Philippine Rain Forest* (New York: Harcourt Brace Jovanovich, 1975).
2. Alvin H. Scaff, "Cultural Factors in Ecological Change on Mindanao in the Philippines," *Social Forces* 27, 2 (December 1948): 119–128.
3. Scaff, "Cultural Factors."
4. Nance, *Gentle Tasaday*, 7–8.
5. Robert McG. Thomas Jr., "Manuel Elizalde, 60, Dies; Defender of Primitive Tribe," *New York Times* (May 8, 1997): nytimes.com/1997/05/08/world/manuel-elizalde-60-dies-defender-of-primitive-tribe.html (accessed 7/4/2015).
6. Benjamin Thomas, "*National Geographic*, PANAMIN and the Stone-Age Tribe," *Dialectical Anthropology* 25, 1 (March 2000): 78.
7. Thomas N. Headland, "Introduction," in Headland, Thomas N., ed. *The Tasaday Controversy: Assessing the Evidence* (Washington, DC: American Anthropological Association, 1992), 9.
8. Nance, *Gentle Tasaday*, 50.
9. B. Thomas, "*National Geographic*, PANAMIN," 81.
10. Headland, "Introduction," 10.
11. Headland, "Introduction," 11; quoting Seth Mydans.
12. B. Thomas, "*National Geographic*, PANAMIN," 78.
13. B. Thomas, "*National Geographic*, PANAMIN," 81.
14. Thomas N. Headland, "Conclusion," in Headland, Thomas N., ed. *The Tasaday Controversy: Assessing the Evidence* (Washington, DC: American Anthropological Association, 1992), 217–218.
15. Carol H. Molony, "The Tasaday Language: Evidence for Authenticity?" in Headland, Thomas N., ed. *The Tasaday Controversy: Assessing the Evidence* (Washington, DC: American Anthropological Association, 1992), 107–116.
16. Traci Watson, "People Without Electricity Don't Get 8 Hours' Sleep Either," *National Geographic* (October 15, 2015): news.nationalgeographic.com/2015/10/20151015-paleo-sleep-time-hadza-san-tsimane-science/.
17. Survival International, "The Most Isolated Tribe in the World?" survivalinternational.org/campaigns/mostisolated.
18. Dan McDougall, "Survival Comes First for the Last Stone Age Tribe World," *The Guardian* (February 11, 2006): theguardian.com/world/2006/feb/12/theobserver.worldnews12.
19. World Health Organization. "Health of Indigenous Peoples." (October 2007). who.int/mediacentre/factsheets/fs326/en/.
20. Andrew Lawler, "Do the Amazon's Last Isolated Tribes Have a Future?" *New York Times* (August 8, 2015): nytimes.com/2015/08/09/opinion/sunday/do-the-amazons-last-isolated-tribes-have-a-future.html?_r=0.

Chapter 43

1. Clifford Irving, *The Hoax* (New York: Hyperion, 2006), vii–viii.
2. Mick Brown, "You Couldn't Make It Up," *The Telegraph* (July 28, 2007): telegraph.co.uk/culture/3666824/You-couldnt-make-it-up.html.
3. Wikipedia, "Howard Hughes," en.wikipedia.org/wiki/Howard_Hughes.
4. Irving, *Hoax*, 4–5.
5. Irving, *Hoax*, 80–88.
6. Irving, *Hoax*, 125.
7. Irving, *Hoax*, 147.
8. Irving, *Hoax*, 151.
9. Irving, *Hoax*, 246.

10. Brown, "You Couldn't Make It Up."
11. Brown, "You Couldn't Make It Up."
12. Wikipedia, "Misha: A Mémoire of the Holocaust Years," en.wikipedia.org/wiki/
    Misha:_A_M%C3%A9moire_of_the_Holocaust_Years (accessed 8/2/2015).
13. Dana Ford and Greg Botelho, "Who Is Rachel Dolezal?" CNN-News (June 17, 2015):
    cnn.com/2015/06/16/us/rachel-dolezal/ (accessed 8/2/2015).

Chapter 44

1. Wikipedia, "Apollo 11 in Popular Culture," en.wikipedia.org/wiki/
   Apollo_11_in_popular_culture.
2. Conspiracy Theories: Separating Fact from Fiction, "The Moon Landings
   Were Faked," Time (2009): content.time.com/time/specials/packages/arti-
   cle/0,28804,1860871_1860876_1860992,00.html.
3. Wikipedia, "Moon Landing," en.wikipedia.org/wiki/Moon_landing.
4. Tony Phillips, "The Great Moon Hoax: Moon Rocks and Common Sense Prove Apollo
   Astronauts Really Did Visit the Moon," NASA Science News (February 23, 2001): sci-
   ence.nasa.gov/science-news/science-at-nasa/2001/ast23feb_2/.
5. Philip Plait, "Fox News and the Apollo Moon Hoax," Bad Astronomy (February 13, 2001–
   June 11, 2011): badastronomy.com/bad/tv/foxapollo.html.
6. John Schwartz, "Vocal Minority Insists It Was All Smoke and Mirrors," New York Times
   (July 13, 2009): nytimes.com/2009/07/14/science/space/14hoax.html.
7. John Schwartz, "Vocal Minority Insists It Was All Smoke and Mirrors," New York Times
   (July 13, 2009): nytimes.com/2009/07/14/science/space/14hoax.html.
8. Ted Goertzel, "Belief in Conspiracy Theories," Political Psychology 15, 4 (December 1994):
   731–742.
9. Jay Windley, "Moon Base Clavius," clavius.org/why.html.
10. Neil deGrasse Tyson, "On the First Moon Landing," YouTube (July 28, 2012): youtube.
    com/watch?v=Q6ClA5f5uu0.
11. Neuman, Scott. "1 in 4 Americans Believes the Sun Goes Around the Earth, Survey Says."
    npr.org/sections/thetwo-way/2014/02/14/277058739/1-in-4-americans-think-the-sun-
    goes-around-the-earth-survey-says (accessed 12/4/2015).
12. National Science Foundation. Science and Engineering Indicators 2014. "Chapter 7: Sci-
    ence and Technology: Public Attitudes and Understanding." nsf.gov/statistics/seind14/
    index.cfm/chapter-7/c7h.htm#s2 (accessed 12/16/2015).

Chapter 45

1. Eric Pace, "Konrad Kujau, 62, 'Hitler Diaries' Swindler," New York Times (September 14,
   2000): nytimes.com/2000/09/14/world/konrad-kujau-62-hitler-diaries-swindler.html.
2. James M. Markham, "Hitler Diaries Plot, If There Was One, Thickens," New York Times
   (July 6, 1985): nytimes.com/1985/07/06/world/hitler-diaries-plot-if-there-was-one-
   thickens.html.
3. Museum of Hoaxes, "The Hitler Diaries," hoaxes.org/archive/permalink/the_hitler_diaries.
4. Eric Rentschler, "The Fascination of a Fake: The Hitler Diaries," New German Critique 90
   (Autumn 2003): 180.
5. Rentschler, "Fascination," 180.
6. "The Currency Converter," Coinmill.com: coinmill.com/DEM_USD.html.
7. Markham, "Hitler Diaries Plot."
8. Allan Hall, "Living in Poverty, the Man Who 'Found' Hitler's Diaries," The Independent
   (April 24, 2008): independent.co.uk/news/world/europe/living-in-poverty-the-man-who-
   found-hitlers-diaries-814757.html.

9. Kate Connolly, "Art Dealer Convicted of Forging Forger's Forgeries," *Guardian* (September 10, 2010): theguardian.com/artanddesign/2010/sep/10/forgeries-conviction-kujau.
10. Rentschler, "Fascination," 180.

Chapter 46

1. "What Happens to the Whistleblowers?" *The Science Show*, Radio National (September 3, 2005): griffith.edu.au/__data/assets/pdf_file/0010/159238/radionat3sept05.pdf.
2. "What Happens?"
3. Roger Lewin, "The Case of the 'Misplaced' Fossils," *Science*, New Series 244, 4902 (April 21, 1989): 277.
4. Lewin, "Case," 278.
5. John A. Talent, "The 'Misplaced' Fossils," *Science*, New Series 246, 4931 (November 10, 1989): 740–741.
6. "Fossils Found in Tibet Revise History of Elevation, Climate," *Science Daily* (June 12, 2008): sciencedaily.com/releases/2008/06/080611144021.htm.
7. Lewin, "Case," 278.
8. Lewin, "Case," 277–278.
9. Constance Holden, "Indian Geologist Suspended," *Science*, New Series 251 (March 15 1991): 1310.
10. "What Happens?"
11. Gary D. Webster, "An Evaluation of the V. J. Gupta Echinoderm Papers, 1971–1989." *Journal of Paleontology* 65, 6 (November 1991): 1006–1008; Gary D. Webster, Carl B. Rexroad, and John A. Talent. "An Evaluation of the V. J. Gupta Conodont Papers." *Journal of Paleontology* 67, 3 (May 1993): 486–493.
12. "What Happens?"
13. John P. A. Ioannidis, "Why Most Published Research Findings Are False," *PLoS* (August 30, 2005): journals.plos.org/plosmedicine/article?id=10.1371/journal.pmed.0020124.

Chapter 47

1. Paul Geraghty, "Doug and Dave: The Crop Circle Hoaxers," Spooky Stuff (October 22, 2012): spookystuff.co.uk/douganddavethecropcirclehoaxers.html.
2. John Roberts, "Trickster." *Oxford Art Journal* 22, 1 (1999): 83–101.
3. Benjamin Radford, "Crop Circles Explained," LiveScience (January 23, 2013): livescience.com/26540-crop-circles.html.
4. "Stoned Wallabies Make Crop Circles," BBC News (June 25, 2009): news.bbc.co.uk/2/hi/asia-pacific/8118257.stm.
5. Alun Anderson, "Britain's Crop Circles: Reaping by Whirlwind?" *Science*, New Series 253, 5023 (August 30, 1991): 961.
6. Jim Schnabel, "Puck in the Laboratory: The Construction and Deconstruction of Hoaxlike Deception in Science," *Science, Technology, & Human Values* 19, 4 (Autumn 1994): 474.
7. Anderson, "Britain's Crop Circles," 962.
8. Richard David Chorley, "Statement of the Chorley Family Concerning Robbert van den Broeke," The Official Website of Colin Andrews (August 19, 2012): colinandrews.net/David_Chorley-Family-Statement-Colin_Andrews-Crop_Circles.html.
9. Schnabel, "Puck," 476.
10. Bernard Dixon, "Mind Boggling," *British Medical Journal* 303, 6808 (October 19, 1991): 999.
11. Roberts, "Trickster," 83.
12. Wynne Parry, "Crop-Circle Artists Becoming High Tech," LiveScience (August 2, 2011): livescience.com/15353-crop-circle-artists-technology-physics-hoax.html.

13. Steve Nolan, "Worst. Crop Circles. Ever." *Daily Mail* (July 31, 2013): dailymail.co.uk/news/article-2381877/Worst-crop-circles-What-happened-patterns-delighted-baffled-world.html.
14. "Why Is the Crop Circle Access Donation Initiative Needed?" Crop Circle Access Centre: cropcircleaccess.com/crop-circle-access-donation-initiative/why-is-an-access-pass-needed/.
15. H.L. Mencken, "The Believing Mind," in *The Bathtub Hoax and Other Blasts & Bravos* (New York: Alfred A. Knopf, 1958), 20–24.

Chapter 48
1. Wikipedia, "Science Wars," en.wikipedia.org/wiki/Science_wars.
2. Alan Sokal, "A Physicist Experiments with Cultural Studies," physics.nyu.edu/faculty/sokal/lingua_franca_v4/lingua_franca_v4.html.

3. Sokal, "A Physicist Experiments."
4, Wikipedia, "C. P. Snow," en.wikipedia.org/wiki/C._P._Snow.
5. Alan Sokal, "Introduction," in Sokal and Bricmont, *Fashionable Nonsense*, 4.
6. Leron Borsten, "What Is Quantum Gravity?" Physicsworld.com (May 9, 2013): physics-world.com/cws/article/multimedia/2013/may/09/what-is-quantum-gravity.
7. Alan Sokal, "Transgressing the Boundaries: Toward a Transformative Hermeneutics of Quantum Gravity," in Sokal and Bricmont, *Fashionable Nonsense* (New York: Picador, 1998), 213.
8. Sokal, "Transgressing."
9. Sokal, "Transgressing," 235.
10. Jonathan Reynolds, "The Sokal Hoax Fifteen Years Later: A Philosophical Reading of the Controversy," *Spike Magazine*: spikemagazine.com/the-sokal-hoax.php.
11. Bruce Robbins and Andrew Ross in "Mystery Science Theatre," *Lingua Franca*, linguaf-ranca.mirror.theinfo.org/9607/mst.html.
12. Andrew Ross, "Reflections on the Sokal Affair," *Social Text*, 50 (Spring 1997): 149–152.
13. Reynolds, "The Sokal Hoax Fifteen Years Later."
14. Dan Fletcher, "Alabama Redefines Pi—1998," *Time* (April 1, 2011): content.time.com/time/specials/packages/article/0,28804,1888721_1888719_1888669,00.html (accessed 8/8/2015).
15. Alison McCook, "Cancer Researcher Cleared of Misconduct," Retraction Watch (December 15, 2015): http://retractionwatch.com/2015/12/15/cancer-researcher-cleared-of-misconduct-inquiry-finds-genuine-error-or-honest-oversight/#more-35279.
16. Robbins and Ross, in "Mystery Science Theatre."

Chapter 49
1. Ban Dihydrogen Monoxide, bandhmo.org/.
2. Wikipedia, "Dihydrogen Monoxide Hoax," en.wikipedia.org/wiki/Dihydrogen_monoxide_hoax.
3. United States Environmental Assessment Center, Dihydrogen Monoxide Research Division, "Dihydrogen Monoxide FAQ," dhmo.org/facts.html.
4. Ban Dihydrogen Monoxide, bandhmo.org/.
5. "Timeline: The Modern Environmental Movement," American Experience, PBS, pbs.org/wgbh/americanexperience/features/timeline/earthdays/.
6. Wikipedia, "Nevada Test Site," en.wikipedia.org/wiki/Nevada_Test_Site.
7. "Timeline," PBS.
8. Wikipedia, "DDT," en.wikipedia.org/wiki/DDT.
9. "Water Works," Snopes.com (March 8, 2015): snopes.com/science/dhmo.asp.

10. Wikipedia, "Dihydrogen Monoxide Hoax," en.wikipedia.org/wiki/Dihydrogen_monoxide_hoax.
11. United States Environmental Assessment Center, Dihydrogen Monoxide Research Division, "Dihydrogen Monoxide FAQ," dhmo.org/facts.html.
12. U.S. Centers for Disease Control and Prevention, "Unintentional Drowning: Get the Facts," cdc.gov/HomeandRecreationalSafety/Water-Safety/waterinjuries-factsheet.html.
13. Wikipedia, "Dihydrogen Monoxide Hoax," en.wikipedia.org/wiki/Dihydrogen_monoxide_hoax.
14. Gerald W. Bracey, "Research," *The Phi Delta Kappan* 79, 5 (January 1998): 406, 408.
15. "Penn and Teller Get Hippies to Sign Water Banning Petition," YouTube (December 6, 2006): youtube.com/watch?v=yi3erdgVVTw.
16. Ban Dihydrogen Monoxide, bandhmo.org/.
17. "DHMO: Your All-Natural Friend," armory.com/~crisper/DHMO/.
18. Jeffrey Kluger, "Why Science Is Winning the Vaccine Wars," *Time* (July 27, 2015): 25.

Chapter 50
1. Wikipedia, "Microsoft Joke," en.wikipedia.org/wiki/Microsoft_joke (accessed 7/24/2015).
2. "Microsoft Buys the Catholic Church," Museum of Hoaxes, hoaxes.org/archive/permalink/microsoft_buys_the_catholic_church (accessed 7/25/2015).
3. Jerome Segura, "Tech Support Scams – Help & Resource Page," Malwarebytes Labs (October 4, 2013): blog.malwarebytes.org/tech-support-scams/.
4. Nate Anderson, "Inside the U.S. Government's War on Tech Support Scammers," *Ars Technica* (May 18, 2014): arstechnica.com/tech-policy/2014/05/stains-of-deceitfulness-inside-the-us-governments-war-on-tech-support-scammers/.
5. Olivia Solon, "What Happens If You Play Along with a Microsoft 'Tech Support' Scam?" *WIRED.Co.UK* (April 11, 2013): wired.co.uk/news/archive/2013-04/11/malwarebytes.
6. Anderson, "Inside."
7. Lance Whitney, "Microsoft Combats Tech Support Scammers with Lawsuit," CNET (December 19, 2014): cnet.com/news/microsoft-combats-tech-support-scammers-with-lawsuit/.
8. Jon Brodkin, "Hello, I'm Definitely Not Calling from India. Can I Take Control of Your PC?" *Ars Technica* (October 3, 2012): arstechnica.com/tech-policy/2012/10/hello-im-definitely-not-calling-from-india-can-i-take-control-of-your-pc/.
9. Brodkin, "Hello."
10. "Microsoft Scam Man Is Sentenced in 'Landmark' Case." BBC News (March 31, 2014): bbc.com/news/technology-26818745.
11. Whitney, "Microsoft Combats Scammers."
12. Hilary George-Parkin, "When Is Fortune-Telling a Crime?" *The Atlantic* (November 14, 2014): theatlantic.com/features/archive/2014/11/when-is-fortunetelling-a-crime/382738/.
13. Robin Pogrebin, "It Seems the Cards Do Lie; a Police Sting Cracks Down on Fortunetelling Fraud," *New York Times* (June 30, 1999): nytimes.com/1999/06/30/nyregion/it-seems-the-cards-do-lie-a-police-sting-cracks-down-on-fortunetelling-fraud.html.
14. George-Parkin, "When Is Fortune-Telling a Crime?"
15. George-Parkin, "When Is Fortune-Telling a Crime?"

Sources: A Word About the Research Process
1. For a codified introduction to information literacy, see the Big6 Skills Overview, developed by Mike Eisenberg and Bob Berkowitz: http://big6.com/pages/about/big6-skills-overview.php.

Index

Author and Series Presenter Biographies

GALE EATON, a former children's librarian at the Boston Public Library and professor at the University of Rhode Island Graduate School of Library and Information Studies, has spent a lifetime with books for children and young adults. Her previous books include *Well-Dressed Role Models: The Portrayal of Women in Biographies for Children; The Education of Alice M. Jordan: Navigating a Career in Children's Librarianship;* and *A History of Civilization in 50 Disasters.* Gale lives in Wakefield, Rhode Island.

PHILLIP HOOSE is the widely acclaimed author of books, essays, stories, songs, and articles, including the National Book Award and Newbery Honor winning book *Claudette Colvin: Twice toward Justice* and the Boston Globe–Horn Book Honor winner *The Boys Who Challenged Hitler: Knud Pedersen and the Churchill Club.* A graduate of Indiana University and the Yale School of Forestry and Environmental Sciences, Hoose was for 37 years a staff member of The Nature Conservancy, dedicated to preserving the plants, animals, and natural communities of the Earth. Find out more at www.philliphoose. com. (Photo by Gordon Chibrowski, Maine Newspapers)